SHED AND GARAGE
PLANS & IDEAS
DREAM IT | BUILD IT

Direct Buy 800/845-9162   openhouse visitors pass

TURN YOUR DREAMS INTO REALITY

The world's largest and first in home improvement retailer—The Home Depot®—together with HomeStyles, the leader of the home- and project-plan industry, provide the inspiration, the plans, the tools and the materials to fulfill your home-building dreams. Select your deck, backyard project or dream home from our inventory of more than 10,000 plans. When you're ready to build, visit www.homedepot.com to locate The Home Depot store nearest you.

For more information on the projects in this book and many others, as well as on thousands of home plans, visit www.DreamIt-BuildIt.com or call 1-888-314-1303.

For additional help with your building or decorating needs, look for these other Home Depot titles:
- *Home Improvement 1-2-3*
- *Outdoor Projects 1-2-3*
- *Decorating 1-2-3*
- *Kitchens & Baths 1-2-3*
- *Wiring 1-2-3*
- *Decks 1-2-3*
- *Landscaping 1-2-3*

More titles are coming soon.

Other titles available in the **Dream-It, Build-It** series:
- *Classic American Home Styles*
- *Deck Plans & Ideas*
- *Backyard Project Plans & Ideas*

HomeStyles
Founders: Jeff Heegaard and Roger Heegaard
Operations and Project Management: Kyle J. Coolbroth
Sales and Marketing: Jim Plucker

Staff for *Shed and Garage Plans & Ideas*
Production Director: Bruce Krause
Managing Editor: Pamela Robertson
Designer: Scott Woodbury
Content: Steve Gramins
Editors: Sara Freund, Josh Kimball
Production: Morgan Brooke, Lynn Colbjornsen

The Home Depot
Marketing Manager: Nathan Ehrlich
Global Product Merchant: Brian Haubenschild
Merchant Assistant: Debbie Cooke
Internet Editor: Anna J. Siefken
Designer: Phil King

St. Remy Media Inc.
President: Pierre Léveillé
Vice President, Finance and Operations: Natalie Watanabe
Managing Editor: Carolyn Jackson
Managing Art Director: Diane Denoncourt
Systems Director: Edward Renaud
Director, Business Development: Christopher Jackson

Staff for *Shed and Garage Plans & Ideas*
Senior Editor: Marc Cassini
Senior Editor, Production: Brian Parsons
Art Directors: Solange Laberge, Francine Lemieux
Writer: Robert Labelle
Illustrators: Gilles Beauchemin, Robert Paquet, Jacques Perrault
Researchers: Lance Blomgren, Aldo Parisi
Photographer: Robert Chartier
Photo Researcher: Linda Bryant
Production Coordinator: Dominique Gagné
Prepress Technician: Jean Angrignon Sirois
Scanner Operator: Martin Francoeur

The following persons also assisted in the preparation of this book:
Danny-Pierre Auger; Ken Balcer, Sandi Construction; Lorraine Doré; Joey Fraser; Pascale Hueber; Roxanne Tremblay

The Home Depot® is a registered trademark of Homer TLC, Inc. The Home Depot® is not affiliated with HomeStyles®.

© Copyright 2001, HomeStyles®. All rights reserved. Printed in U.S.A. The trademark HomeStyles is registered in the U.S. Patent and Trademark Office by Gruner and Jahr, Inc., and is used under license therefrom.

ISBN 1-56547-121-0

HomeStyles
Saint Paul, Minnesota

St. Remy Media Inc.
Montreal, Quebec

FOREWORD

It starts with a dream. A dream where there's a place for everything and everything is in its place—whether the family car, the lawn mower or a collection of garden tools.

Today's home owners envision sheds and garages as more than glorified storage bins. These structures need to have a flair, style and character that enables them to blend in with the family home and become an extension of the home. The shed and garage plans and ideas in this book will help you transform your dreams into reality.

Who better to bring you this book than the world's largest home-improvement retailer—The Home Depot—in conjunction with the leader of the home- and project-plan industry, HomeStyles?

Working together, we have developed a truly unique and valuable book that addresses your needs as a do-it-yourselfer. This book includes 16 of the most popular shed and garage plans in full detail from HomeStyles, coupled with the suggested materials lists so that you may visit your local Home Depot store and purchase the materials to complete your project. In addition, you'll find lots of ideas that will inspire you to create the perfect outdoor structure.

"To accomplish great things, we must not only act, but also dream; not only plan, but also believe."
Anatole France, writer and Nobel laureate
(Photo: courtesy Raynor Worldwide)

Contents: THE IDEAS

Dream Your Project	9
1 Plan the Structure	**22**
Legal Considerations	22
Location, Location, Location	23
What Kind of Shed?	24
What Kind of Garage?	26
The Road to Building the Structure	28
2 Structure Basics	**30**
Underpinnings	32
Exterior Skin	34
Raise the Roof	36
Windows and Doors	38
Walls, Ceilings and Woodwork	40
3 Fancy Add-ons	**42**
Accessories	42
Adding a Deck or Landing	43
Structures that Shed Water	44
The Comforts of Home	45
Storage	46

Contents: The Plans

4 Our Most Popular Shed and Garage Plans — **48**

- The Tucson & Sierra — **49**
- The Monroe & Jackson — **62**
- The Charleston & Viceroy — **76**
- The Cedarville & Springfield — **90**
- The Boulder — **103**
- The Emerson — **110**
- The Carlton — **117**
- The Adams — **124**
- The Marquis — **131**
- The Windsong — **138**
- The Morton — **145**
- The Clinton — **152**

Picture Credits — **159**

Glossary — **160**

INTRODUCTION

Overflowing flower boxes and a classic Americana white picket fence give this playhouse a sense of home. Practicality, however, is not forgotten: The gutter and downspout assembly go a long way in making the structure weatherwise.
(Photo: Jean-Claude Hurni)

DREAM YOUR PROJECT

Building a shed or garage to your specifications has a multitude of payoffs. You will not only enlarge your storage space, but also improve your property aesthetically and increase its value. But where can you get the information and inspiration you need to build the project of your dreams? The plans, ideas and photos in this book are a great starting point. The plans and ideas will fulfill the information side of the equation, while the photos will supply plenty of inspiration. The photos aren't necessarily tied to the plans; rather, they are intended to inspire you by providing vivid examples of creative shed and garage design. Whether it's a harmonious blend of roofing and siding, a distinctive door and window design or overflowing window boxes that blur the boundary between garden and shed, the following pages—along with the helpful employees at The Home Depot—will guide you in putting a personal stamp on your chosen plan. At the end of the process, you may find yourself sitting in your yard, admiring your new shed or garage—just the right setting to lie back and…dream!

Blue-painted wood trim frames the two windows and door of this spacious garden shed, lending the structure a unified design. Wreaths, hanging plants and colorful potted annuals harmonize with the traditional strap hinges of the door, accentuating the shed's rustic style.
(Photo: Jean-Claude Hurni)

INTRODUCTION

Double doors and a wide ramp make this shed ideal for wheeling in unwieldy items such as a riding mower and a wheelbarrow. The arched double windows give the shed a symmetrical facade.
(Photo: courtesy Handy Home Products)

INTRODUCTION

The gabled roof of this attractive toolshed makes it the perfect companion to an older country home. The blue-gray clapboard siding set off by white trim sounds a note of traditional harmony.
(Photo: Jean-Claude Hurni)

These simple poolside changing cabanas with matching arched doorways are enhanced by the choice of building material. Handsome redwood paneling with accompanying brass light fixtures lend the buildings a rich tone.
(Photo: Jean-Claude Hurni)

OPPOSITE PAGE:
This greenhouse shed is a perfect home for plants. With one side of the roof topped by glass instead of shingles, sun-hungry plants inside get plenty of natural light. The vent built into the gable wall lets air circulate inside the shed, ensuring that the plants do not suffer from wilting heat.
(Photo: courtesy Handy Home Products)

The back of this shed is tailor-made for storing wood. The roof overhang shelters the logs from rain while the open wall enables air to circulate.
(Photo: Jean-Claude Hurni)

Wide weathered-gray clapboard gives this shed the appearance of a traditional farm building. Its utilitarian structure also provides this yard area with a backdrop for climbing plants and an attractive rest spot.
(Photo: Jean-Claude Hurni)

INTRODUCTION

INTRODUCTION

INTRODUCTION

The robust appearance of this finished knotty-pine shed belies its mobility. Built on skids, the structure can easily be moved to another locale. The small awning windows are hinged at the bottom, ventilating the interior space while preventing water seepage.
(Photo: courtesy Kloter Farms, Inc. / photo by Fred Bird Photography)

This storage shed doubles as a playhouse. High doors allow easy access and a small patio just outside the entrance provides a spot for toys and playthings. The gambrel roof imparts a country flavor to the shed, helping it blend into its backyard setting.
(Photo: courtesy Handy Home Products)

Window muntins, shutters, well-tended flower boxes and a "front-porch" area give this shed the look of a mini-house. But appearances can be deceiving. The double doors provide easy access for the storage of large garden tools and machinery.
(Photo: courtesy Kloter Farms, Inc. / photo by Fred Bird Photography)

INTRODUCTION

OPPOSITE PAGE:
This two-car garage addition provides its owners with an ideal locale for an outdoor recreational space. The large deck with an overhead and privacy screens is kept far away from ground moisture and is easily accessed from an upper section of the house by way of an adjoining stairway.
(Photo: Jean-Claude Hurni)

ABOVE:
With its front door set behind the front of the house, this one-car garage avoids clashing with the home's facade. The matching red siding, pale trim and decorative scrollwork at the apex of the gables help create the impression that the garage is part of the house rather than an appendage.
(Photo: Jason Miller)

It is possible to build a spacious garage without overwhelming your house. This detached model with old-fashioned barn doors complements the older structures of this neighborhood. A working set of trap doors to the "hayloft" completes the farmyard effect.
(Photo: Jean-Claude Hurni)

INTRODUCTION

Consider future needs when selecting a garage design. This three-door structure can accommodate two cars as well as a boat or an RV, items you may only own years from now. Or, the third bay can be converted into a sports or leisure area.
(Photo: courtesy Garages by Opdyke)

The hip roof of this three-car garage creates an architectural complement to the adjoining home. The red brick facade with its covering of ivy further links it to the complete home structure.
(Photo: courtesy Raynor Worldwide)

INTRODUCTION

A little can do a lot. The cupola crowning this detached garage gives the structure a classic design touch. A pair of lights make the front door area safe and secure at night, and the roof overhang, along with an unobtrusive gutter and downspout system, keeps roof runoff away from the door.
(Photo: courtesy Garages by Opdyke)

INTRODUCTION

Surrounded by trees, this stand-alone single garage blends in well with its environment. The dormer and shapes of the windows add to its simple, eclectic character.
(Photo: Jean-Claude Hurni)

One way to downplay the visual impact of a garage is by designing the structure with smaller doors. A single loading-dock door on this attached two-car garage might have clashed with the style of the house. Outfitting the structure with a pair of single doors makes it appear less imposing.
(Photo: courtesy Garages by Opdyke)

Clever application of recesses and arches as well as the offset lines of the walls and roof keep this prominent triple garage from overwhelming the house.
(Photo: courtesy Raynor Worldwide)

This garage has several design touches that help it stand out. The red of the brick echoes the cupola on the roof and the wrought-iron door hinges are reflected in the two light fixtures.
(Photo: courtesy Garages by Opdyke)

PLAN THE STRUCTURE

If the featured sheds or garages on the preceding pages have whet your appetite for a similar structure on your own property, now is the time to start some serious planning. This chapter will help you select a shed or garage plan that fits your budget, time frame and individual needs. Before beginning the process, however, you need to answer these questions:

• What type, size and style of shed or garage is best? As shown in the plans starting on page 49, there is a wide range of designs to consider. Your choice should depend on your design sense as well the uses you intend for the structure.

• How will I pay for the project? This may not be an important issue with a shed that will cost a few hundred dollars, but can be significant with a garage costing several thousand.

• Do I have the time? A simple shed can go up over a weekend, but a garage can take weeks or months. You need to set aside a reasonable amount of time for construction.

• Where should I locate the structure? As shown below and on page 23, you want to pick a spot that will be convenient and aesthetically pleasing, balanced against any legal restrictions on the location of a shed or garage.

Legal Considerations

Planning your new shed or garage should include a visit to your local building-permit department. In most cases, you will need to obtain a building permit before starting construction. The permit shows that your plans comply with local building codes and any legal restrictions that could affect your project. Some of these restrictions are illustrated in the drawing at right.

• **Why do you require a building permit?** In most areas, you cannot legally build a structure larger than 100 square feet on your property without one. A building permit allows your municipality to ensure your project will be safe and structurally sound. The first step is to take your plans to the building-permit department—better still, have your contractor do it and get the needed permits in his name. This way, he'll be liable if the work does not comply with the codes. If your project involves bringing electricity or water to the structure, you may need individual permits for the electrical and plumbing work. Bear in mind that obtaining a permit is only half the battle. After the work is completed, the building-permit department will inspect the project to confirm that you followed your plans. If any of the work is substandard, you will be required to redo it—even if that means dismantling the shed or garage.

IN THE ZONE: Restrictions You Should Know About

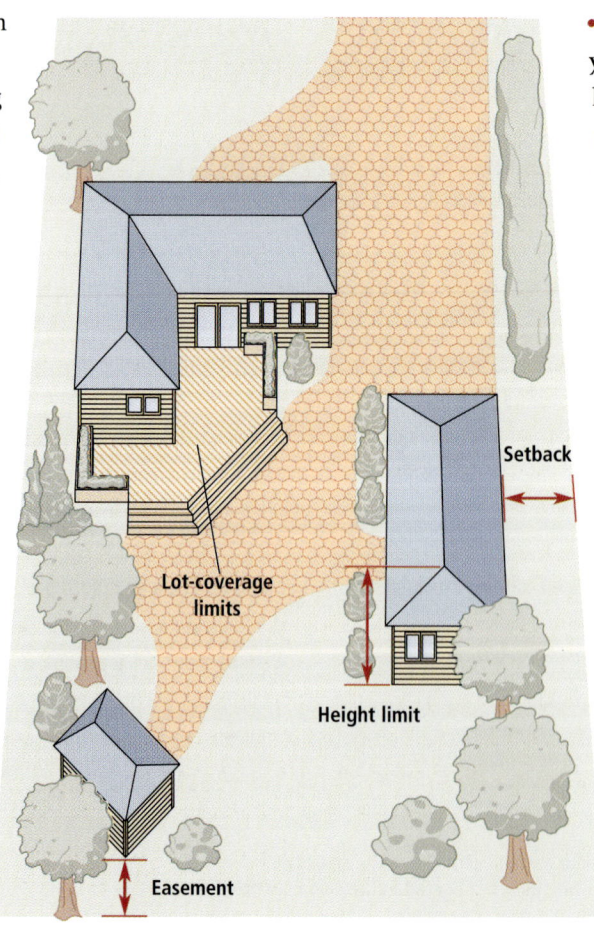

• **What legal restrictions can affect your plans?** Zoning bylaws can set a limit on the height of a structure, the proportion of your property the structure will cover and the setback  (or how close the structure is to your property line). Architectural controls can throw roadblocks in your way if you live in a neighborhood with tight controls over new construction. You may have to submit your plans to a review board to ensure your plans meet architectural standards.

• **Deed restrictions.** Check your property deed for any limits on the design or location of your project. Your property might, for example, include an easement—a section that must be left accessible for others to use.

CHAPTER 1

Location, Location, Location

The illustration at right shows typical locations for a garage and shed. Here, a detached garage sits alongside and behind the front of the house at the end of a straight driveway and a shed occupies a corner of the backyard. While this arrangement may work for you, it's a good idea to explore your needs and preferences before deciding on the location of a shed or garage. There's a lot to consider.

FINDING A HOME FOR A GARAGE
Builders usually advise home owners to locate a garage so it won't overpower or clash with their home's facade. This means siting the structure away from the front of the house, choosing a spot along the side or at the rear. You can even orient the garage so the door lines up with the side or rear of the house rather than with the front. These solutions are easier to carry out with a detached garage, but even if you opt for an attached design, there are ways of helping the garage blend visually with the home. For example, a two-car garage will appear less overpowering if it has two doors rather than a single loading-dock style door. Two doors add to construction costs (you'll need two garage-door openers, for example), so you can opt for a single-door design to save some money and camouflage the door by painting it the same color as the garage's exterior siding. Another solution is to go with a one-car garage if that's all you really need. Although a single-car garage won't add as much to your home's value as a larger structure, it will have less visual impact on the home.

Consider how a new garage will affect sight lines from the house. You don't want to locate a garage so it blocks a nice view.

When you build a new garage, you'll need a driveway leading to it, so you have to consider its location as well. Make sure the driveway doesn't cut across an area that is used for other activities such as play or leisure.

LOCATING A SHED
A shed will only be a valuable addition to your property if it is put in the right place. Keep the following factors in mind as you select a location for your new shed:
- **Convenience:** Choose a spot that will be handy for people using the shed and getting items in and out of it. Locate a potting shed, for example, near the garden and a play shed for storing children's toys near their play area. If cumbersome tools and supplies, such as a riding mower or wheelbarrow, will regularly be taken into and out of the shed, locate the structure so there are no sharp turns to negotiate.

SITE INSIGHT: Where to Place a Shed or Garage

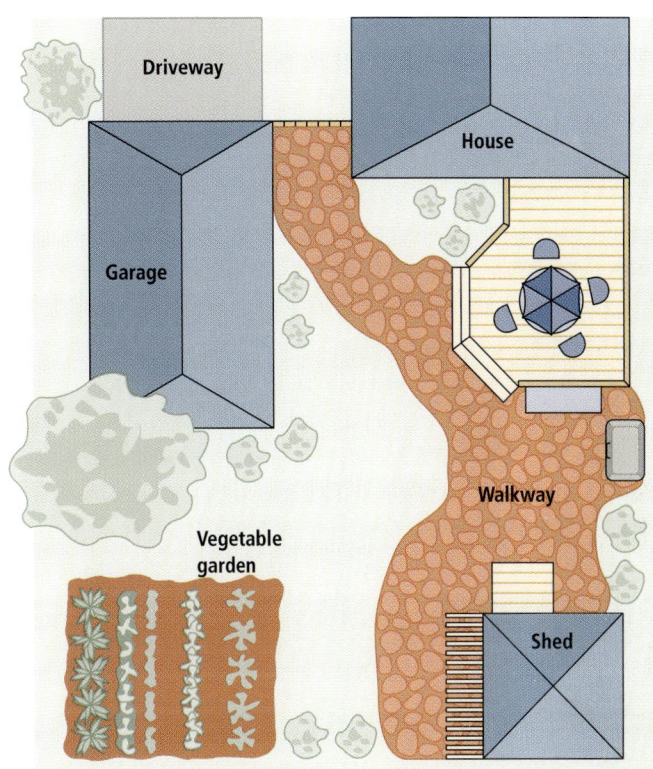

- **Heat and light:** A shed that spends a good part of the day in the sun will be warmer and brighter than a shaded structure. Orient a shed with windows facing south for optimal heat and light. A shed's location can also affect other sections of a yard; don't place a shed, for instance, where it will block sunlight to a vegetable garden.
- **Traffic patterns:** Consider the route people will take to and from the shed. Locate the shed so traffic patterns do not interfere with other backyard activities. This will be particularly important if you plan to lay a paved or gravel path to the shed. It can help to sketch out your property and draw the traffic patterns for different shed locations.
- **Sight lines:** How will a new shed contribute to your view of the backyard and to the property's overall appearance? Depending on where the shed is situated, the structure can become the yard's focal point or fade into the background. You may also want to consider how the shed location will impact your neighbors' views.
- **Building considerations:** Select a spot for your shed so erecting it will go as smoothly as possible. A flat and firm site with good drainage is best, with enough space all around for clearance of tools and materials.

CHAPTER 1

What Kind of Shed?

A shed's size, design, features, and overall appearance is determined by and large by its purpose. The illustrations below and on page 25 provide a sampling of the major types of sheds, from the basic utility and convenience shed to the greenhouse shed and playhouse. Thinking about how you will use the shed can help you choose one of the designs beginning on page 49.

If all you want is a structure for storing backyard tools and equipment, for example, then a basic utility and convenience shed may be all that you need. Even so, try to estimate the space that the various items to be stored will occupy so you choose a design that is large enough. If the shed will also serve as a workshop, the structure will need to be larger. It may also need windows to let in air and light and amenities such as electricity and plumbing. A shed that will be used as a children's playhouse needs wide doors, functional windows and perhaps even a front porch or attached deck. A pool shed can encompass such features as a dressing room, storage space and a serving area.

Give some thought to how you will outfit the shed interior. A storage shed will need shelves, cabinets and wall hooks while a workshop shed might be equipped with a workbench.

A GALLERY OF SHED TYPES

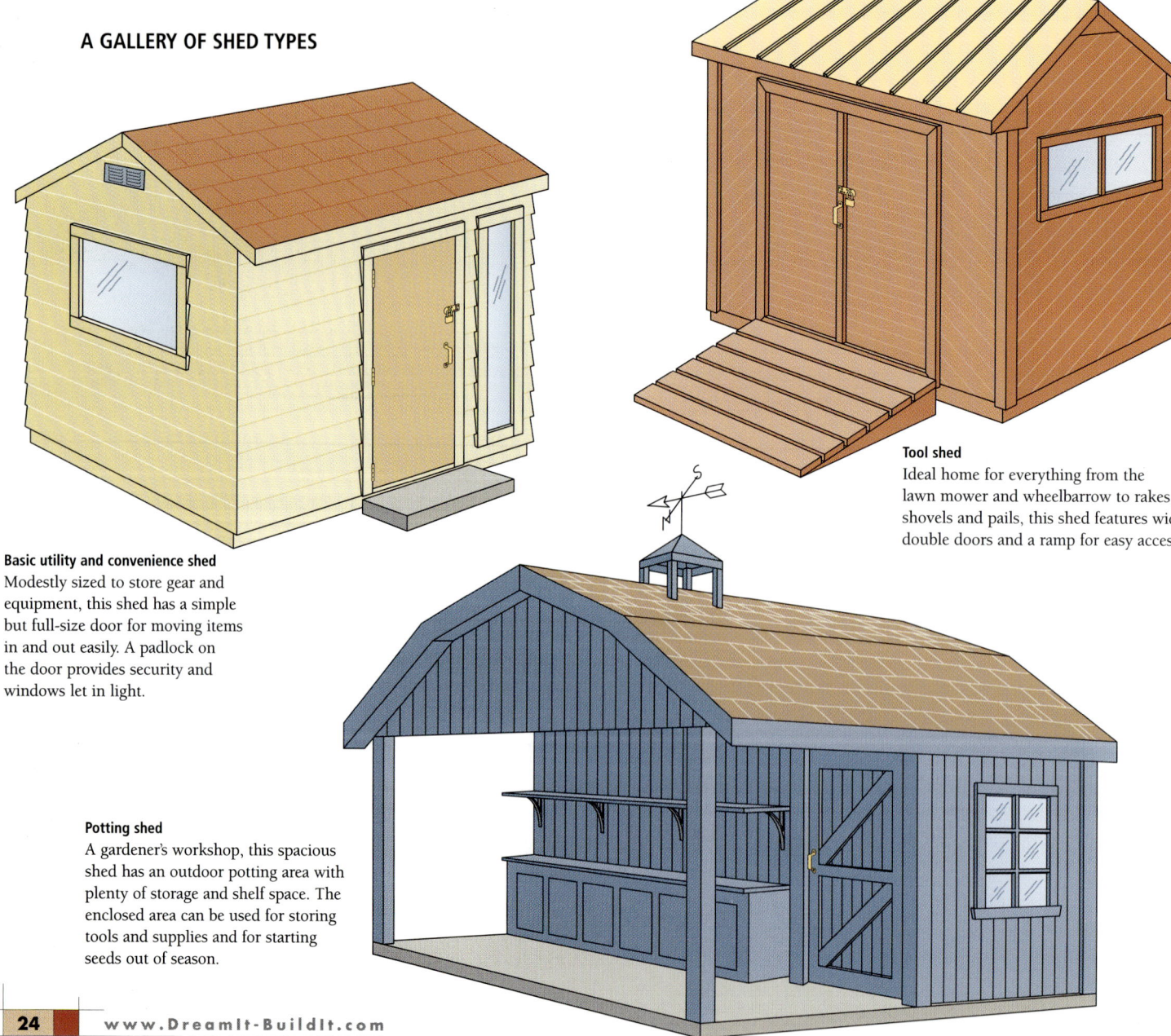

Basic utility and convenience shed
Modestly sized to store gear and equipment, this shed has a simple but full-size door for moving items in and out easily. A padlock on the door provides security and windows let in light.

Tool shed
Ideal home for everything from the lawn mower and wheelbarrow to rakes, shovels and pails, this shed features wide double doors and a ramp for easy access.

Potting shed
A gardener's workshop, this spacious shed has an outdoor potting area with plenty of storage and shelf space. The enclosed area can be used for storing tools and supplies and for starting seeds out of season.

CHAPTER 1

Greenhouse
Perfect for growing plants that can't be exposed to the elements, this shed features skylights and windows that ensure a bright, sunny interior.

Playhouse
A house in miniature, this playhouse has everything children could want: a spacious interior, realistic features and an enclosed porch for snacks or board games.

Wood shed
A basic structure with one side removed, this shed shelters firewood from the elements while allowing air to circulate around the logs to promote drying.

Pool shed
This shed is a stepping-stone between home and pool. An outdoor shower accommodates bathers before and after swimming, a spacious interior stores tools and supplies, and louvered windows provide privacy.

www.homedepot.com   25

CHAPTER 1

What Kind of Garage?

Most people believe that choosing a garage plan is straightforward. A single-car family needs a one-car garage, a two-car family needs a double garage and so on. But a garage can be more than just a stable for the family minivan. It's a good idea to peer into your crystal ball and try to anticipate future needs. Maybe a teenager will soon be needing a car to get to college out of town. Perhaps you plan to acquire an RV that will need a place of its own. Maybe you've been thinking of expanding your home's living space: Why not kill two birds with one stone and build a garage with an upper floor? This additional space can be anything from a playroom, storage area or guest room to a workshop or rental apartment. Yet another option is to build a garage with more ground-floor area than you need and use the additional space for leisure or sports activities.

The typical car needs a 14- by 22-foot garage; two cars require 24 by 24 feet, so anything larger than these leaves additional space that can be put to some other use.

MODIFYING A PLAN

If the idea of changing a garage or shed plan to better suit your needs or design preferences appeals to you, HomeStyles Design Services will work with you to modify one of their plans. The experts at HomeStyles Design Services can make changes quickly, conveniently and cost-effectively. Contact HomeStyles Design Services by e-mail at **projectmods@homestyles.com** or by phone at **1-888-314-1303** to discuss the changes you would like to make. You can even fax a rough sketch and a specific list of your changes. Either way, they'll call you back with an estimate.

A GALLERY OF GARAGE TYPES

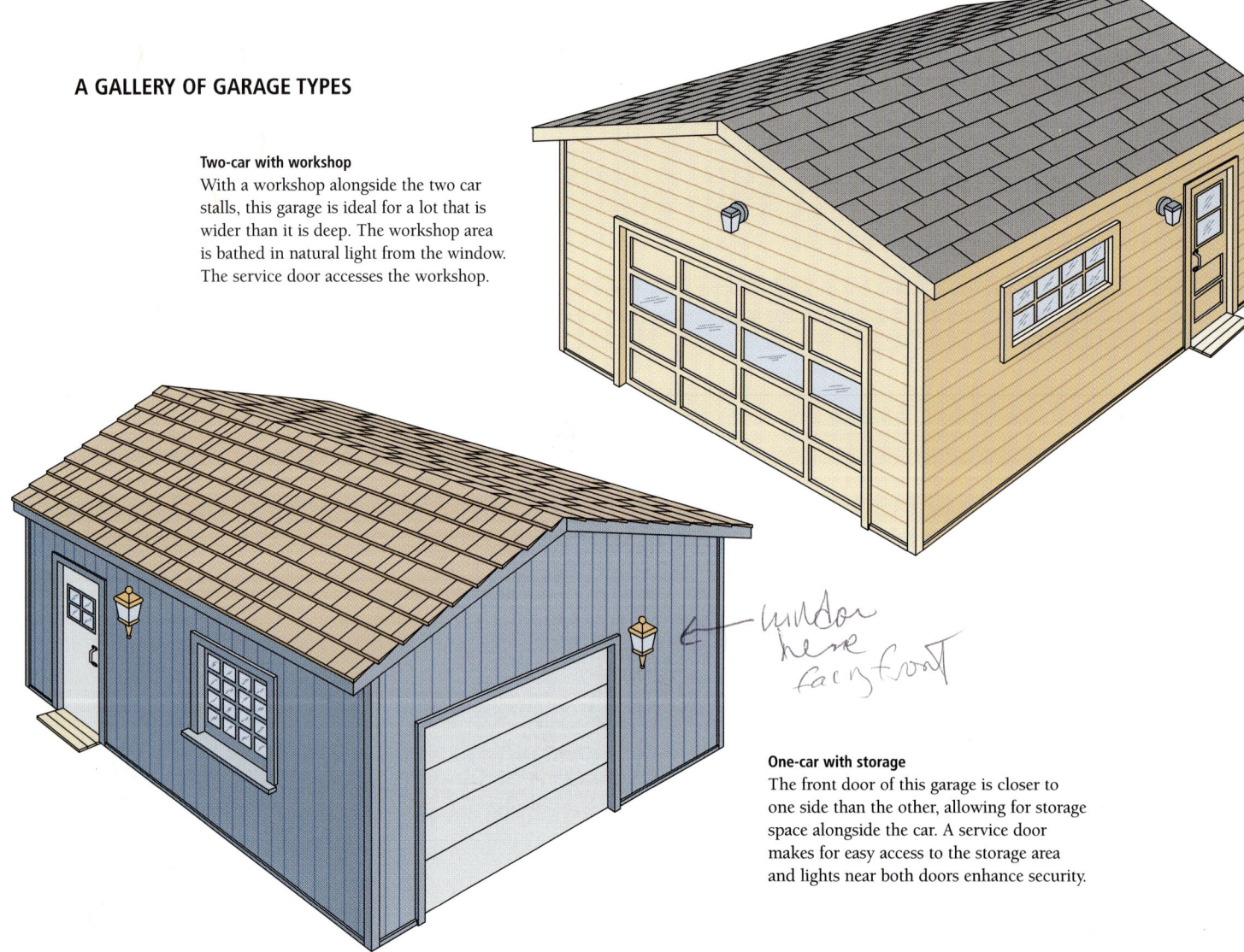

Two-car with workshop
With a workshop alongside the two car stalls, this garage is ideal for a lot that is wider than it is deep. The workshop area is bathed in natural light from the window. The service door accesses the workshop.

One-car with storage
The front door of this garage is closer to one side than the other, allowing for storage space alongside the car. A service door makes for easy access to the storage area and lights near both doors enhance security.

www.DreamIt-BuildIt.com

CHAPTER 1

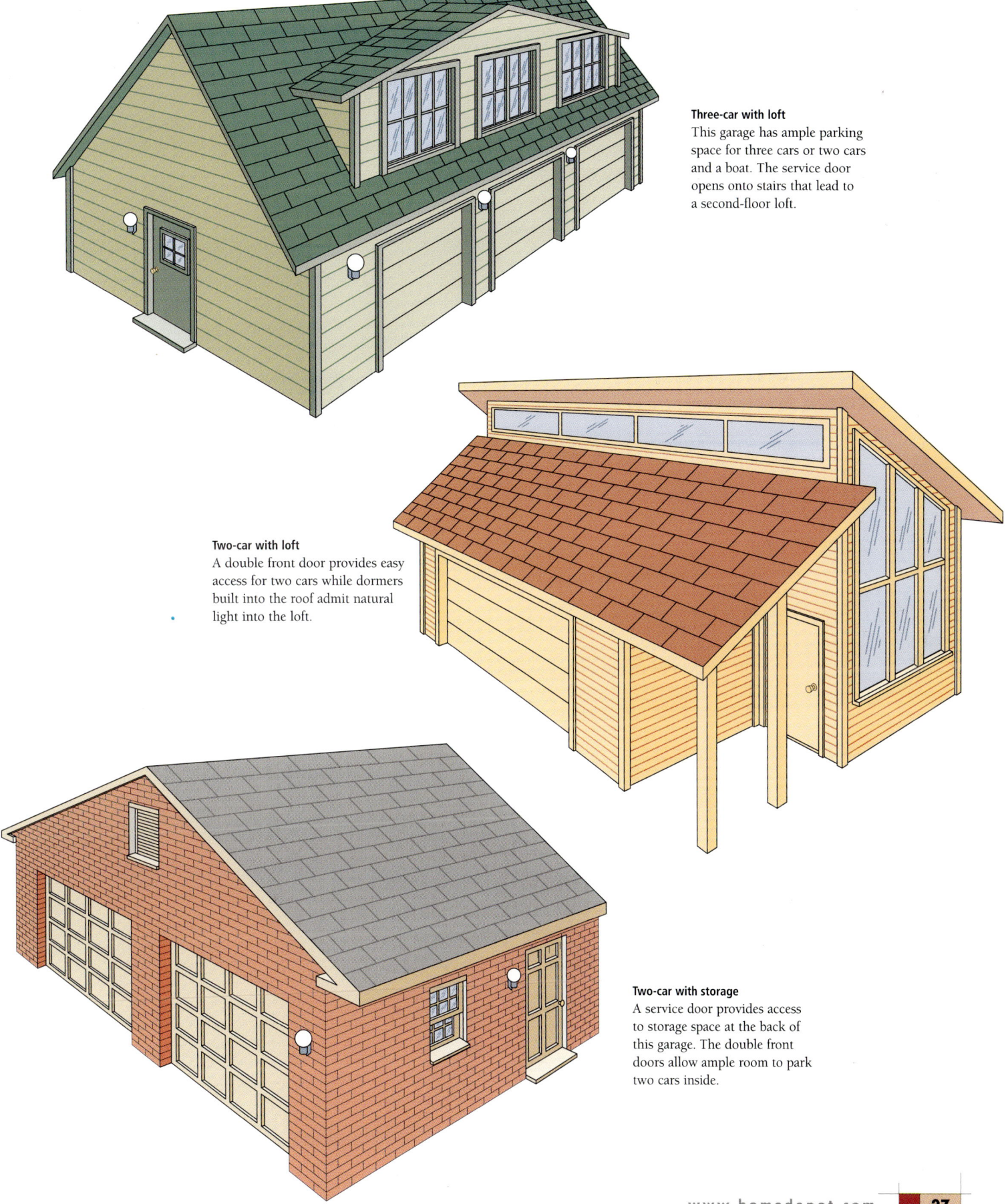

Three-car with loft
This garage has ample parking space for three cars or two cars and a boat. The service door opens onto stairs that lead to a second-floor loft.

Two-car with loft
A double front door provides easy access for two cars while dormers built into the roof admit natural light into the loft.

Two-car with storage
A service door provides access to storage space at the back of this garage. The double front doors allow ample room to park two cars inside.

www.homedepot.com

CHAPTER 1

The Road to Building the Structure

In addition to choosing a shed or garage plan, you have to decide whether you will tackle the structure yourself or hire a contractor. (Chances are, though, you're more likely to attempt the building of a shed on your own than a garage.) These two pages are not intended to provide an in-depth, step-by-step how-to guide to constructing a shed or garage. Rather, the idea is to give you an appreciation of the process and the basic steps involved so that you can choose to execute certain parts of the construction and contract others out. Although this book focuses on building design and style, the often overlooked issue of attending to construction details has a huge impact on the appearance of a shed or garage.

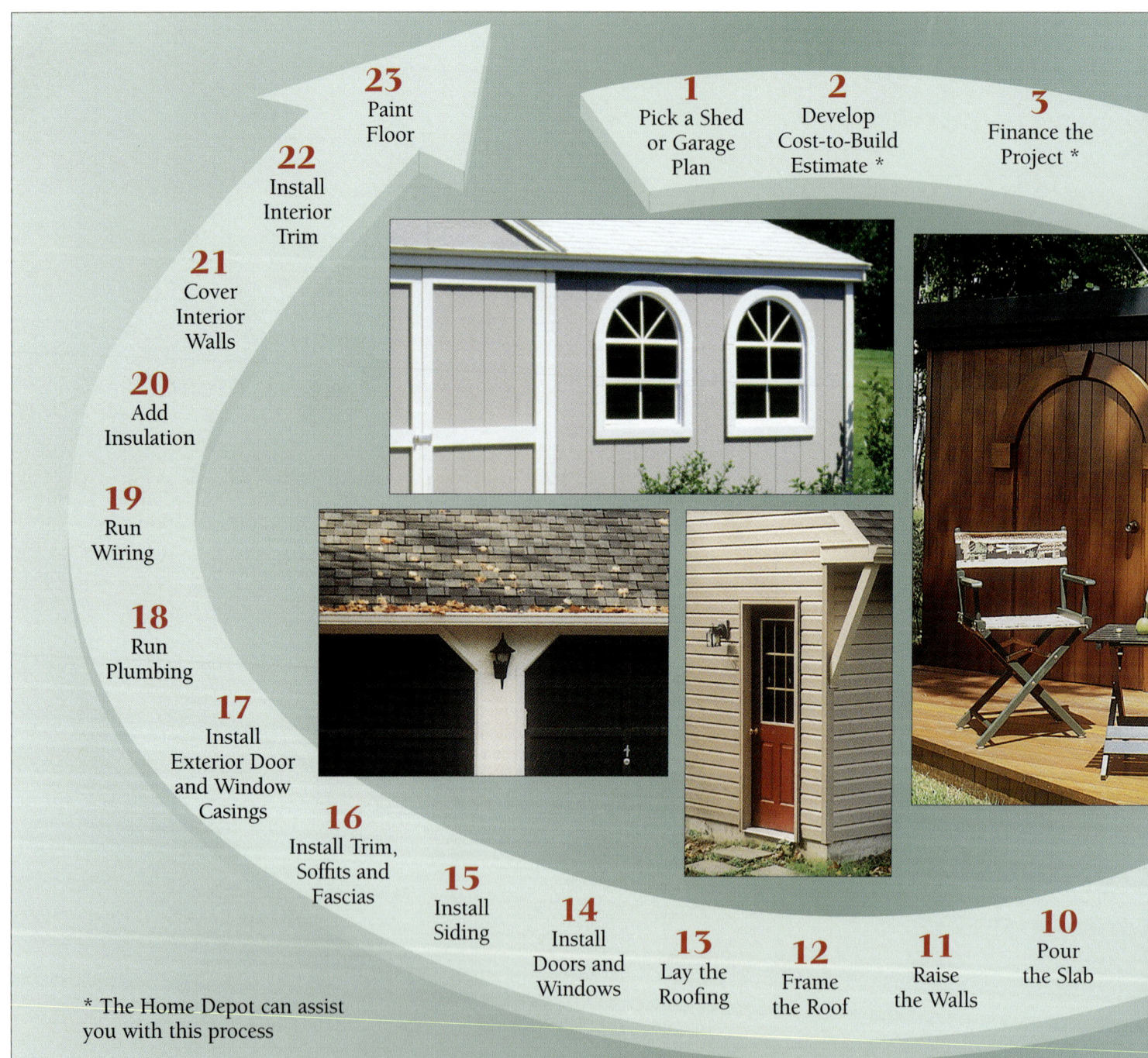

1. Pick a Shed or Garage Plan
2. Develop Cost-to-Build Estimate *
3. Finance the Project *
10. Pour the Slab
11. Raise the Walls
12. Frame the Roof
13. Lay the Roofing
14. Install Doors and Windows
15. Install Siding
16. Install Trim, Soffits and Fascias
17. Install Exterior Door and Window Casings
18. Run Plumbing
19. Run Wiring
20. Add Insulation
21. Cover Interior Walls
22. Install Interior Trim
23. Paint Floor

* The Home Depot can assist you with this process

CHAPTER 1

A Well-Connected Shed or Garage

A shed or garage is subjected to a great deal of physical stress. The weather beats on it year after year. The ground under it constantly shifts. And if you live in hurricane country, annual storms put every structural joint to the test. And years from now, the structure is supposed to look as good as the day it was built.

Simpson Strong-Tie makes steel connectors designed to connect, support and strengthen joints in sheds and garages. From joist hangers that strengthen floors to hurricane ties that anchor the roof to the walls, **Simpson Strong-Tie** connectors make building easier. In addition to adding strength and safety, connectors cut down on the number of nails required for installation and eliminate the need for complicated construction techniques such as toenailing—driving a nail into one piece at a 45-degree angle so the nail tip penetrates an adjoining piece. Although connectors were once optional parts of construction projects, they are now required by building codes in some areas.

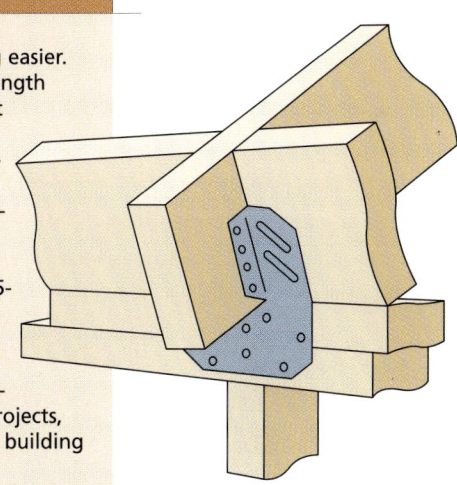

4 Take Your Plan to Building-Permit Department

5 Hire a Contractor (if necessary)

6 Buy Materials *

7 Lay Out the Site

8 Pour the Footings

9 Build the Foundation

FINANCE OPTIONS

The Home Depot offers several great finance options for your home improvement needs. Apply at any store for a Home Depot Consumer, Home Improvement Loan, or Commercial Credit Account. For your convenience, you can also apply online at www.homedepot.com for a Consumer or Commercial Credit Account. Receive a decision within minutes and get started on building your dreams at The Home Depot!

MANAGING MONEY AND TIME

Money. Unless you can finance your project with ready cash, you'll need to take out a loan to pay for materials and labor. For most people, borrowing against the equity that they've built up in their home is a good bet. Interest rates are generally lower than for other types of loans and, in the U.S. at least, interest payments are tax deductible. Here are three types of loans worth considering:

- **Home-equity credit line.** This flexible loan option allows you to borrow funds as you need them. The credit limit can be as high as 25 percent more than your home's value, less the amount still owing on the mortgage, but you only pay interest on the money you withdraw. Available from banks and credit unions, credit lines are a good choice if you plan to complete the project over the course of several months.

- **Home-equity loan.** Once known as second mortgages, these loans pay out a lump sum of money at a fixed interest rate. Much like mortgages, home-equity loans are available at fixed interest rates and can be repaid in as few as five years or as many as 30 years.

- **Extended mortgage.** This option allows you to add the cost of your project to your mortgage amount when you purchase a house or at mortgage renewal time.

Time. Building projects generally take longer to complete than expected. That shed you hope to put up in a weekend may take a week. And your new garage may take months to build rather than weeks. Here are a few tips to keep time on your side:

- Don't schedule your project at a time when it may interfere with a family event, such as a birthday barbecue.

- Select and order all the materials you need before starting to build and make sure everything has been delivered.

- If you plan to tackle the project yourself, schedule the work for vacation time.

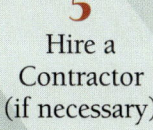

CHAPTER 2

STRUCTURE BASICS

This chapter will guide you in putting your own personal design stamp on a new shed or garage. You'll need to make choices about everything from window and door styles to roofing and siding options.

If you plan to build your new shed or garage yourself, you will of course need to know how the various components of the structure fit together. But even if you intend to hand the project over to a contractor once you've chosen a plan, it's a good idea to become acquainted with the parts of a shed or garage. This will not only help you select the plan that best fits your needs, but it will also enable you to speak intelligently with your contractor as the project evolves.

THE PARTS OF A SHED:
Building Blocks of Design

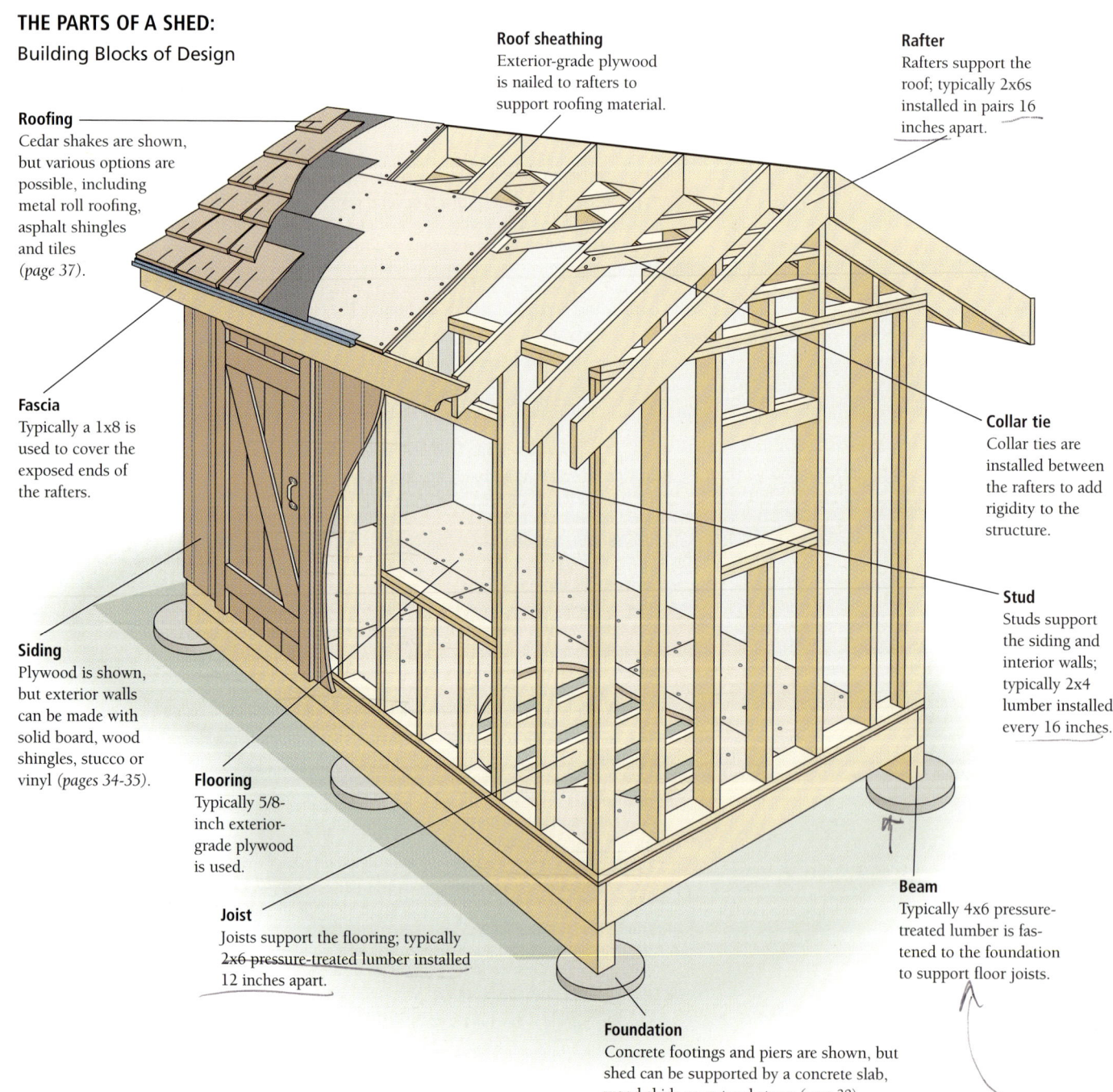

Roofing
Cedar shakes are shown, but various options are possible, including metal roll roofing, asphalt shingles and tiles (page 37).

Fascia
Typically a 1x8 is used to cover the exposed ends of the rafters.

Siding
Plywood is shown, but exterior walls can be made with solid board, wood shingles, stucco or vinyl (pages 34-35).

Flooring
Typically 5/8-inch exterior-grade plywood is used.

Joist
Joists support the flooring; typically 2x6 pressure-treated lumber installed 12 inches apart.

Roof sheathing
Exterior-grade plywood is nailed to rafters to support roofing material.

Foundation
Concrete footings and piers are shown, but shed can be supported by a concrete slab, wood skids or natural stone (page 32).

Rafter
Rafters support the roof; typically 2x6s installed in pairs 16 inches apart.

Collar tie
Collar ties are installed between the rafters to add rigidity to the structure.

Stud
Studs support the siding and interior walls; typically 2x4 lumber installed every 16 inches.

Beam
Typically 4x6 pressure-treated lumber is fastened to the foundation to support floor joists.

CHAPTER 2

THE PARTS OF A GARAGE:
An Anatomy of Style

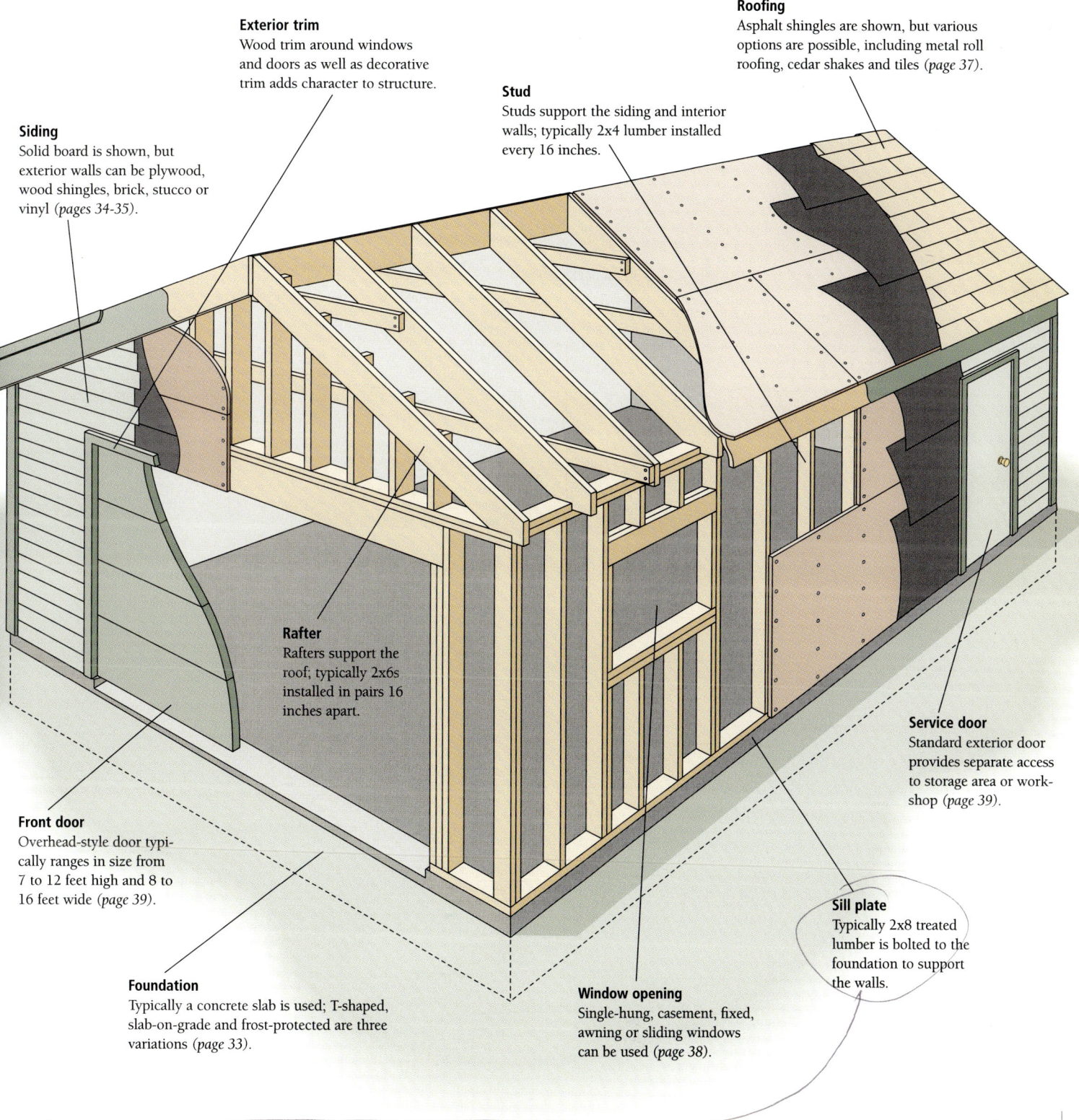

Exterior trim
Wood trim around windows and doors as well as decorative trim adds character to structure.

Roofing
Asphalt shingles are shown, but various options are possible, including metal roll roofing, cedar shakes and tiles *(page 37)*.

Stud
Studs support the siding and interior walls; typically 2x4 lumber installed every 16 inches.

Siding
Solid board is shown, but exterior walls can be plywood, wood shingles, brick, stucco or vinyl *(pages 34-35)*.

Rafter
Rafters support the roof; typically 2x6s installed in pairs 16 inches apart.

Service door
Standard exterior door provides separate access to storage area or workshop *(page 39)*.

Front door
Overhead-style door typically ranges in size from 7 to 12 feet high and 8 to 16 feet wide *(page 39)*.

Foundation
Typically a concrete slab is used; T-shaped, slab-on-grade and frost-protected are three variations *(page 33)*.

Window opening
Single-hung, casement, fixed, awning or sliding windows can be used *(page 38)*.

Sill plate
Typically 2x8 treated lumber is bolted to the foundation to support the walls.

www.homedepot.com   31

CHAPTER 2

Underpinnings

Whichever plan you choose, your new shed or garage will need to be supported by a solid foundation.

SHED FOUNDATIONS

The illustrations below show four foundation options for sheds. Each one has a unique design and appearance, and each has advantages and disadvantages. With the **skid** foundation, a shed can be moved after construction because it is not fixed to the ground. This foundation involves less expense than one using concrete since the shed rests on just two wood skids. It also entails less labor, though there is some work involved. You have to ensure good water drainage under and around the shed by digging a trench under each skid and filling it with gravel.

Concrete footings and piers, the type of foundation represented in the plans in this book, provide a more durable and immovable foundation than skids. This option involves digging a hole for each pier below the frost line, pouring a concrete footing, embedding the pier in the footing and fastening 4x6 beams atop the piers. Both skids and concrete piers are paired with wood floors: Joists sit atop the skids or beams and plywood flooring is fastened to the joists.

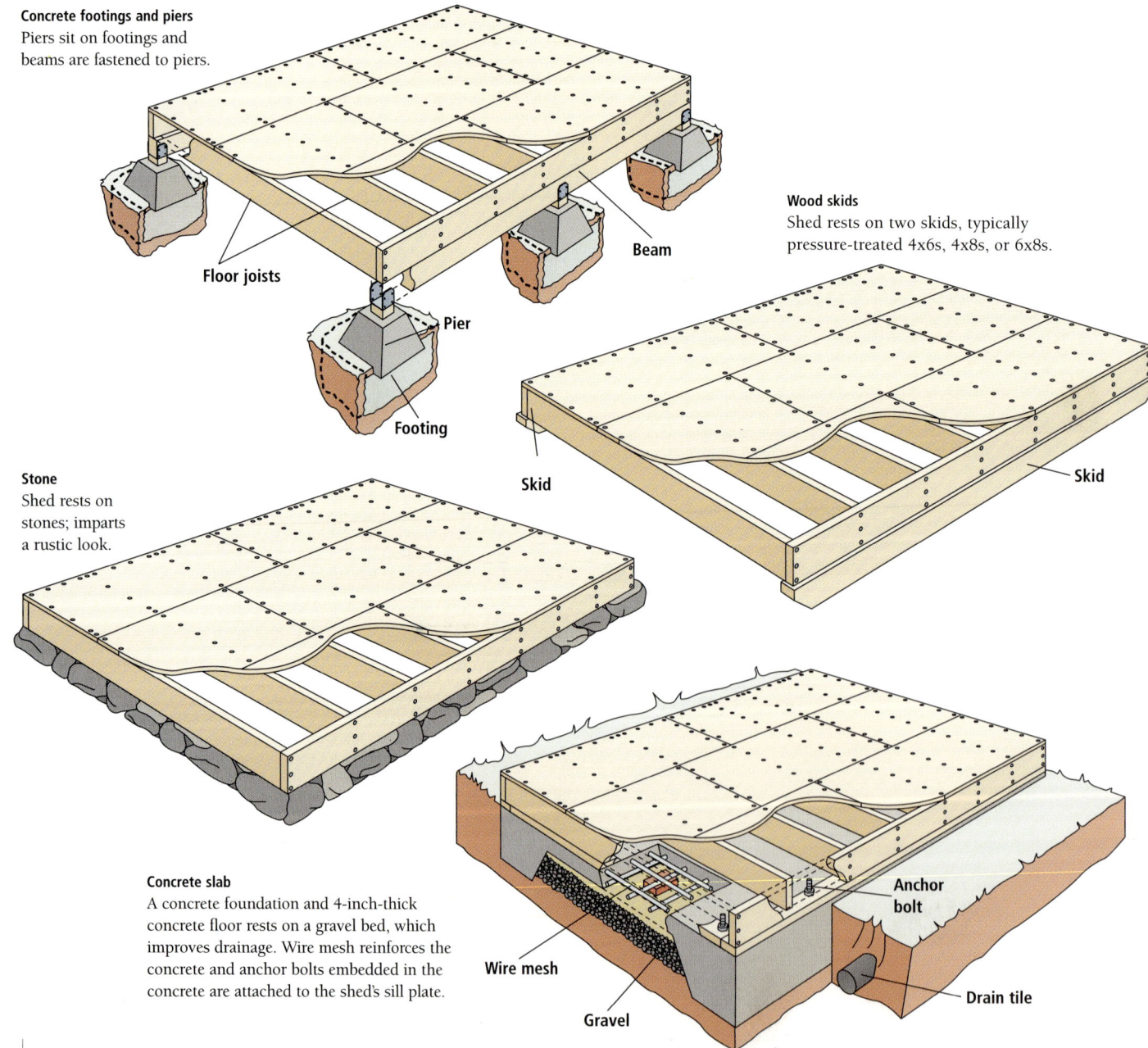

Concrete footings and piers
Piers sit on footings and beams are fastened to piers.

Wood skids
Shed rests on two skids, typically pressure-treated 4x6s, 4x8s, or 6x8s.

Stone
Shed rests on stones; imparts a rustic look.

Concrete slab
A concrete foundation and 4-inch-thick concrete floor rests on a gravel bed, which improves drainage. Wire mesh reinforces the concrete and anchor bolts embedded in the concrete are attached to the shed's sill plate.

Even more costly and labor intensive—but also more durable—is the **concrete slab** foundation. At 4 inches thick, a slab means you'll need to have the concrete delivered by a ready-mix truck. However, a slab comes with some hidden savings. It offers an all-in-one foundation and floor and puts the floor close to the ground, which may eliminate the need for a ramp.

If you like the rustic design of old country sheds, you can support the structure with a **stone** foundation. Similar to skids, this option can be the least costly of all, particularly if you have a lot of stone on your property.

GARAGE FOUNDATIONS

Garages require a concrete slab foundation. Three common choices are shown below, although you may be limited by where you live. In areas that do not experience frost, the simplest option is a **slab-on-grade** foundation, a 4-inch-thick slab with thicker, reinforced edges. In areas prone to freezing, you can opt for a **T-shaped** foundation—a slab framed by a foundation wall that goes down below the frost line—or a **frost-protected** foundation. This option, which is a version of the slab-on-grade foundation with insulated edges, should only be used for a heated garage.

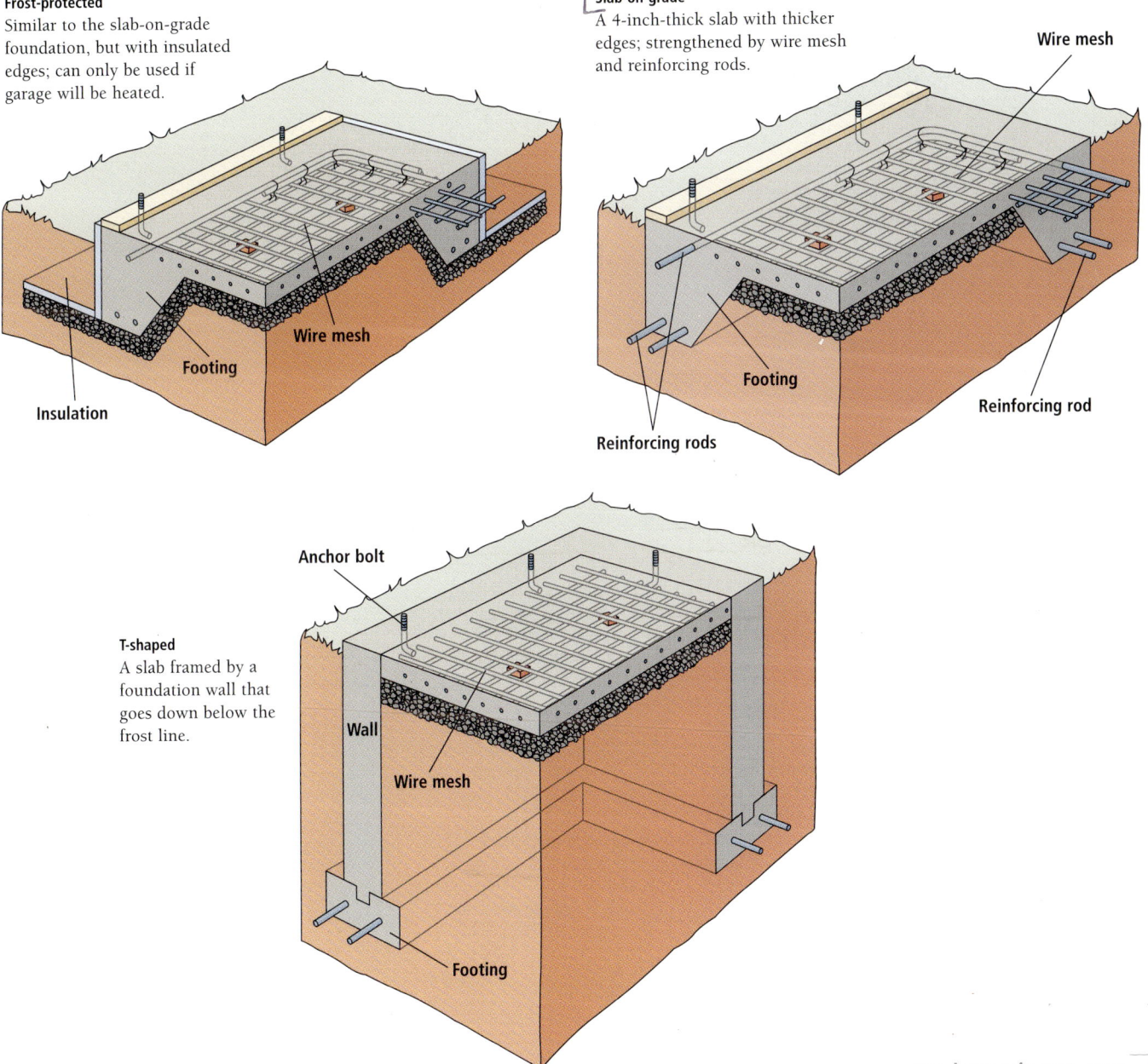

Frost-protected
Similar to the slab-on-grade foundation, but with insulated edges; can only be used if garage will be heated.

Slab-on-grade
A 4-inch-thick slab with thicker edges; strengthened by wire mesh and reinforcing rods.

T-shaped
A slab framed by a foundation wall that goes down below the frost line.

CHAPTER 2

Exterior Skin

As you raise the walls of your shed or garage, you will have two closely connected concerns: framing and sheathing, which impact the solidity of the structure, and siding, which influences design and appearance. Keep in mind that it is during the wall-framing stage that you will be thinking about and creating window and door openings. Try to locate and size these openings to harmonize with the doors and windows of your house.

The chart below compares the main types of sheathing used on sheds and garages, looking at the rigidity and insulating value of each along with other pros and cons. The photographs on page 35 show common wood siding choices for sheds and garages—including solid board, plywood, and cedar shingles—as well as vinyl siding. If it suits your design, you can apply a finish, such as paint or a preservative, to wood siding.

WALL SHEATHING	SIZES	RIGIDITY	INSULATING VALUE	PROS AND CONS
Exterior-grade plywood	Thickness of 1/2 inch or 15/32 inch typically used; sold in 4- x 8-foot panels	Superior	Poor	Can be installed vertically or horizontally; does not require diagonal bracing on wall
Exterior fiberboard	Available in thickness of 1/2 inch or 25/32 inch; sold in 2- x 8-foot panels	Moderate	Good	Easy to handle and install; requires diagonal bracing on wall
Exterior gypsum boards	Available in thickness of 1/2 inch; sold in 2- x 8-foot panels	Superior	Poor	Can be installed vertically or horizontally; siding must be nailed to studs
Rigid foam insulating boards	Sold in 4- x 8-foot and 4- x 9-foot panels	Poor	Superior	Adds no rigidity; siding must be nailed to studs

READING THE SHED AND GARAGE PLANS

Knowing how to interpret the plans in this book will help you choose the shed or garage that's best for you. The plans are all produced to professional standards, clearly indicating the layout, size and position of all the elements making up each structure. They are all drawn to scale, which varies from plan to plan. Most of them include the following elements:

- The **RENDERING** is an artist's representation of the shed or garage.

- The **PLAN VIEW** shows an overhead view of the shed or garage. It includes exterior dimensions and some details such as the sizes of studs, windows and doors.

- Next on shed plans is the **PIER LAYOUT**. It indicates the positions and distances between the concrete piers that support the structure. Also shown is the process by which these measurements are found—with mason's lines elevated on batterboards. An equivalent feature on garage plans is the **FOUNDATION PLAN**. This layout shows the concrete slab that supports the structure as well as the sill plates to which the walls are attached.

- On shed plans, the **FRAMING PLAN** shows the dimensions and types of materials for the understructure. The abbreviation **O.C.** refers to "on center," meaning that all measurements shown are taken from the center of each structural element to the center of the next one.

- Both shed and garage plans have **ELEVATIONS**, also referred to as side views, which indicate vertical dimensions as well as types and sizes of materials.

- **DETAILS** reveal the wall and roof structures shown from the side. A below-ground cutaway of the foundation is also shown. This view, combined with the other details of the structure, includes all the necessary materials and dimensions for the shed or garage.

Although you will very likely find a plan in this book that suits your needs and design sense, none of the plans is cast in stone. It's possible to make adjustments to the size or shape of a shed or garage. A rule of thumb for adjusting a plan is to work from the top down, beginning with the roof and walls, then making the necessary changes to the understructure. Work through all adjustments with a professional architect or builder who will be able to recommend appropriate structural changes.

CHAPTER 2

SKIN CARE: PAINTS AND PRESERVATIVES

If you're covering your shed or garage with wood siding, you'll need to apply a finish, both for appearance and protection. There are basically two choices: paint and wood preservatives. Your main concern, particularly with a garage, is to choose a product that matches or harmonizes with the finish of your house.

Paints: This is a good choice for covering unattractive siding. Paints fall into two categories: water-based (latex) and solvent-based (oil or alkyd). Latex paints are more environmentally friendly than solvent-based ones—in some areas, oil and alkyd paints are no longer available—and some siding manufacturers recommend latex. Paints come in three sheens: gloss, semi-gloss and flat. A good paint job can last about five years.

Wood preservatives: Preservatives are a popular choice with attractive wood such as cedar because they don't obscure the grain and character of the wood. Like paints, preservatives come in water- and solvent-based formulations. Although they don't cover surfaces as completely as paints, preservatives do alter the color of wood to varying degrees. For that reason, they are referred to as stains. Depending on how much you want to stain the wood, preservatives come in three versions. Transparent stains add little color, often intensifying the wood's original hue. Semi-transparent stains add color without obscuring the wood grain. Solid-color stains provide almost as much cover as paints. Most wood preservatives need to be reapplied once every couple of years, which means more maintenance than with painted structures.

(Photo: courtesy Hickory Dickory Decks)

DECIDING ON SIDING

Vinyl
This type of siding is relatively inexpensive, easy to install and requires virtually no maintenance; however, it is only available in a few colors and is subject to fading over time.

Solid board
Various types of solid board siding are available, including clapboard, tongue-and-groove and shiplap, which imparts a rustic flavor to a shed or garage.

Plywood
Sold as T1-11 siding, this option serves double-duty as wall sheathing and siding. Because of its large panel size (up to 4 feet wide and 8, 9 or 10 feet long), plywood siding can be installed rapidly.

Cedar shingles
A good choice for creating a rustic look, cedar shingles are relatively expensive and more challenging to install than other types of siding, especially around doors and windows.

WOOD PURCHASING POLICY

The Home Depot is committed to building a better world through sustainable business practices. Responsible wood purchasing is one step toward sustainability and presents a tremendous opportunity to meet our customers' demand for wood products while sustaining the forests for generations to come.

To learn more about The Home Depot's wood purchasing policies, please visit our web site at **www.homedepot.com**.

PRESSURE-TREATED LUMBER

Safety Alert!

Always wear eye protection, a dust mask and long clothes when cutting and handling pressure-treated lumber. Be sure you are working safely by checking out the important handling tips at **www.epa.gov/opp00001/citizens/1file.htm**.

CHAPTER 2

Raise the Roof

Most of the sheds and garages in the plan section of this book are topped with the ubiquitous gable roof, which slopes on two sides. This roof gets its name from the triangular gables at each end wall. One exception is the hip-roofed garage on page 110. Hip roofs slope on all four sides. Added features, such as clerestory windows *(page 103)*, dormer windows, cupolas and weather vanes, lend some variety to the designs. In addition, not all gable roofs are sloped the same way. In general, the steeper the slope, the more room there is overhead for storage or even a second floor. The illustrations below show how gable and hip roofs are framed.

It's in your choice of roofing material where you can really put your personal design stamp on a new shed or garage. Most of the plans in this book feature asphalt-shingle roofs, but there are other choices, including clay or concrete tiles, wood shakes and shingles, and metal roll roofing. A sampling of these options is illustrated on the opposite page.

ROOF FRAMING

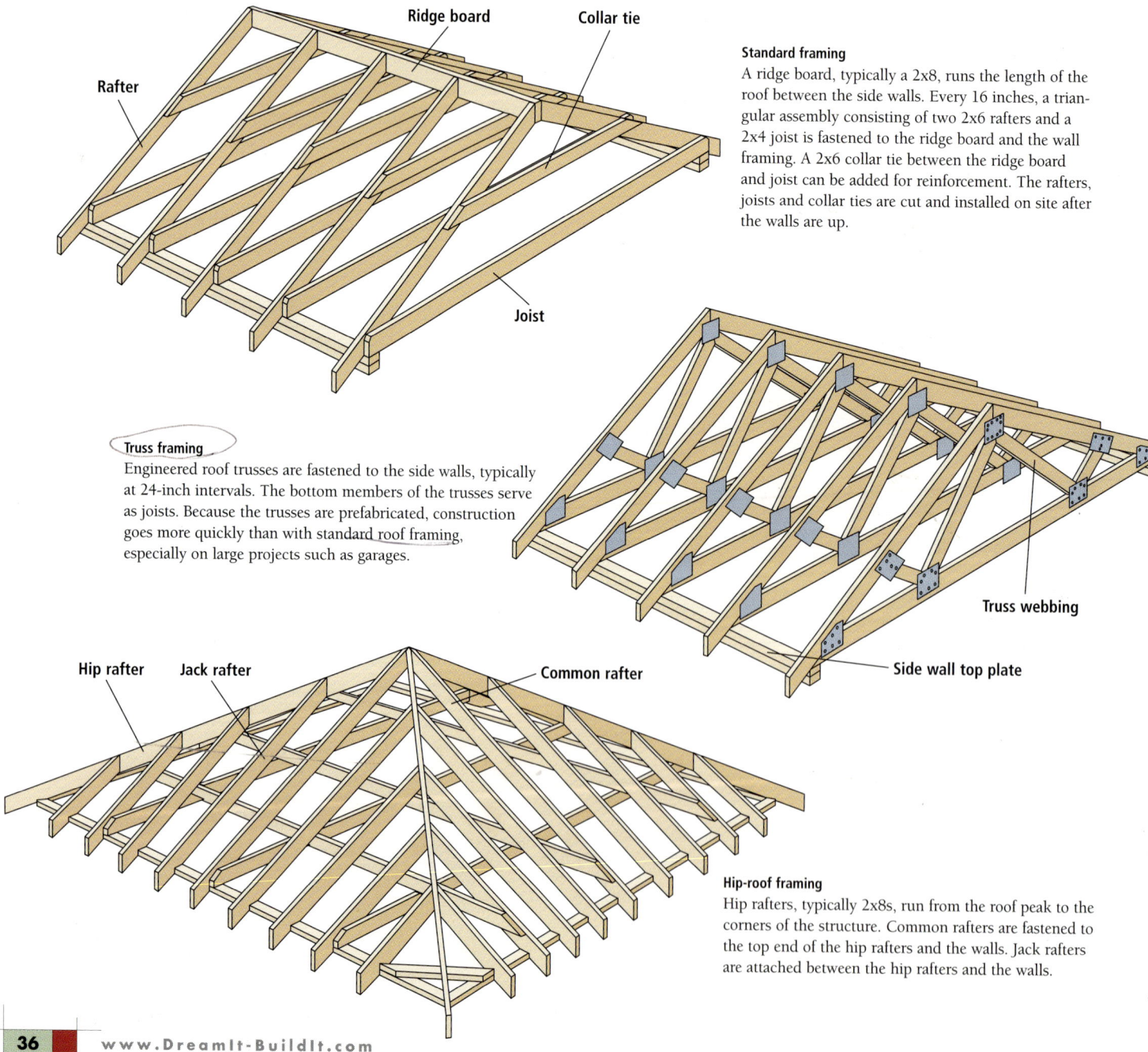

Standard framing
A ridge board, typically a 2x8, runs the length of the roof between the side walls. Every 16 inches, a triangular assembly consisting of two 2x6 rafters and a 2x4 joist is fastened to the ridge board and the wall framing. A 2x6 collar tie between the ridge board and joist can be added for reinforcement. The rafters, joists and collar ties are cut and installed on site after the walls are up.

Truss framing
Engineered roof trusses are fastened to the side walls, typically at 24-inch intervals. The bottom members of the trusses serve as joists. Because the trusses are prefabricated, construction goes more quickly than with standard roof framing, especially on large projects such as garages.

Hip-roof framing
Hip rafters, typically 2x8s, run from the roof peak to the corners of the structure. Common rafters are fastened to the top end of the hip rafters and the walls. Jack rafters are attached between the hip rafters and the walls.

CHAPTER 2

metal

ROOF MATERIALS

Roof tiles
Tiles are ideal for a traditional or Southwestern-style appearance. The concrete type is less costly than clay. Tiles are more time-consuming to install than shingles, but they can last for up to 100 years. Two varieties of tiles are shown here: undulating (*top*) and square (*bottom*). Your local Home Depot has a wide range of high-quality roofing materials in a range of decorative colors.

Cedar shakes
Provide a rustic look. Their advantage is that with proper care they can last for up to 30 years.

Asphalt shingles
Inexpensive, easy to install and virtually maintenance-free. Available in a wide range of colors, asphalt shingles can last for 15 to 20 years.

The muted earthy color of the asphalt-shingle roofing on this shed keeps the bold red door and cupola from overpowering the structure.
(Photo: Jean-Claude Hurni)

Focus on Appearance and Performance

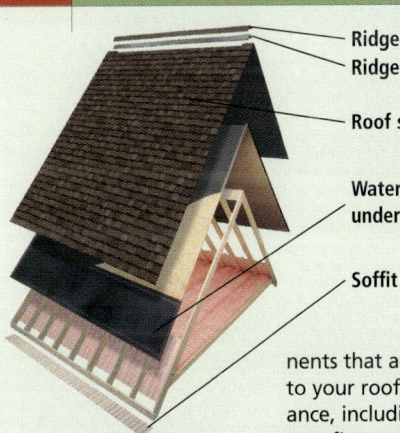

- Ridge shingles
- Ridge vent
- Roof shingles
- Waterproofing underlayment
- Soffit vent

Your home's roof, siding and trim play a major role in the overall appearance and performance of your home. It's the first impression people have of your home and your first line of defense against the elements.

Although your shingles make up the most visible part of your roof, **Owens Corning** makes several other components that are essential to your roof's performance, including waterproofing, ventilation and hip and ridge products. Once you've chosen quality roofing products, you're ready to select color scheme and style. There are many different options available.

Owens Corning also offers a wide selection of high-quality vinyl siding in different profiles, finishes and colors to complement your roof and coordinate with your overall exterior.

www.homedepot.com   37

CHAPTER 2

Windows and Doors

All sheds and garages are outfitted with doors and all but the most basic designs also feature windows. Windows not only let light into the structure, but those that can be opened enable air to be circulated. As you consider different window and door types, bear in mind that your choices should match or harmonize with their counterparts used for the house. Most of the plans in this book feature single-hung windows, but other options are shown in the illustrations at right, including fixed (or picture) windows, casement, horizontal slider, and awning.

The same range of choice applies to doors. If you are building a garage, you'll need a sectional door for the front. Single doors are available for one- and two-car garages, but double doors can also be used for multiple-bay structures. In either case, a garage-door opener is a convenience you probably won't want to do without. You'll also need an entry door for a shed and, depending on your design, a garage. Besides basic solid doors, you can choose a wood- or glass-panel door, as shown on page 39. In some areas, building codes may require a self-latching fire-resistant door for a garage.

Visit your local Home Depot store for a wide range of door and window options.

Windows on the world
Single-hung windows have two sashes, but only the bottom one moves up and down. Fixed windows don't open, but they can feature a variety of shapes or be mounted directly above a single-hung unit for decorative effect. Casement and awning windows have sashes that open outward, whereas horizontal sliders typically have two sashes that move in tracks.

Single-hung

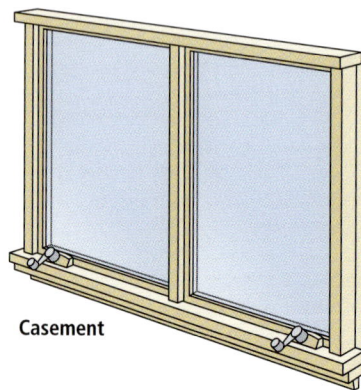
Casement

Awning

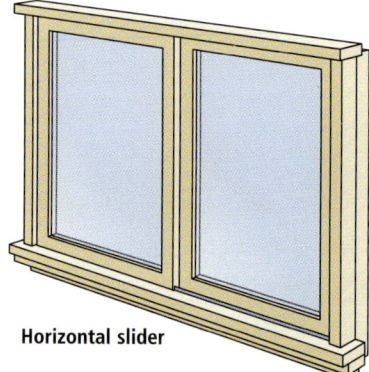
Horizontal slider

Fixed (rectangular)

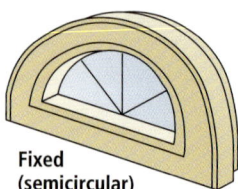
Fixed (semicircular)

The glass panels on this shed door echo the multiple-pane windows that flank the door on each side. White shutters and matching flower boxes framing the door lend the structure a homey character, while the arched window on the side wall imparts a touch of class and style.
(Photo: courtesy Summerwood Products)

CHAPTER 2

The front doors on this garage do more than just let the family cars in and out. The decorative strap hinges on the outer faces give the garage a Victorian touch. The bold red color of the doors is matched by the service door on the side. Such unifying design touches make this garage aesthetically pleasing.
(Photo: courtesy Garages by Opdyke)

Behind closed doors
In wood panel doors, rails and stiles frame wood panels; glass panel doors are made the same way, with glass panels instead of wood. The glass panels can be sized and configured to match windows. Some models feature both wood and glass panels. Panel doors are generally available with wood or metal veneer, combining strength and an attractive appearance. Flush doors are commonly made by covering a panel door with plywood veneer.

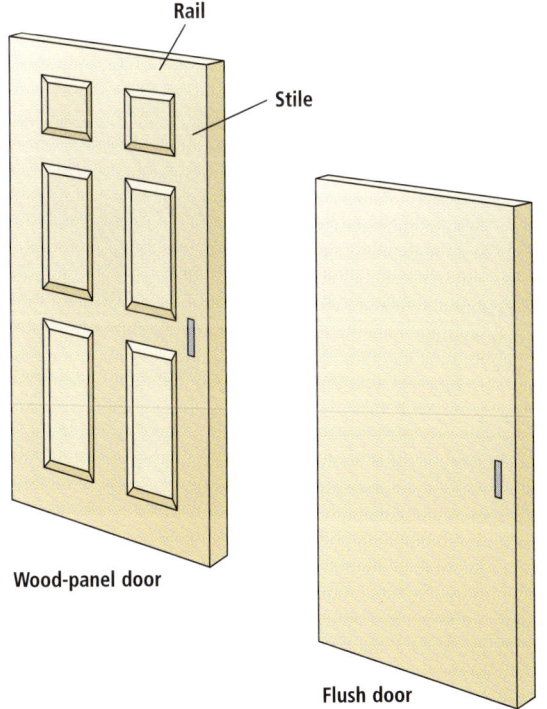

Wood-panel door

Flush door

Glass- and wood-panel door

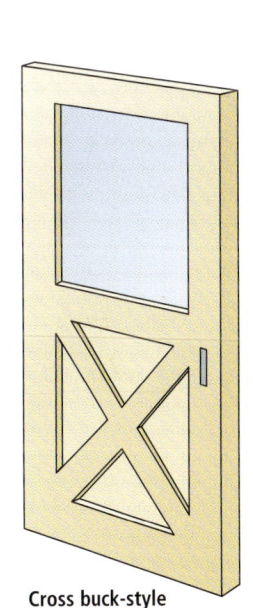

Cross buck-style glass-panel door

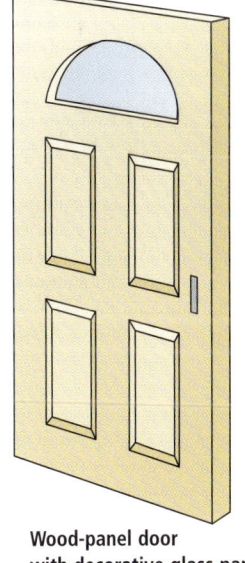

Wood-panel door with decorative glass panel

CHAPTER 2

Walls, Ceilings and Woodwork

Decorative wood trim can make a simple shed the focal point of backyard design. The gable end of this shed roof is finished with solid board siding in a fanfold design and the top corners of the porch overhead are dressed up with intricate scrollwork.
(Photo: courtesy Jamaica Cottage Shop)

Once you've got your shed or garage closed off to the elements, it's time to turn your attention to interior design. You can always leave framing members exposed—in fact, the spaces between studs and rafters can always be converted into storage areas—but for a more finished look, it's a good idea to hang drywall inside your shed or garage. Check local building codes; you may be required to hang fire-rated (type X) drywall in a wood-framed garage to help retard the spread of fire.

With the drywall hung and the joints between panels finished, it's time to paint the interior of your shed or garage. A good choice is latex paint, which dries quickly and requires only water for cleanup. In a garage that will be housing cars or a shed where you will store flammable substances, consider fire-retardant paint. High temperatures transform this paint into a foam that slows the spread of fire. The chart below compares different paint sheens—there's one for every design sense.

You can add character to a garage by installing trim and molding along the walls and floor. And as the photograph at left shows, exterior wood trim can breathe life into a shed. Check out your local Home Depot store for a sampling of the different types of molding and trim available.

INTERIOR PAINT	ADVANTAGES	DISADVANTAGES	APPLICATIONS
High gloss	Most resistant to staining; highly durable; cleans easily	Sheen will eventually fade, often in patches; light glares off surface; blemishes on surface are highlighted	Walls; door and window frames and casing
Semigloss	Durable; cleans easily; allows more time to apply special effects	Flaws on surface are highlighted	Walls, doors and wood trim
Satin and eggshell	Both sheens dry to a soft finish; more durable and resistant to staining than flat; cleans easily	Not as durable as semigloss or high gloss; can be damaged by water	Wood trim
Flat	Dries to a matte finish; downplays blemishes on surface; absorbs light rather than giving off glare	Has a softer finish and may scuff easily	Ceilings and walls

Keeping It Warm

Rigid-board insulation
Moisture resistant, this type does not require a moisture barrier; but it is flammable so it generally must be covered with drywall; offers an R-value of between 4.4 and 5 per inch of thickness.

Fiberglass batt
Fiberglass insulation is available in rolled blankets or batts, as shown here; blankets are ideal for insulating a garage quickly. Both forms are available in 14½-inch widths and in thicknesses between 3½ and 7 inches, and offer an R-value of between 3.1 and 3.7 per inch of thickness.

Insulation isn't only a worthwhile investment for your shed or garage if you live in a cold climate. Certainly, it will make interior spaces more comfortable and reduce heating costs in winter. But insulation will also help keep your shed or garage cooler in hot weather.

The best time to insulate a shed or garage is during construction, usually when the outer shell is closed off and you haven't yet covered the wall and roof framing with drywall. As shown in the photographs on this page, there are two main types of insulation you can use for the sheds and garages featured in this book.

Fiberglass insulation comes in two forms: rolled blankets and batts, which are precut into 4- or 8-foot-long rectangles. Blankets are preferable for insulating a large space quickly, but otherwise, blankets and batts share the same characteristics. They are the standard choice for insulating wood-framed walls and rafters. Whichever of the two you choose, get the type with a vapor barrier; placed on the warm side of the structure, the vapor barrier prevents moisture from condensing on cold surfaces. Blankets and batts come in standard 14½-inch widths to fit snugly between studs and in thicknesses between 3½ and 7 inches. The colder your climate, the thicker you need. Fiberglass doesn't quite provide the same insulating value per inch as rigid board insulation, but it's less expensive. In addition, although fiberglass can irritate your skin and lungs during installation—it's advisable to wear a dust mask, gloves and long sleeves—it is fire resistant, which is a plus for a garage or shed where you will store flammable materials.

Rigid-board insulation (known technically as extruded polystyrene) is the standard choice for insulating masonry walls. It is moisture resistant, so it does not require a vapor barrier. The main disadvantage of rigid insulation is its flammability; it gives off toxic fumes when it burns. Building codes generally require installation of ½-inch drywall over rigid insulation for fire protection.

Visit your local Home Depot when the time comes to choose insulating materials for your new shed or garage.

CHAPTER 3

FANCY ADD-ONS

Accessories

Who says a shed has to be plain and simple? A flower box brimming with annuals adds color and character to this basic tool shed. Shutters framing the window impart a welcoming, homey feel and the traditional strap hinges and latch on the door convey a rustic charm.
(Photo: courtesy Summerwood Products)

Although functionality may be your first priority when designing a shed or garage project, there is a wide range of accessories that can personalize the structure. Options include ramps (for wheeling heavy items up to the door), window boxes and shutters, porch lights, weather vanes and cupolas. As shown on page 43, you can even add a deck or landing to a shed.

Keep in mind when designing your shed or garage project that subtle accents can sometimes become the crowning touch of the structure, packing a powerful design punch. Although a cupola, for example, may appear to serve no apparent purpose, a model with louvered openings will help ventilate your shed or garage, carrying warm air and humidity up and out of the structure. And while porch lights can add a decorative touch to your design, they also enhance both safety and security by clearing the way in and out of a shed or garage at night and by discouraging intruders.

Likewise, a ramp is a virtual necessity for a shed that will house heavy equipment such as lawn tractors, snow throwers or wheelbarrows. Be sure to design the ramp wide enough to accommodate the equipment—36 inches is typically adequate—and build with pressure-treated lumber since the ramp will be in contact with the ground or close to it.

You'll find an extensive variety of add-ons to outfit your new shed or garage at your local Home Depot store.

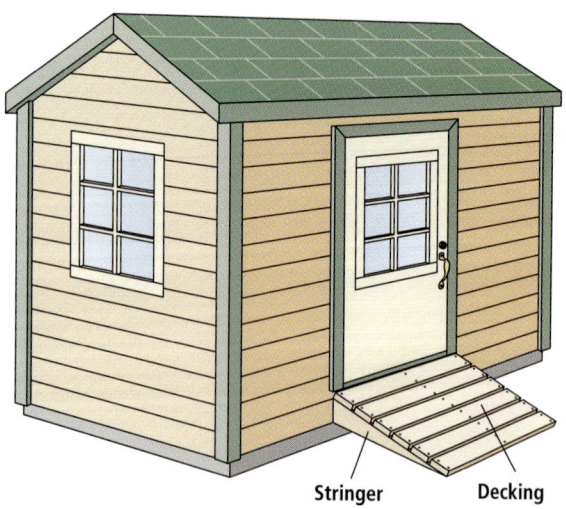

Adding a ramp
For a shed that will store large wheeled items such as a riding mower or a wheelbarrow, a ramp in front of the door is a valuable addition. Built as wide as the door, a ramp is typically made with 2x6 decking on 2x4 stringers. The stringers are fastened to a 2x4 nailer which, in turn, is bolted to the shed framing.

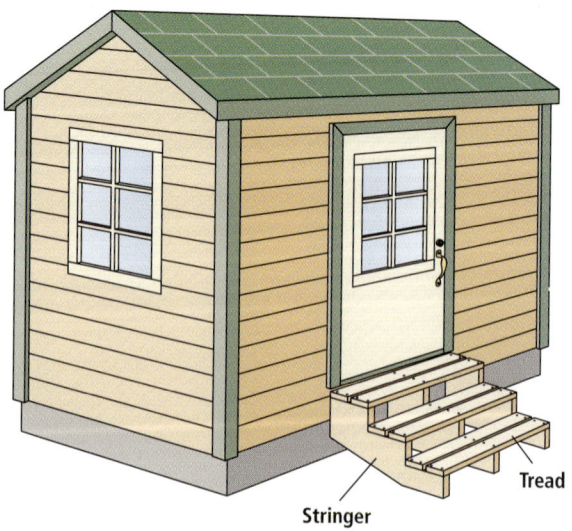

Adding stairs
For a shed that will store items that can be carried in and out, stairs are an invaluable addition if the door threshold is more than a few inches above ground level. Here, treads of 2x6 decking are fastened to 2x10 stringers, which are attached to the shed framing.

Adding a Deck or Landing

This shed has the inviting feel of a cabin in the woods. Part of the shed's allure comes from its spacious size, but several other features make it more than just a backyard warehouse. Matching single-hung windows open up the interior to light and air, with curtains to ensure privacy and shade the interior from direct sunlight. The low-level deck is a valuable add-on that provides a spot for relaxing in the open air.
(Photo: courtesy Handy Home Products)

Floating Foundation Deck System

Over the life of a deck—even one attached to a shed—the frost heave that occurs in winter can lift posts from their original positions, causing significant damage to the structural integrity of the deck. The standard method for preventing this damage is to anchor the posts to concrete piers dug and poured down to the frost line, with deeper and wider concrete footings at the bottom.

With no holes to dig and no concrete to mix, **DekBrands** floating foundation deck system offers an easier and less expensive solution to frost-heave damage. As shown in the illustration, the system uses precast piers that sit on top of the ground, moving up and down to accommodate frost movement. The **DekBrands** floating foundation deck system is strong, durable and safe. Designed in accordance with all national building codes, it far exceeds minimum structural construction requirements when built according to plan.

Structures that Shed Water

The number one cause of water infiltration into a building, whether a house, a garage or a shed, is poor drainage around the perimeter of the structure. One part of the solution is to make sure the ground around your new shed or garage slopes away from the walls. Another part of the answer is a system of gutters and downspouts designed to collect the water that runs off the roof and carry it away from the structure. The illustration below shows a typical setup.

Gutters are available in two main materials: aluminum and vinyl. Although either type will do the trick of removing water runoff from your new shed or garage, each material has its own characteristics. Aluminum, for example, can be painted whereas vinyl cannot. Vinyl gutters and downspouts are usually available only in white, so aluminum may be a better choice if you have a specific color design in mind. On the plus side, vinyl is less expensive and easier to install.

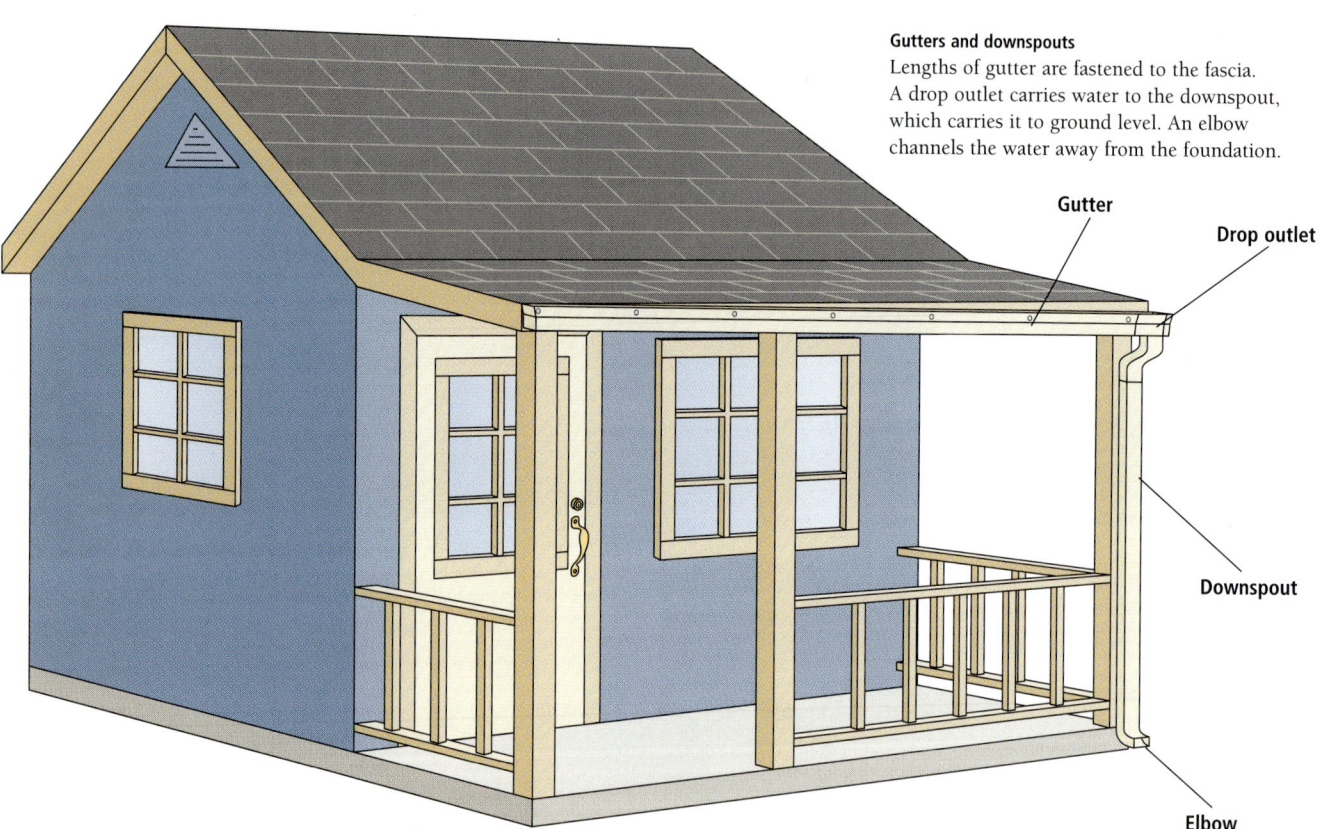

Gutters and downspouts
Lengths of gutter are fastened to the fascia. A drop outlet carries water to the downspout, which carries it to ground level. An elbow channels the water away from the foundation.

Gutter
Drop outlet
Downspout
Elbow

A "Tuff" Alternative for Overheads

An overhead is a great way to shield a shed or garage door or landing from the elements. An overhead doesn't have to be made of a traditional material such as wood. Corrugated polycarbonate sheets manufactured by **Suntuf** offer many of wood's advantages and possess several benefits that wood cannot match. Combining light weight with strength, **Suntuf** sheets resist wind and hail as well as physical abuse and they won't distort in hot weather or become brittle in winter. They are available in a wide variety of transparent, translucent and opaque colors to suit most designs. And while transparent and translucent sheets transmit light with the clarity of glass, all three types provide protection from harmful ultraviolet rays. This makes **Suntuf** sheets a good choice for an overhead above a door or landing that will be exposed to direct sunlight.

Perhaps best of all, **Suntuf** sheets don't require professional installation. If you can build a shed yourself, then you can install these sheets. They are easy to handle and can be cut and drilled with standard tools.

(Photo: courtesy Suntuf / Elizabeth Benham)

CHAPTER 3

The Comforts of Home

If you plan to incorporate a workshop or living quarters in your new shed or garage, you will need to run electricity and plumbing to the structure. The scope of your project will determine how extensive a wiring and plumbing job you have in store. For a modest backyard shed, you may only need to run a single electrical circuit from your house to the shed to power lights and perhaps an outlet. For a garage with a workshop and a second-story apartment, on the other hand, the work will be more extensive. On the plumbing side of the ledger, you'll need to extend water supply pipes to the garage for a sink, an outdoor faucet and perhaps a bathtub or shower stall. Drain-waste and vent (DWV) pipes will also be required. You will also need to run several electrical circuits to the structure, at least one for lighting and one or more additional ones for tool and appliance outlets, a garage-door opener and a hot-water heater. Depending on the capacity of your existing service panel, this can mean replacing the panel with a larger one and/or installing a subpanel in the new garage.

Lighting adds to the inviting whimsy of this minitiature home.
(Photo: courtesy Limestone Trail Company Ltd.)

Don't allow the plumbing and wiring needs of your new shed or garage to become an afterthought. You need to plan and decide what you want to do early on. With a garage, for instance, the DWV piping must be installed even before the foundation is poured. And electrical wiring is almost always installed before the interior walls are closed in.

In most cases, you will need individual permits for plumbing and electrical extensions. As mentioned on page 22, it's advisable to have your general contractor or your plumbing and electrical contractors apply for the permits so they—and not you—are responsible for making sure the work conforms to the applicable codes.

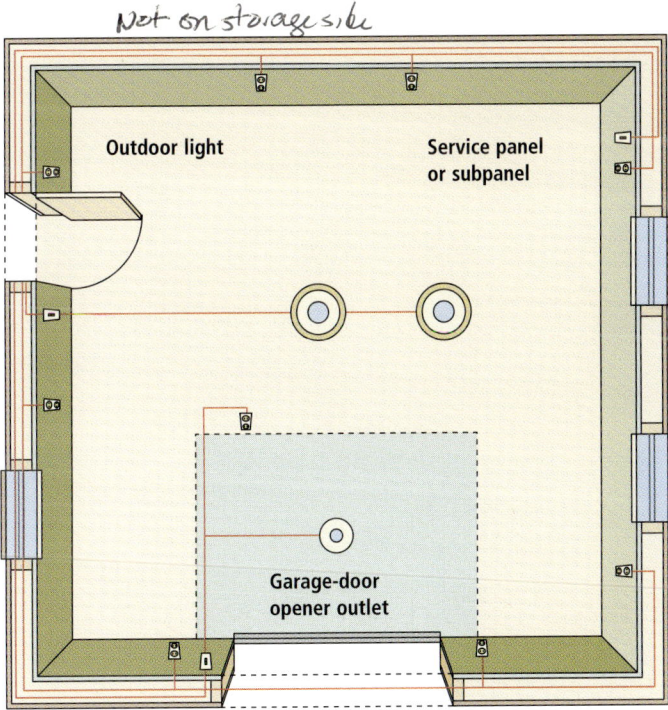

Shed some light
The illustration above depicts a typical wiring layout for a garage. The drawing shows the locations of indoor and outdoor light fixtures, two outlets for garage-door openers, another outlet in a storage or workshop area and a service panel or subpanel at the service door.

WIRING 1-2-3

Learn how to install new fixtures, run cable, add circuits or rewire and detach old wires in The Home Depot's *Wiring 1-2-3*. In addition, find out how to select the best materials for your shed, garage or other project and how to avoid common mistakes.

www.homedepot.com 45

CHAPTER 3

Storage

The need for storage—whether for the lawn mower or the family car—is probably what prompted your desire to design and build a shed or garage in the first place. Knowing how you will use a new shed or garage and what you will store in it can help you choose the most appropriate structure for your needs (*pages 24-27*) and help you select the most ideal shed or garage plan for you.

Making efficient use of the storage space inside a shed or garage takes some planning. Without a little forethought, your storage strategy will become haphazard, turning your new shed or garage into a disorganized repository for tools, clothing and discarded items.

There is a lot you can do to maximize the storage potential of a shed or garage. For example, many of the plans in this book include construction details for adding shelves and cupboards along the walls of the structures. Shelves and cupboards are ideal for reducing clutter and organizing all sorts of items, from tools and toys to out-of-season clothing and sports equipment, without cutting into the floor space in a shed or garage. They can also be locked, making them useful for keeping chemicals and other potentially hazardous materials out of the reach of children.

Don't overlook the space between a garage ceiling and the roof of your car. Racks anchored to the ceiling or roof rafters

A place for everything
With one wall lined with garden tools and cabinets along adjoining walls, this garage features a well-organized storage system.

can be used to store lumber, skis or even bicycles. Keep the following pointers in mind as you develop a storage system for your new shed or garage:

• Store like items together. For example, if a shed will be used to store both gardening and home-repair tools, plan on keeping the gardening implements in one section of the space and the repair tools in another.

• Let the size and weight of an item determine how you store it. For example, big and heavy objects should be set on the floor, whereas flat or thin items can be hung on a wall. Place small items in drawers, cabinets or bins, and suspend large, light objects from the ceiling or roof rafters.

• Plan your storage so that the placement of items makes it easier to carry out the activities for which they are used. Consider the people who will use the storage space. Storage areas for children's toys, for example, should be low to the ground and within easy reach. Also consider how frequently belongings are used. Those that are used often should be more accessible than items that sit idle most of the time.

• Consider rotating your storage system according to the seasons. By reorganizing your storage two or three times a year, you can make snow shovels, skates and skis more accessible in winter and move bikes, garden tools and basketballs to the foreground when there is no snow on the ground.

(Photo: courtesy Knape & Vogt Manufacturing)

Reach for the Top

Whether you are working on the roof or installing an electrical box in the ceiling, you'll need a sturdy ladder to get to the right height. **Werner Co.**, the professional's choice, makes a variety of climbing equipment for your building needs.

Safety is paramount when working at heights. If you are using a stepladder, follow these pointers:

• Use a ladder that is 2 feet longer than the height you need to stand.
• Place the ladder on firm, flat ground, open the legs fully and lock the spreader braces.
• Don't stand higher than the third step from the top.

(Photos: courtesy Werner Co.)

CHAPTER 4

Our Most Popular Shed and Garage Plans

In the pages that follow we present our most popular shed and garage plans. Our selection includes a variety of storage options and styles so that you can adapt your project to your yard, your needs and even the style of your home. Who says that a storage shelter has to look like a warehouse? Our Southwestern-style garage and charming country-style sheds let you complement your home with a storage solution that you'll want seen in plain view. Each shed, garage and carport plan included in this book is followed by a complete construction plan and material list. Depending on the complexity of the structure, the following drawings are included:

- Plan Rendering
- Pier Layout
- Elevations
- Plan View
- Framing Plan
- Details

Once you've selected the plan that you'd like to build, take the material list to your local Home Depot store to purchase everything you'll need to begin construction. To get more information on these plans or to see our other project plans, visit us at www.DreamIt-BuildIt.com, where you'll find these additional building aides:

- A comprehensive list of recommended materials
- A tools list
- "Build-It Guide" with illustrations
- Tips on how to build your project smarter and safer
- A glossary of project-related building terms

To see the quality of our complete project plans, download our FREE doghouse plan. Our site also offers the largest on-line inventory of home plans. Call 1-888-314-1303 for more information.

"He who plans and follows out that plan, carries a thread that will guide him through the maze of the most busy life. But where no plan is laid, chaos will soon reign."
Victor Hugo
(Photo: Jean-Claude Hurni)

DISCLAIMER

Building Codes: Variations in building codes, specific local development covenants or site conditions may require modification to the design of the project plans and other information contained in this publication. You are ultimately responsible for complying with all applicable permit, building codes and other regulatory requirements. Be sure to review the plans with your local building inspector and acquire all appropriate building permits before starting your project. The project plans have been designed in accordance with the Uniform Building Code (UBC 1997).

Accuracy: There always exists a possibility for errors or omissions in the project plans and other information contained in this publication. Therefore, you and/or your building contractor(s) shall assume the responsibility of verifying all conditions and dimensions contained within a project plan prior to the start of construction. Please report any discrepancies to HomeStyles, Inc. at 1-888-314-1303 for verification and/or correction before proceeding with construction. You and/or your building contractor(s) shall assume responsibility for errors that are not reported. HomeStyles' warranty for errors and omissions is limited to, and may not exceed, the amount of fees collected for the design services related to the purchase of these plans. The Home Depot, Inc. and its directors, officers, employees, affiliates and subsidiaries specifically disclaim all warranties and conditions of any kind.

Liability: Neither The Home Depot, Inc. and its directors, officers, employees, affiliates and subsidiaries nor HomeStyles shall have any liability or responsibility for your action or inaction in connection with any project plan or any other information contained in this publication or for any damage or liability that arises during the construction and/or use of any project or project plan. Always read and observe all of the safety precautions provided by any tool or equipment manufacturer and follow all accepted safety procedures.

Materials Lists: Materials Lists are based upon the drawings contained in this plan set. Actual quantities may vary based upon actual site conditions.

CHAPTER 4

THE TUCSON   HPM-1404
Dimensions for this shed are 10' X 8'.
80 sq. ft.

THE TUCSON & SIERRA

With their tiled roofs and stucco exteriors, these Southwestern-style sheds are distinctive and durable. Each shed features three stylish arched windows and handy double doors to allow for storage of wide items. The front ramp makes moving large items in and out convenient. What differentiates this handsome pair is the addition of a big workbench and built-in cabinets in the larger shed (Sierra).

THE SIERRA   HPM-1304
Dimensions for this shed are 14' X 10'.
140 sq. ft.

www.homedepot.com   49

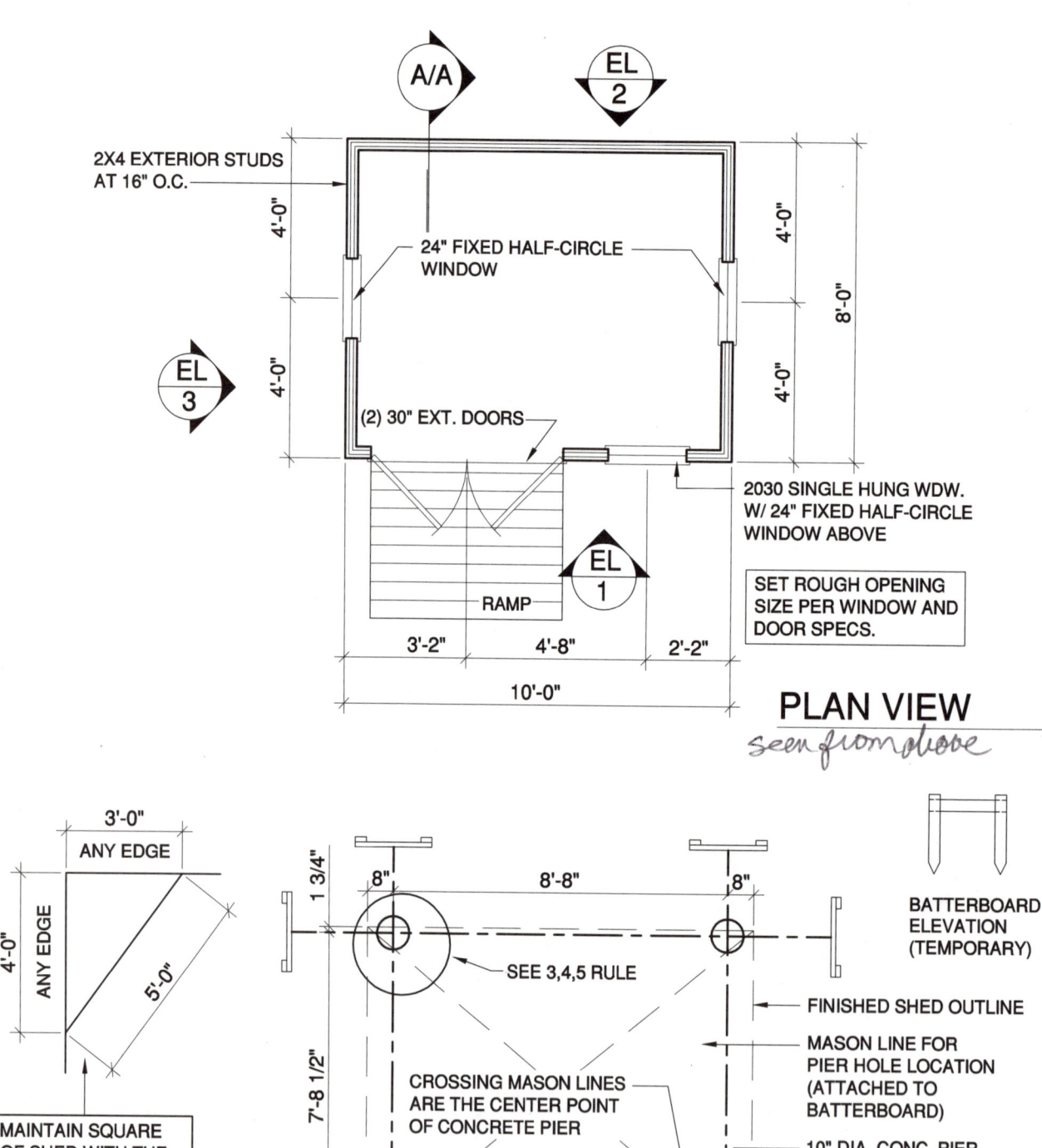

Tucson — Elevation and Framing Plan

Scale: 1/4" = 1'-0"

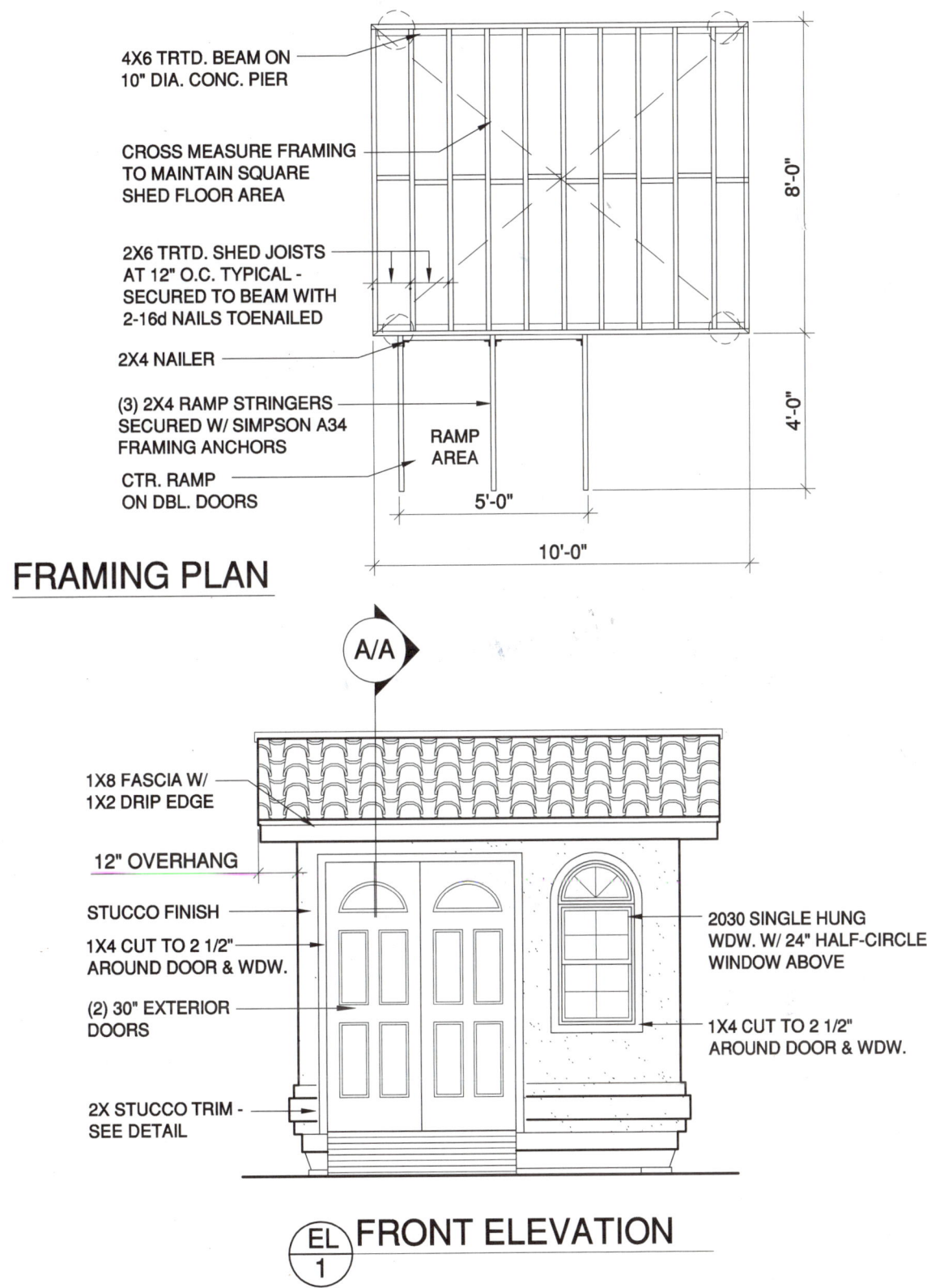

FRAMING PLAN

- 4X6 TRTD. BEAM ON 10" DIA. CONC. PIER
- CROSS MEASURE FRAMING TO MAINTAIN SQUARE SHED FLOOR AREA
- 2X6 TRTD. SHED JOISTS AT 12" O.C. TYPICAL - SECURED TO BEAM WITH 2-16d NAILS TOENAILED
- 2X4 NAILER
- (3) 2X4 RAMP STRINGERS SECURED W/ SIMPSON A34 FRAMING ANCHORS
- CTR. RAMP ON DBL. DOORS
- RAMP AREA
- 8'-0"
- 4'-0"
- 5'-0"
- 10'-0"

FRONT ELEVATION (EL/1)

- 1X8 FASCIA W/ 1X2 DRIP EDGE
- 12" OVERHANG
- STUCCO FINISH
- 1X4 CUT TO 2 1/2" AROUND DOOR & WDW.
- (2) 30" EXTERIOR DOORS
- 2X STUCCO TRIM - SEE DETAIL
- 2030 SINGLE HUNG WDW. W/ 24" HALF-CIRCLE WINDOW ABOVE
- 1X4 CUT TO 2 1/2" AROUND DOOR & WDW.

Tucson — Elevations and Details

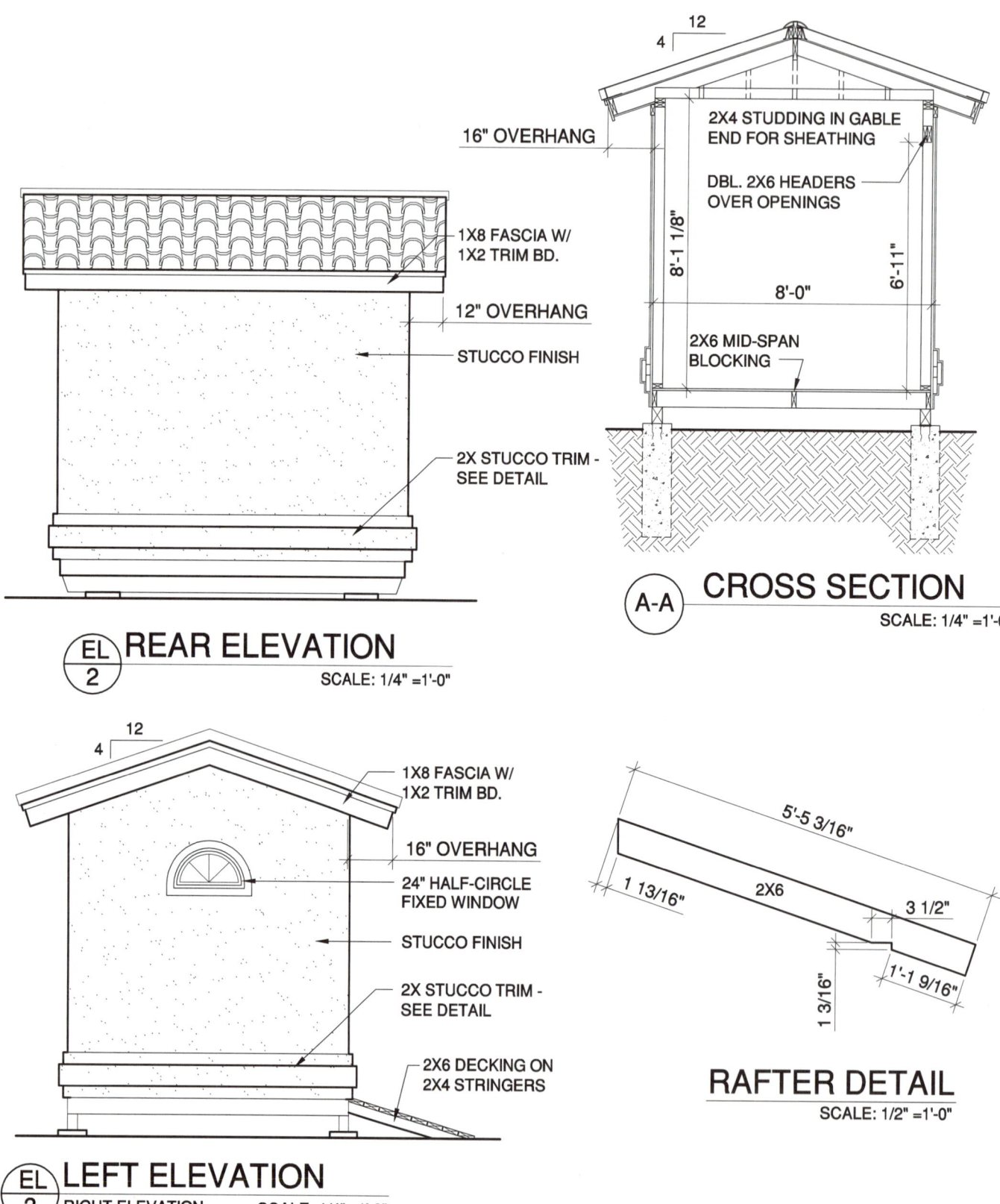

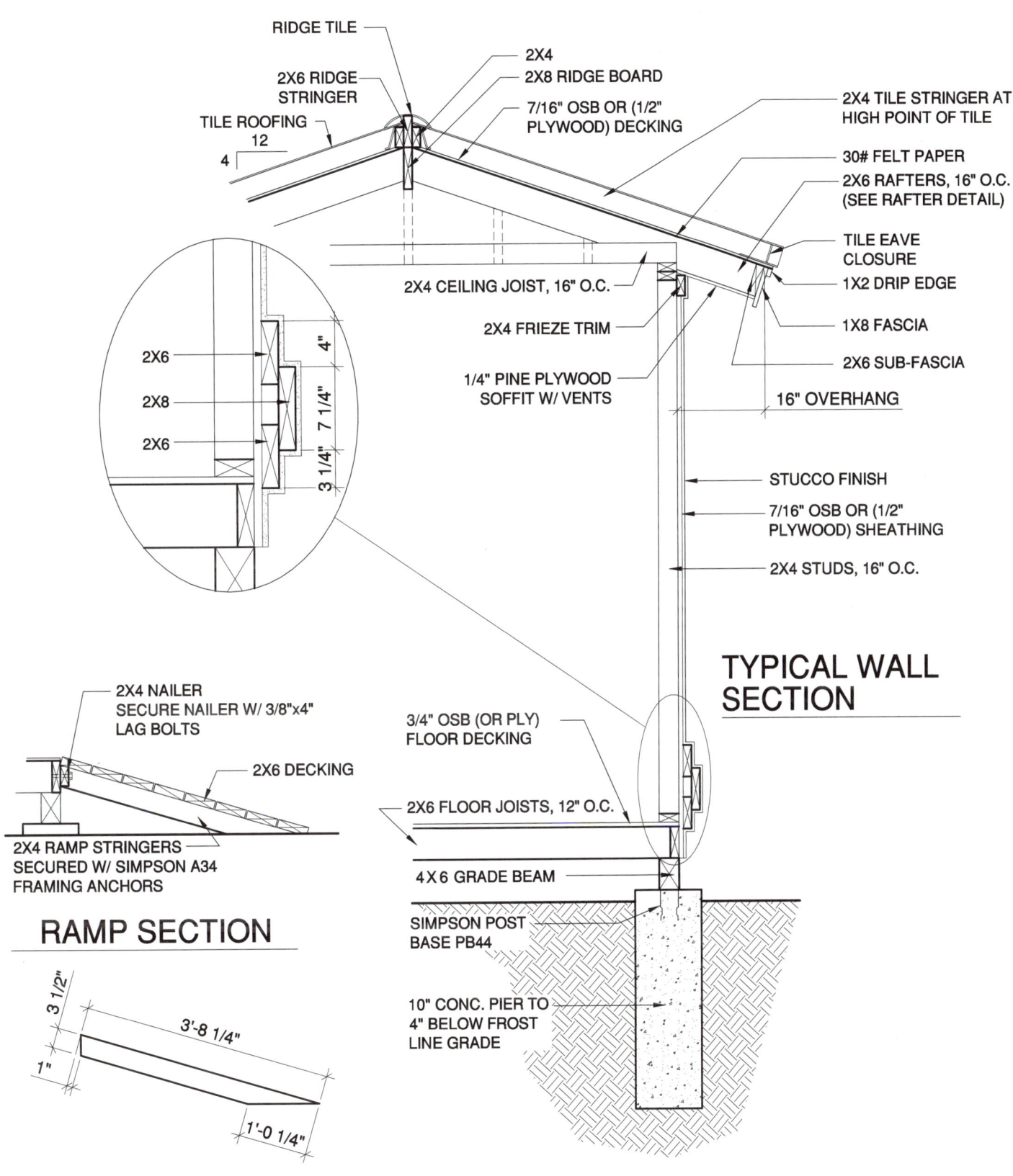

Tucson Material List

FOUNDATION

Item	Location	Qty	UM
60# Concrete Mix	Pier	20	BG
10"x 48" Fiber Tube	Pier	4	EA
2x4 - 10' Std. & Btr.	Batterboard	5	EA
Post Base (PB 44)	Pier	4	EA
1/2" Hex. Hd. Nut	Post Base	8	EA
1/2"x4-1/2" Bolt	Post Base	8	EA
1/2" Washer	Post Base	16	EA
Crushed Gravel	Pier	4	CF

FLOOR

Item	Location	Qty	UM
4x6 - 12' Treated	Beam	2	EA
2x4 - 10' Treated	Nailer/Stringer	2	EA
2x6 - 8' Treated	Floor Joist	11	EA
2x6 - 10' Treated	Jst./Blkg./Rmp.	7	EA
3/4" T & G OSB (PLY.)	Floor Decking	3	EA
Framing Anchor (A34)	Flr. Frmg.	8	EA
3/8"x4" Lag Screws	Nailer	4	EA
3/8"x1-1/2" Washer	Nailer	4	EA
5# 16d Galv. Nails	General Framing	1	EA
5# 8d Ctd. Box Nails	General Framing	1	EA
1# 2-1/2" Ctd. Ext. Screws	General Framing	1	EA
Construction Adhesive	Floor Decking	2	TB

WALL FRAMING

Item	Location	Qty	UM
2x4 - 96" Stud Grade	Stud	39	EA
2x4 - 8' Treated	Bottom Plate	2	EA
2x4 - 10' Treated	Bottom Plate	2	EA
2x4 - 8' Std. & Btr.	Top/Cap Plate	4	EA
2x4 - 10' Std. & Btr.	Top/Cap Plate	4	EA
2x4 - 96" Stud Grade	Blocking	11	EA
2x6 - 8' Std. & Btr.	Header	2	EA
2x6 - 10' Std. & Btr.	Header	2	EA
7/16 OSB (Ply.)	Wall Sheathing	10	EA
5# 16d Galv. Nails	General Framing	2	EA
5# 8d Ctd. Box Nails	General Framing	2	EA
1x6 - 10' Std. & Btr.	Bracing	6	EA
40"x 97' Bldg. Paper	Wall Covering	1	RL
5# 1/2" Roofing Nails	Wall Covering	1	EA

CEILING/ROOF

Item	Location	Qty	UM
2x4 - 8' Std. & Btr.	Clg. Jst./Rake	18	EA
2x4 - 96" Stud Grade	Gable Wall	1	EA
2x4 - 10' Std. & Btr.	Frieze	2	EA
2x4 - 12' Std. & Btr.	Ridge Blocking	2	EA
2x6 - 8' Std. & Btr.	Rafter	18	EA
2x6 - 10' Std. & Btr.	Stucco Trim	4	EA
2x6 - 12' Std. & Btr.	Stucco Trim	4	EA
2x6 - 12' Std. & Btr.	Sub-Fascia/Ridge	3	EA
2x4 - 10' Std. & Btr.	Fascia/Soffit Nailer	7	EA
2x8 - 12' Std. & Btr.	Rdg. Bd./Trim	5	EA
1x2 - 8' S4S Vert. Grn.	Drip Edge	7	EA
1x8 - 10' #2 & Btr.	Fascia	4	EA
1x8 - 12' #2 & Btr.	Fascia	2	EA
7/16" OSB (Ply.)	Roof Decking	5	EA
2x2 - 8' Std. & Btr.	Rake Tile Stringer	4	EA
2x4 - 8' Std. & Btr.	Tile Stringer	28	EA
135 SF Roof Tile	Roof	2	SQ
Ridge Tile	Ridge	12	LF
Ridge Cover Starter Tile	Ridge	2	EA
Rake Tile (End Band)	Rake	24	LF
Eave Closure	Eave	40	EA
Top Fixture	Ridge	40	EA
30-lb. Asphalt Rfg. Felt	Roofing	1	RL
Galv. Drip Edge	Roof Edge	7	EA
5# 8d Ctd. Box Nails	General Framing	2	EA
5# 10d Bright Box Nails	General Framing	2	EA
5# 16d Galv. Nails	General Framing	1	EA
5# 1/2" Roofing Nails	Roofing Felt	1	EA
1-3/4" Stainless Nails	Roof Tile	40	LB
5# 6d Galv. Box Nails	General Framing	1	EA
5# 6d Galv. Finish Nails	Siding/Soffit	1	EA

EXTERIOR TRIM & ACCESSORIES

Item	Location	Qty	UM
80# One Coat Stucco	Wall	24	BG
Furred Stucco Netting	Wall	1	RL
1/2"x10' Casing Bead	Window/Door	5	EA
10' 1A Stucco Corner Bead	Corner	22	EA
5-1/2" #7 Fnd. Sill Screen	Sill	4	ea
1x4 - 8' Std. & Btr.	Window Trim	5	EA
1/4" Plywood (Sanded)	Soffit Material	2	EA
14x6 Metal Soffit Vent	Soffit	4	EA
(2) 30"x 80" Exterior Door	Exterior Door	1	EA
2030 SH Window	Window	3	EA
24" Half-Circle Window	Window	3	EA
Lockset/Deadbolt/Pin	Exterior Door	1	EA
5# 6d Galv. Finish Nails	Soffit	2	EA
5# 8d Galv. Finish Nails	Window/Door	1	EA
10 oz. - Paintable Caulk	Trim	3	TB
1-1/4"x 2" Brickmold	Exterior Door	3	EA
4" - 10' "Z" Flashing	Window/Door	2	EA

SIERRA — Plan View and Pier Layout

Scale: 1/4" = 1'-0"

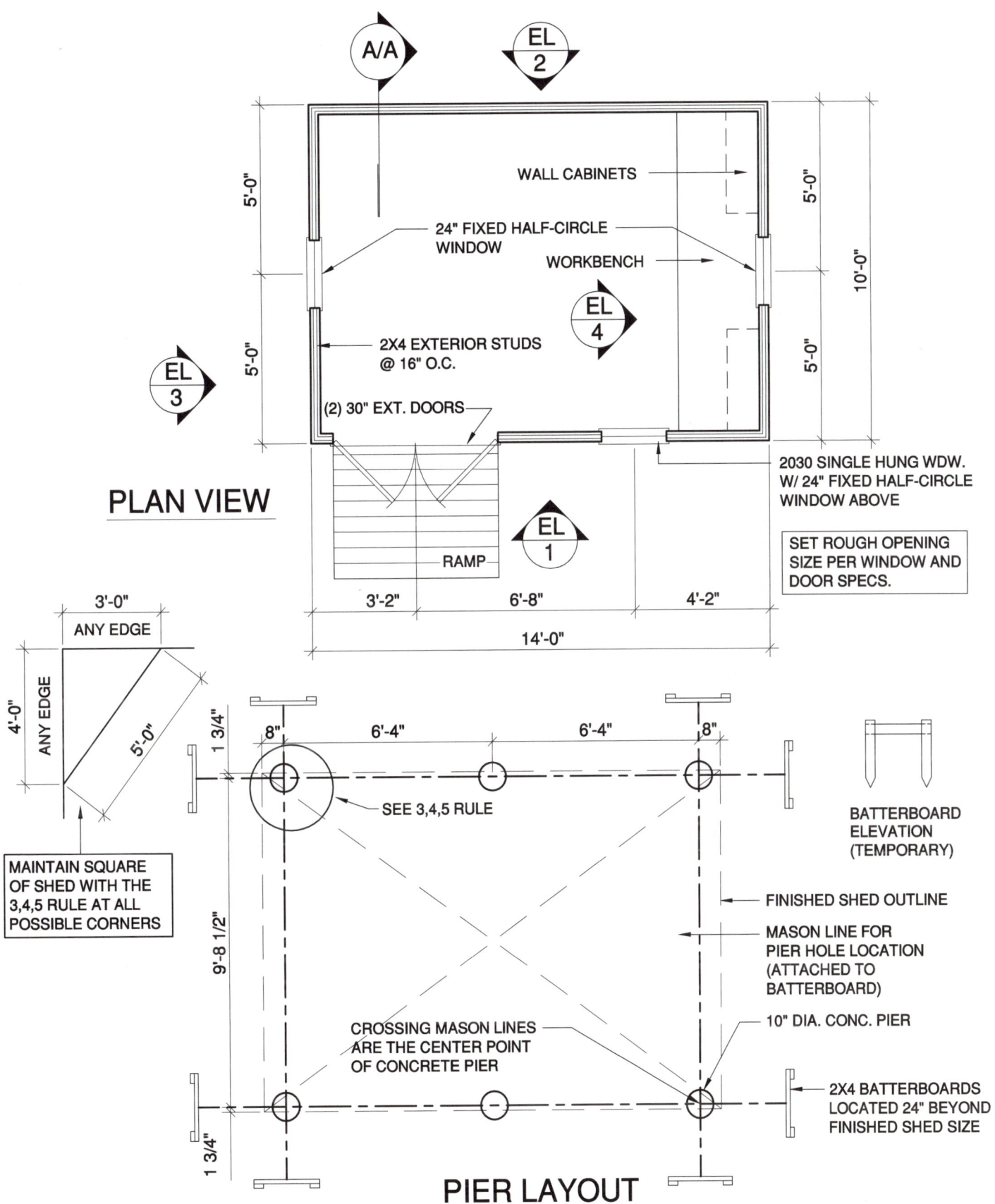

www.homedepot.com 55

SIERRA
Framing Plan and Elevation
Scale: 1/4" = 1'-0"

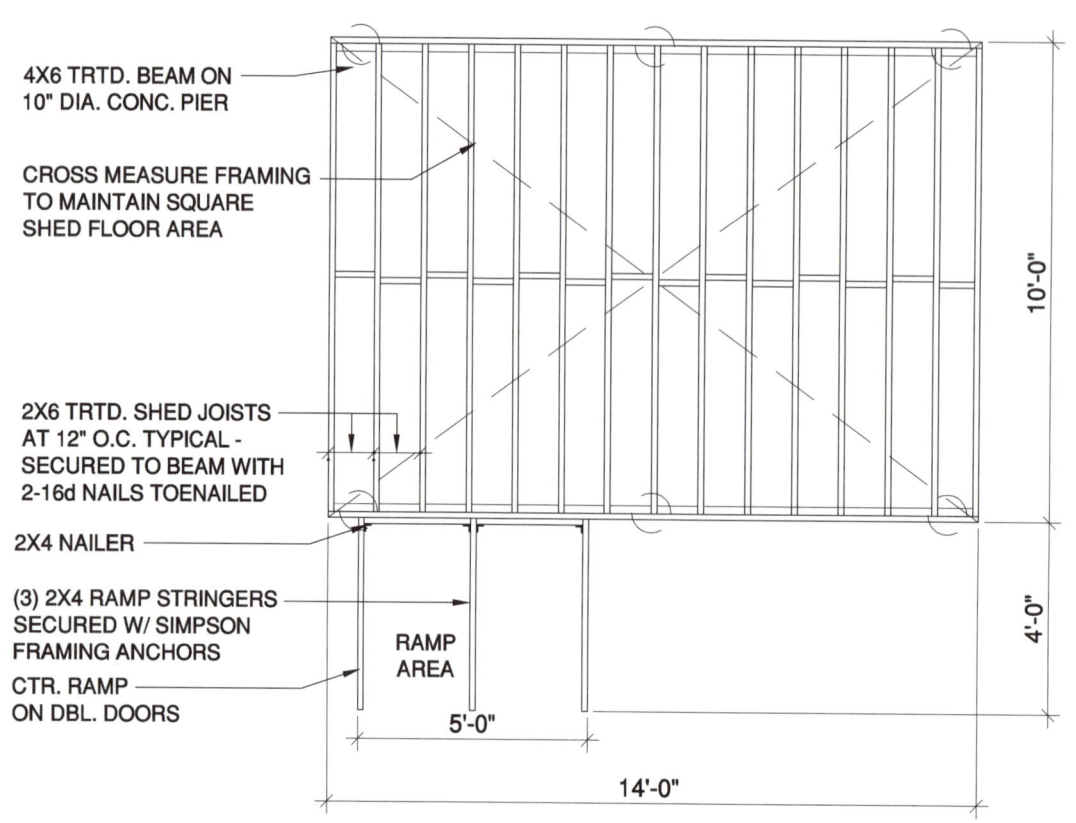

FRAMING PLAN

- 4X6 TRTD. BEAM ON 10" DIA. CONC. PIER
- CROSS MEASURE FRAMING TO MAINTAIN SQUARE SHED FLOOR AREA
- 2X6 TRTD. SHED JOISTS AT 12" O.C. TYPICAL - SECURED TO BEAM WITH 2-16d NAILS TOENAILED
- 2X4 NAILER
- (3) 2X4 RAMP STRINGERS SECURED W/ SIMPSON FRAMING ANCHORS
- CTR. RAMP ON DBL. DOORS
- RAMP AREA
- 10'-0"
- 4'-0"
- 5'-0"
- 14'-0"

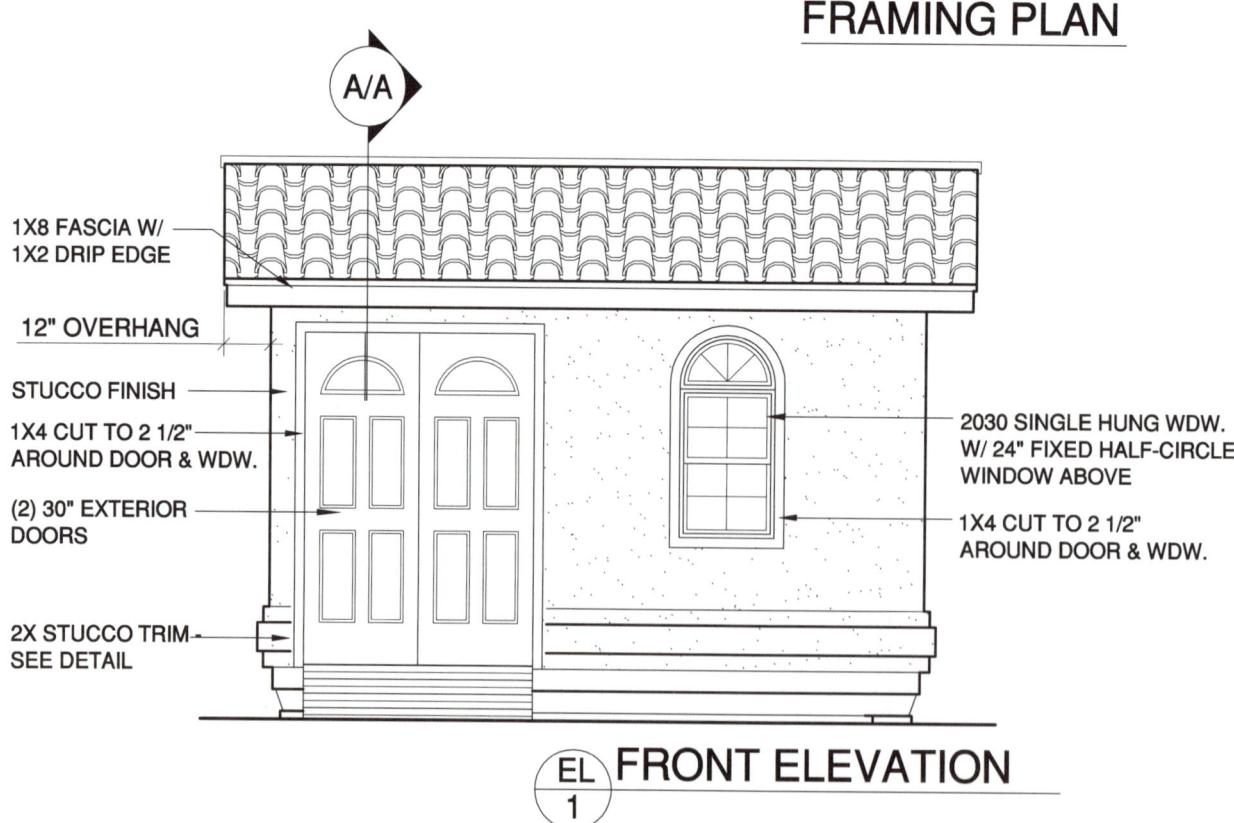

FRONT ELEVATION (EL 1)

- 1X8 FASCIA W/ 1X2 DRIP EDGE
- 12" OVERHANG
- STUCCO FINISH
- 1X4 CUT TO 2 1/2" AROUND DOOR & WDW.
- (2) 30" EXTERIOR DOORS
- 2X STUCCO TRIM SEE DETAIL
- 2030 SINGLE HUNG WDW. W/ 24" FIXED HALF-CIRCLE WINDOW ABOVE
- 1X4 CUT TO 2 1/2" AROUND DOOR & WDW.

SIERRA — Elevations

Scale: 1/4" = 1'-0"

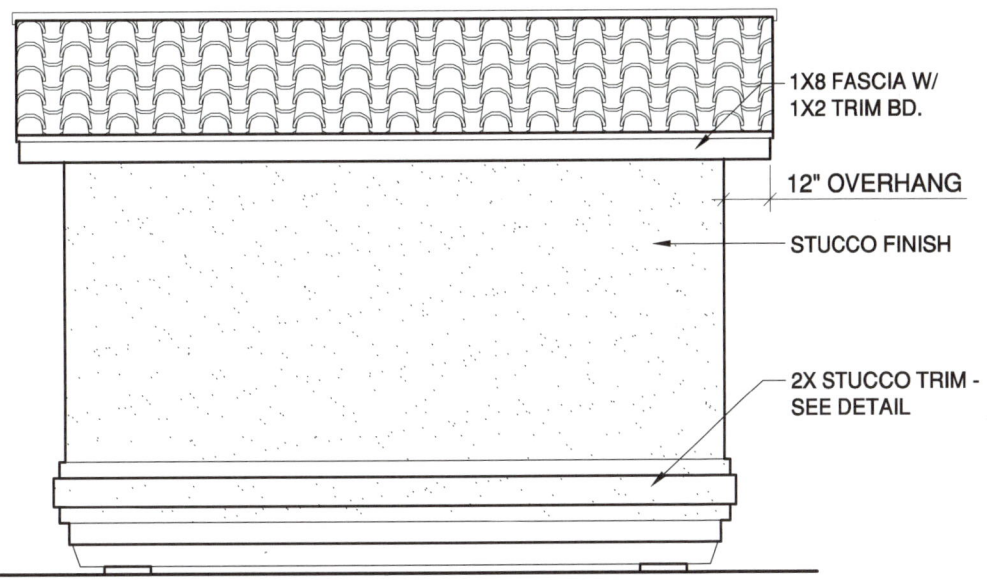

EL 2 — REAR ELEVATION

- 1X8 FASCIA W/ 1X2 TRIM BD.
- 12" OVERHANG
- STUCCO FINISH
- 2X STUCCO TRIM - SEE DETAIL

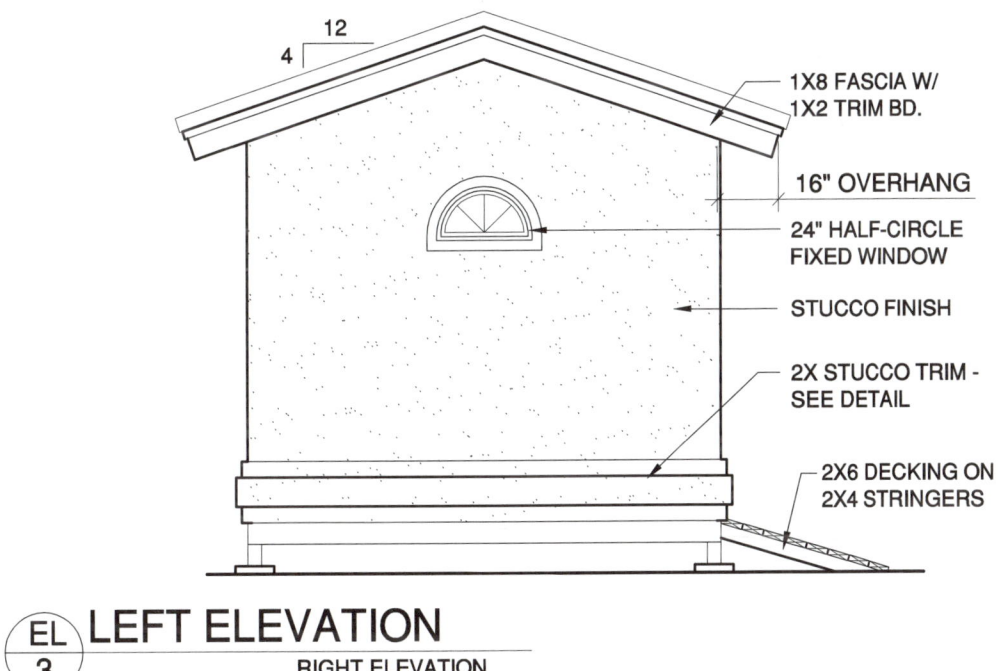

EL 3 — LEFT ELEVATION
RIGHT ELEVATION REVERSE OF LEFT

- 4 / 12
- 1X8 FASCIA W/ 1X2 TRIM BD.
- 16" OVERHANG
- 24" HALF-CIRCLE FIXED WINDOW
- STUCCO FINISH
- 2X STUCCO TRIM - SEE DETAIL
- 2X6 DECKING ON 2X4 STRINGERS

www.homedepot.com 57

SIERRA — Section and Detail

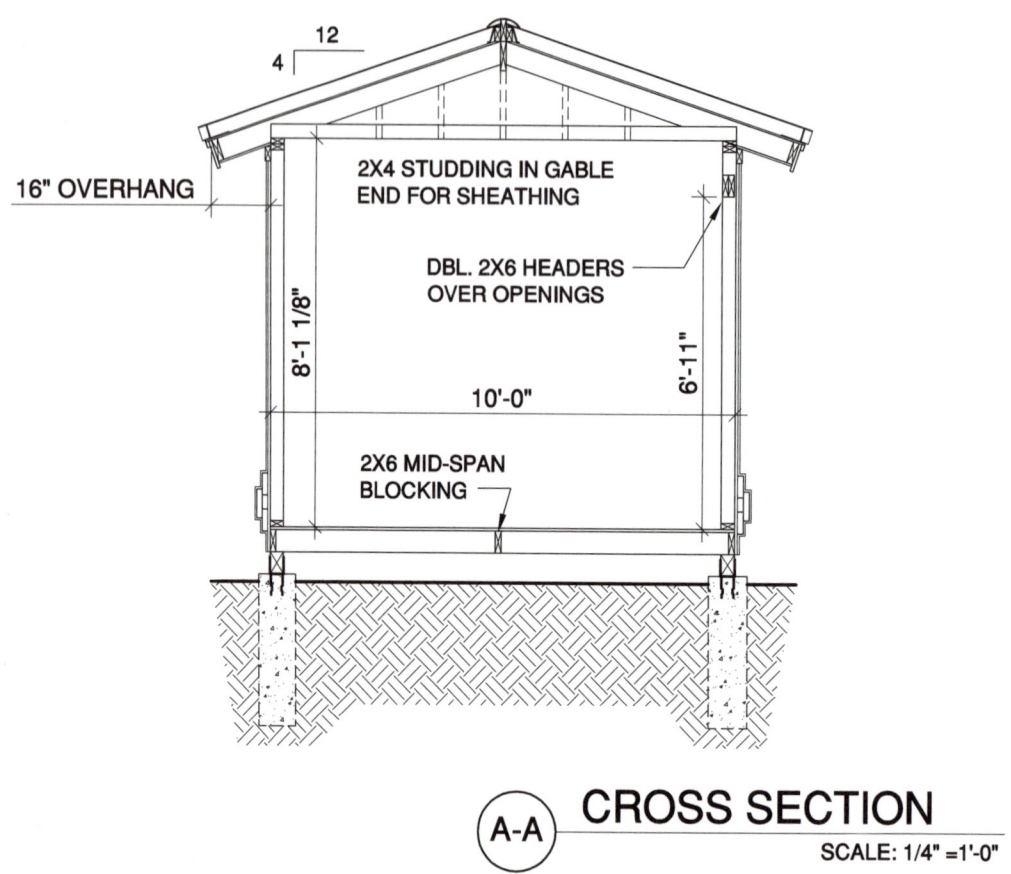

A-A CROSS SECTION
SCALE: 1/4" = 1'-0"

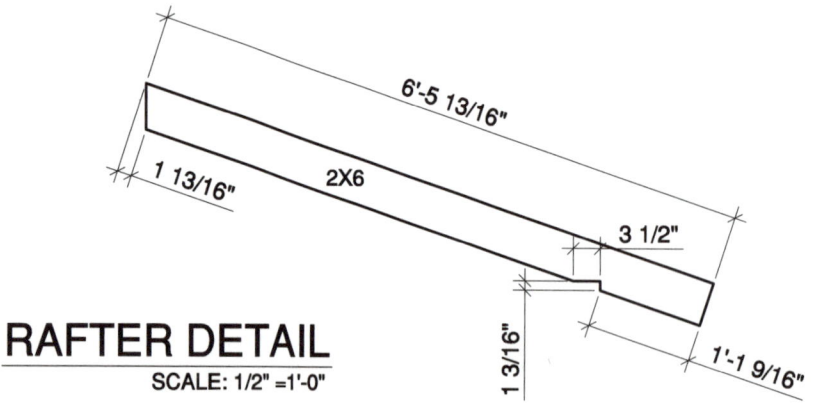

RAFTER DETAIL
SCALE: 1/2" = 1'-0"

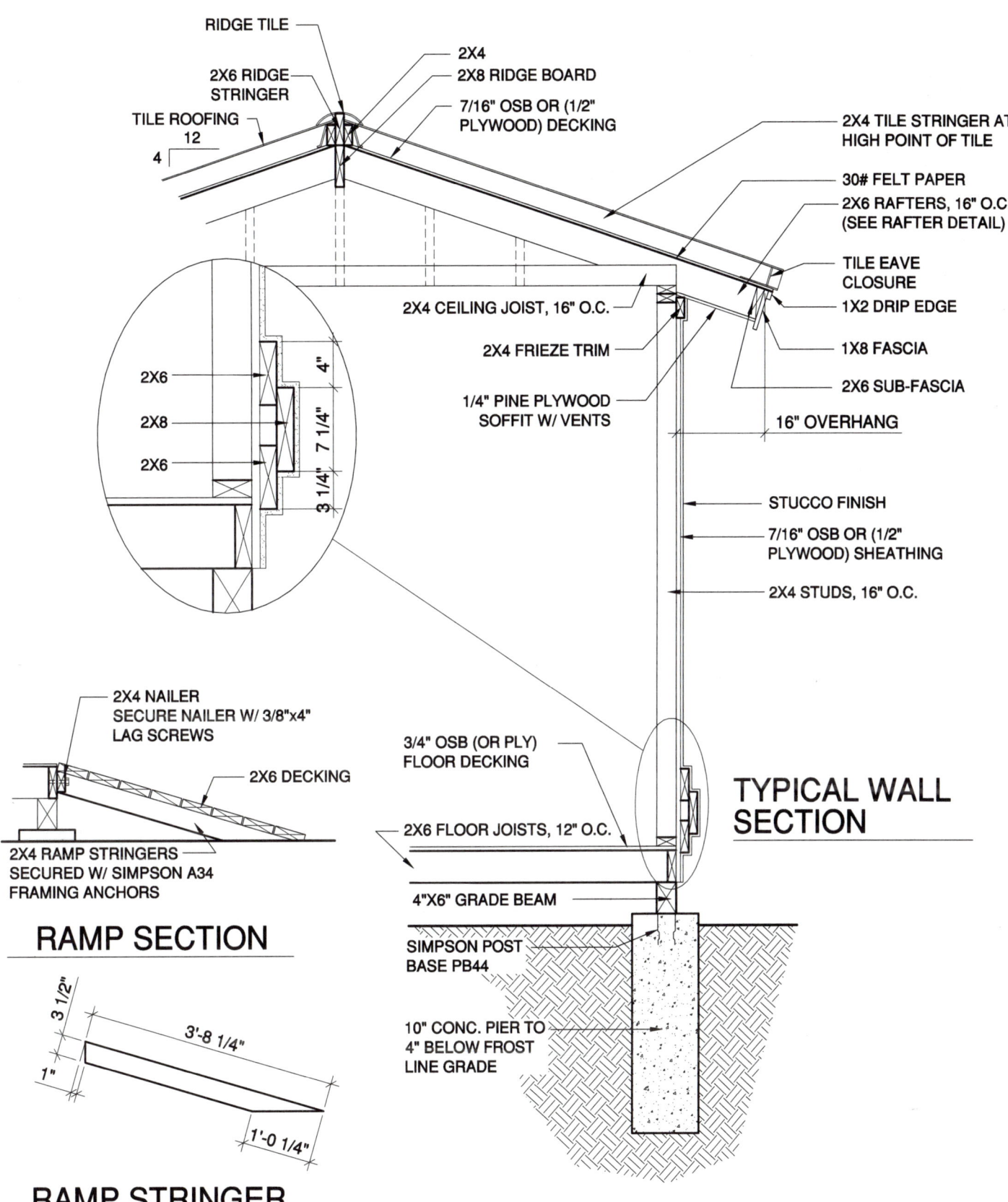

SIERRA — Workbench Layout

Scale: 1/2" = 1'-0"

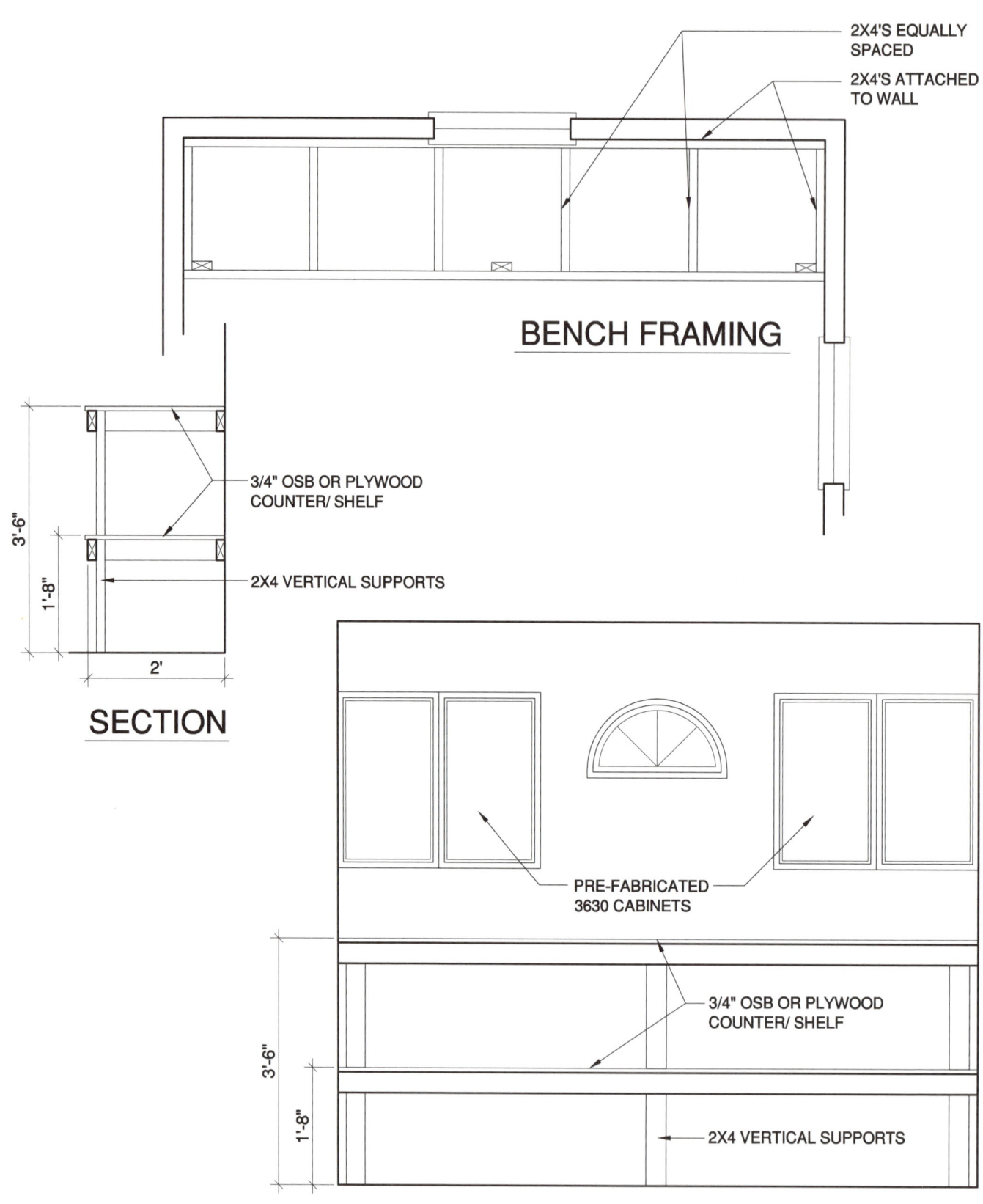

SIERRA — Material List

FOUNDATION

Item	Location	Qty	UM
60# Concrete Mix	Pier	30	BG
10"x 48" Fiber Tube	Pier	6	EA
2x4 - 10' Std. & Btr.	Batterboard	5	EA
Post Base (PB44)	Pier	6	EA
1/2" Hex. Hd. Nut	Post Base	12	EA
1/2"x4-1/2" Bolt	Post Base	12	EA
1/2" Washer	Post Base	24	EA
Crushed Gravel	Pier	12	BG

FLOOR

Item	Location	Qty	UM
4x6 - 8' Treated	Beam	4	EA
2x4 - 10' Treated	Nailer/Stringer	2	EA
2x6 - 10' Treated	Flr. Jst./Deck	19	EA
2x6 - 12' Treated	Hdr. Jst./Blkg.	3	EA
3/4" T & G OSB (PLY.)	Floor Decking	5	EA
Framing Anchor (A34)	Flr. Frmg./Stair	8	EA
3/8"x4" Lag Screws	Nailer	4	EA
3/8"x1-1/2" Washer	Nailer	4	EA
5# 16d Galv. Nails	General Framing	1	EA
5# 8d Ctd. Box Nails	General Framing	1	EA
1# 2-1/2" Ctd. Ext. Screws	General Framing	1	EA
Construction Adhesive	Floor Decking	2	TB

WALL FRAMING

Item	Location	Qty	UM
2x4 - 96" Stud Grade	Stud	46	EA
2x4 - 10' Treated	Bottom Plate	2	EA
2x4 - 16' Treated	Bottom Plate	2	EA
2x4 - 10' Std. & Btr.	Top/Cap Plate	4	EA
2x4 - 14' Std. & Btr.	Top/Cap Plate	4	EA
2x4 - 96" Stud Grade	Cripple/Sill/Blkg.	9	EA
2x6 - 8' Std. & Btr.	Header	2	EA
2x6 - 10' Std. & Btr.	Header	2	EA
7/16" OSB (Ply.)	Wall Sheathing	14	EA
5# 16d Galv. Nails	General Framing	2	EA
5# 8d Ctd. Box Nails	General Framing	2	EA
1x6 - 10' Std. & Btr.	Bracing	6	EA
40"x 97" Bldg. Paper	Wall Covering	2	RL
5# 1/2" Roofing Nails	Wall Covering	1	EA

CEILING/ROOF

Item	Location	Qty	UM
2x4 - 8' Std. & Btr.	Rake	9	EA
2x4 - 10' Std. & Btr.	Ceiling Joist	12	EA
2x4 - 96" Stud Grade	Gable Wall	2	EA
2x4 - 14' Std. & Btr.	Frieze	2	EA
2x4 - 16' Std. & Btr.	Ridge Stringer Blkg.	2	EA
2x6 - 8' Std. & Btr.	Rafter	24	EA
2x6 - 12' Std. & Btr.	Stucco Trim	4	EA
2x6 - 16' Std. & Btr.	Stucco Trim	4	EA
2x6 - 16' Std. & Btr.	Sub-Fascia/Ridge	3	EA
2x8 - 12' Std. & Btr.	Stucco Trim	2	EA
2x8 - 16' Std. & Btr.	Ridge Bd./Trm. Bd.	3	EA
1x2 - 8' C & Btr. S4S	Drip Edge	8	EA
1x8 - 10' Std. & Btr. S4S	Fascia	5	EA
1x8 - 12' Std. & Btr. S4S	Fascia	2	EA
7/16" OSB (Ply.)	Roof Decking	7	EA
2x2 - 8' Std. & Btr.	Rake Tile Stringer	4	EA
2x4 - 8' Std. & Btr.	Tile Stringer	30	EA
214 SF Roof Tile	Roof	3	SQ
Ridge Tile	Ridge	16	LF
Ridge Cover Starter Tile	Ridge	2	EA
Rake Tile (End Band)	Rake	28	LF
Eave Closure	Eave	50	EA
Top Fixture	Ridge	50	EA
30-lb. Asphalt Rfg. Felt	Roofing	1	RL
5# 8d Ctd. Box Nails	General Framing	2	EA
5# 10d Bright Box Nails	General Framing	2	EA
5# 16d Galv. Nails	General Framing	1	EA
5# 1/2" Roofing Nails	Roofing Felt	1	EA
1-3/4" Stainless Nails	Roof Tile	60	LB
5# 6d Galv. Box Nails	General Framing	1	EA
5# 6d Galv. Finish Nails	Soffit	1	EA

EXTERIOR TRIM & ACCESSORIES

Item	Location	Qty	UM
80# One Coat Stucco	Wall	33	BG
Furred Stucco Netting	Wall	1	RL
1/2"x10' Casing Bead	Window/Door	5	EA
10' 1A Corner Bead	Corner	28	EA
5-1/2" #7 Fnd. Sill Screen	Sill	5	EA
1x4 - 8' Std. & Btr.	Window Trim	5	EA
1/4" Plywood (Sanded)	Soffit Material	2	EA
14x6 Metal Soffit Vent	Soffit	4	EA
(2) 30"x80" Exterior Door	Exterior Door	1	EA
2030 SH Window	Window	3	EA
24" Half-Circle Window	Window	3	EA
Lockset/Deadbolt/Pin	Exterior Door	1	EA
2x4 - 8' Std. & Btr.	Work Bench	5	EA
2x4 - 10' Std. & Btr.	Work Bench	4	EA
36"x30" White Wall Cabinet	Over Bench	2	EA
White Door Package 'H'	Wall Cabinet	4	EA
3/4" OSB Sq. Edge (Ply.)	Bench Top	2	EA
5# 6d Galv. Finish Nails	Soffit	2	EA
5# 8d Galv. Finish Nails	Window/Door	1	EA
10 oz. - Paintable Caulk	Trim	3	TB
1-1/4"x2" Brickmold	Exterior Door	3	EA
4" - 10' "Z" Flashing	Window/Door	2	EA

CHAPTER 4

THE MONROE   HPM-1400
Dimensions for this shed are 10' X 8'. 80 sq. ft.

THE MONROE & JACKSON

Available in two sizes, the larger of these charming and rustic sheds adds an extra double-door access as well as a built-in workbench and cabinets to the interior. Outside, each shed features a functional front porch with space to stack firewood, pot plants or just relax after a hard day's work! With their shingled roofs, these great sheds offer the same shelter and security as your home.

THE JACKSON   HPM-1300
Dimensions for this shed are 14' X 10'. 140 sq. ft.

MONROE — Plan View, Pier Layout and Framing Plan

Scale: 1/4" = 1'-0"

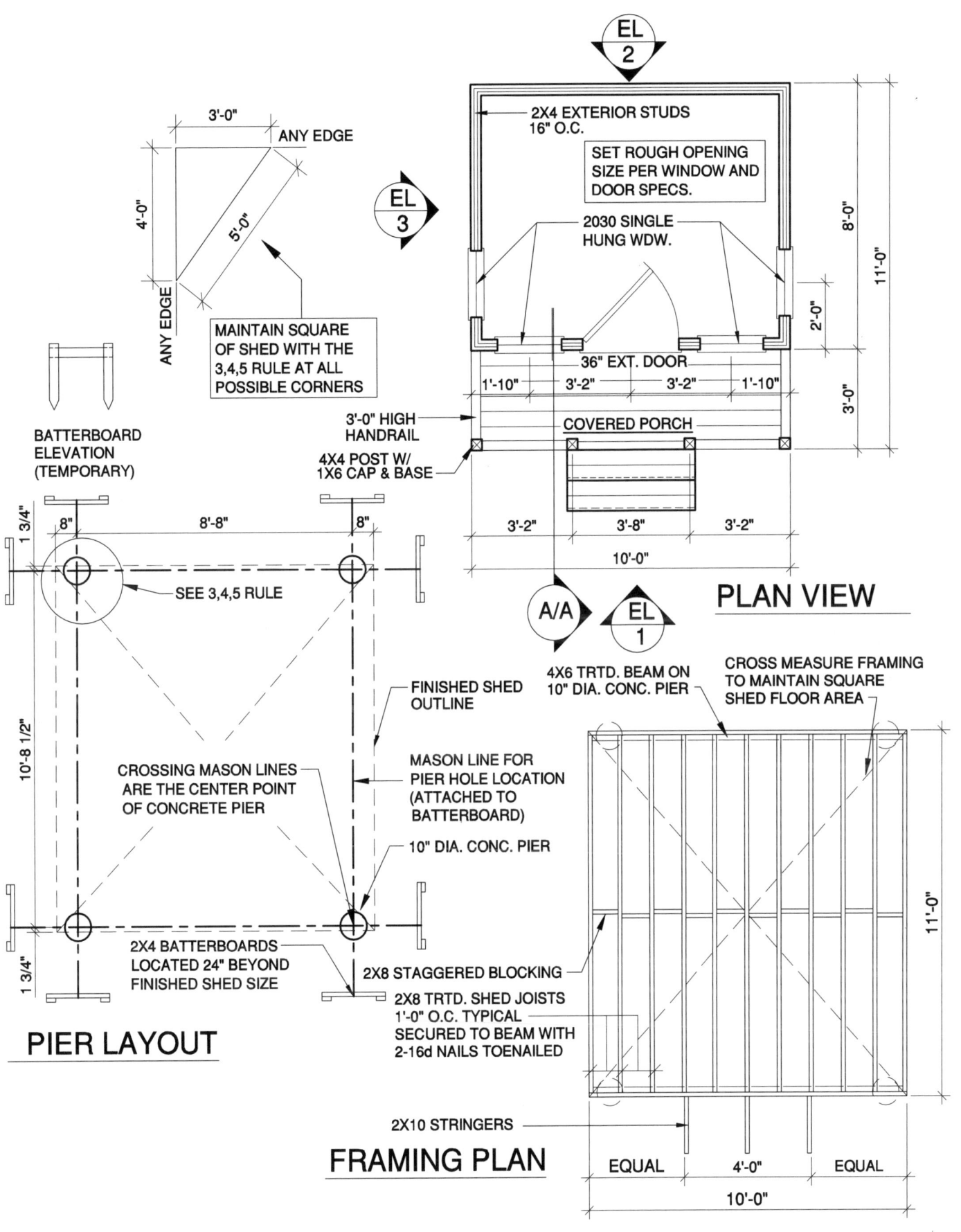

www.homedepot.com

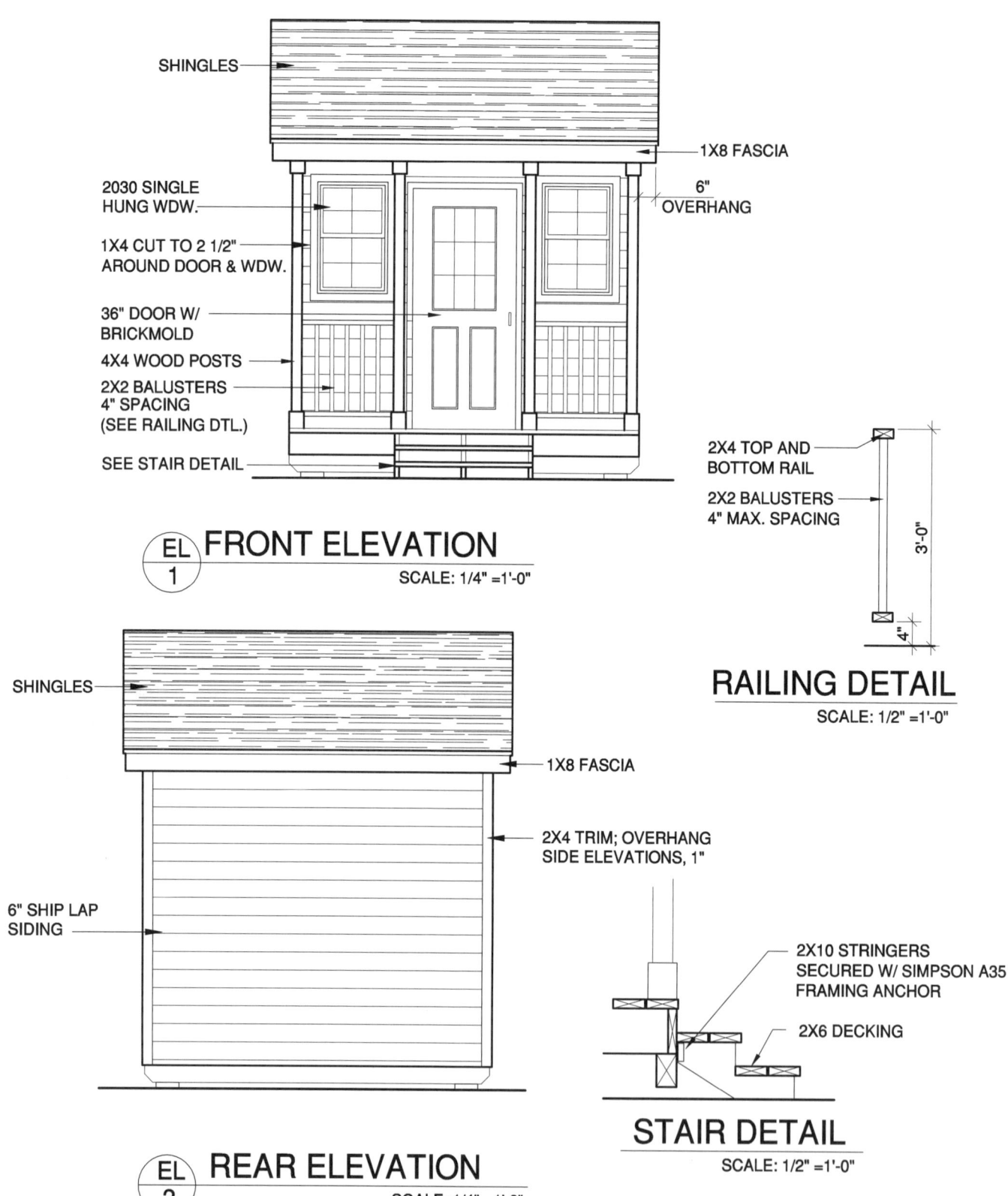

MONROE — Elevation and Section

Scale: 1/4" = 1'-0"

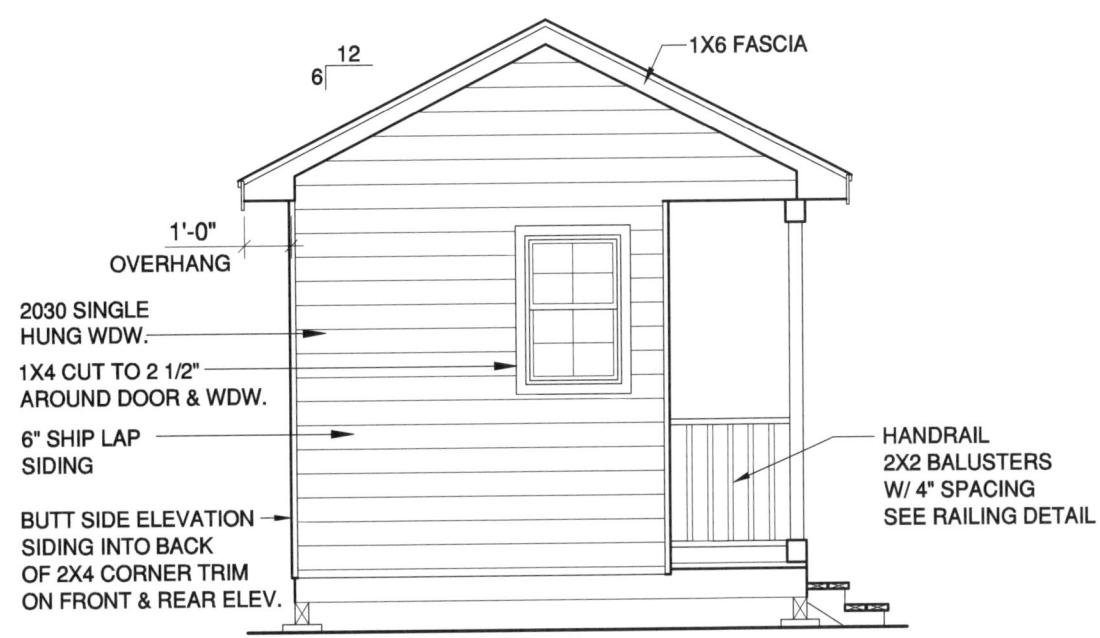

LEFT ELEVATION
EL/3

RIGHT ELEVATION REVERSE OF LEFT

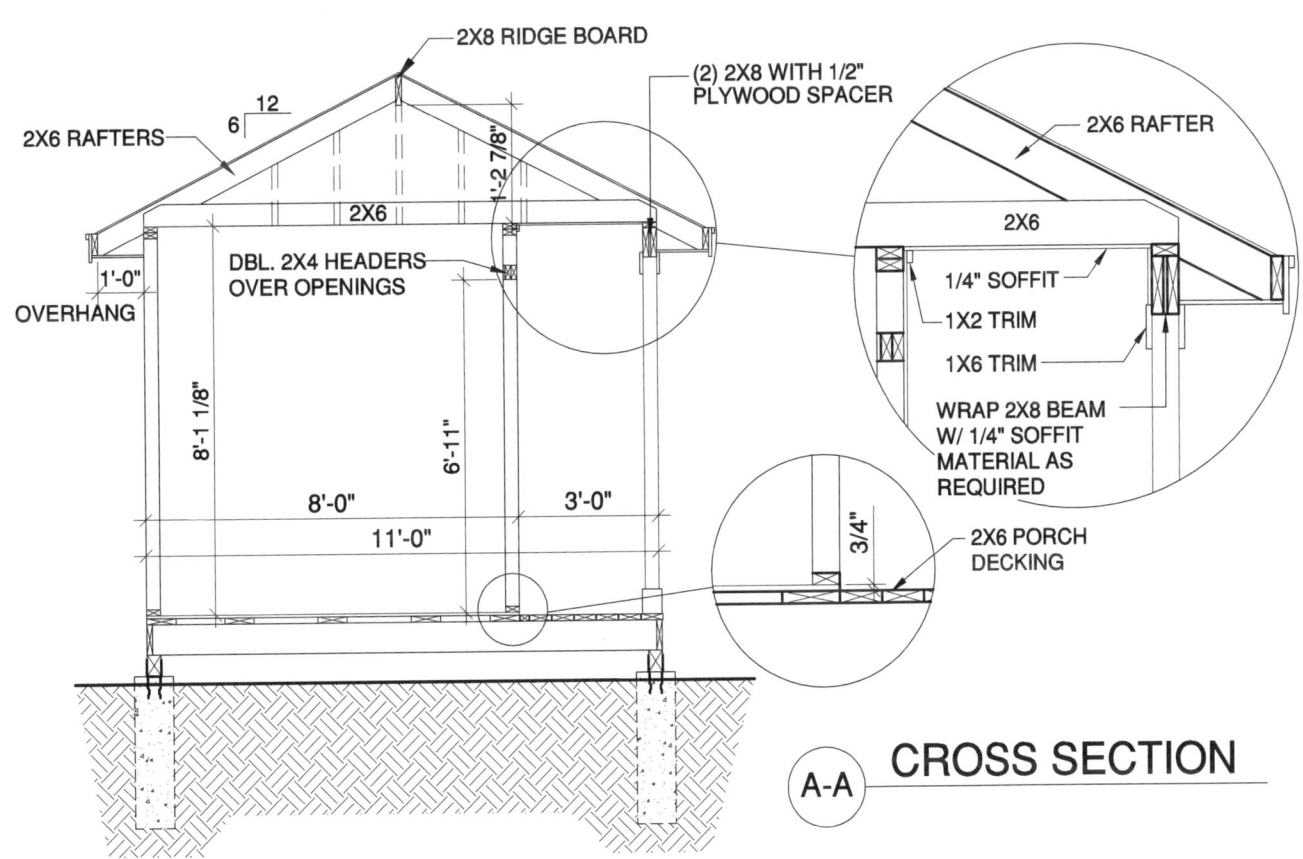

CROSS SECTION
A-A

www.homedepot.com

Monroe — Details

Scale: 1/2" = 1'-0"

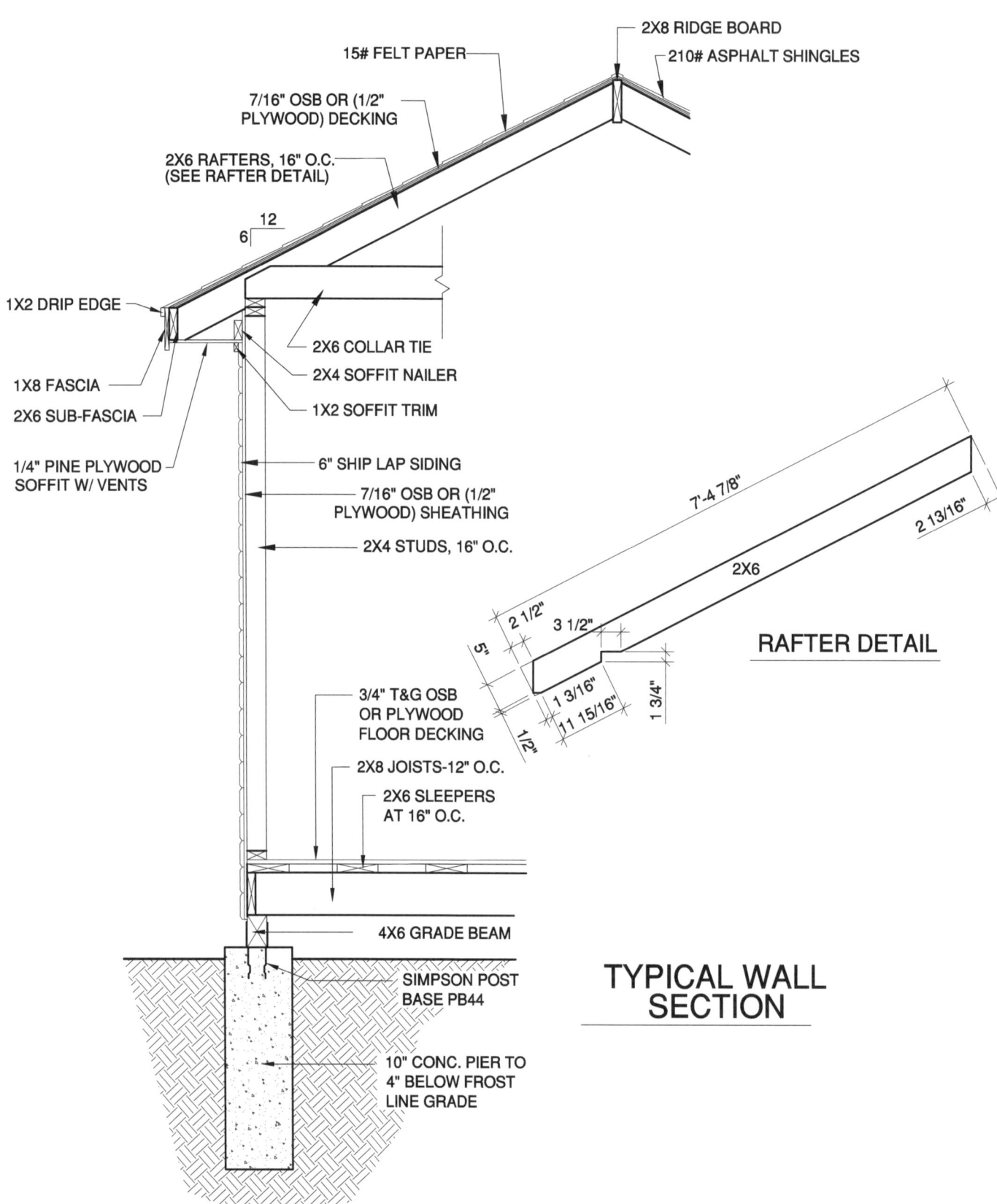

TYPICAL WALL SECTION

RAFTER DETAIL

Monroe — Material List

FOUNDATION

Item	Location	Qty	UM
60# Concrete Mix	Pier	20	BG
10"x 48" Fiber Tube	Pier	4	EA
2x4 - 10' Std. & Btr.	Batterboard	5	EA
Post Base (PB44)	Pier	4	EA
1/2" Hex Hd. Nut	Post Base	8	EA
1/2"x4-1/2" Bolt	Post Base	8	EA
1/2" Washer	Post Base	16	EA
Crushed Gravel	Pier	8	BG

FLOOR

Item	Location	Qty	UM
4x6 - 12' Treated	Beam	2	EA
2x8 - 10' Treated	Header Jst./Blkg.	3	EA
2x8 - 12' Treated	Floor Jst./End Jst.	11	EA
2x10 - 8' Treated	Stringer	1	EA
Framing Anchor (A34)	Stringer/Hdr. Joist	8	EA
2x6 - 8' Treated	Stair Tread	2	EA
2x6 - 10' Treated	Sleeper/Decking	14	EA
3/4" OSB (Ply.)	Floor Decking	3	EA
5# -16d Galv. Nails	General Framing	1	EA
5# - 8d Ctd. Box Nails	General Framing	1	EA
1# - 2-1/2" Ctd. Ext. Screws	General Framing	1	EA
Construction Adhesive	Floor Decking	2	TB

WALL FRAMING

Item	Location	Qty	UM
2x4 - 8' Treated	Bottom Plate	2	EA
2x4 - 10' Treated	Bottom Plate	2	EA
2x4 - 96" Stud Grade	Stud/Crpl./Gable	53	EA
2x4 - 96" Stud Grade	Hdr./Sill/Blocking	5	EA
2x4 - 8' Std. & Btr.	Top/Cap Plate	4	EA
2x4 - 10' Std. & Btr.	Top/Cap Plate	4	EA
7/16" OSB (Ply.)	Wall Sheathing	11	EA
1x6 - 10' Std. & Btr.	Bracing	6	EA
40"x 97' Building Paper	Wall Covering	2	RL
5# 6d Galv. Nails	General Framing	2	EA
5# 8d Ctd. Box Nails	General Framing	2	EA
5# 1/2" Roofing Nails	Wall Covering	1	EA

CEILING/ROOF

Item	Location	Qty	UM
2x6 - 12' Std. & Btr.	Collar/Sub-Fascia	11	EA
2x6 - 8' Std. & Btr.	Rafter	18	EA
2x4 - 8' Std. & Btr.	Rake	8	EA
2x4 - 10' Std. & Btr.	Bm. Plt./Soffit Nlr.	3	EA
2x8 - 12' Std. & Btr.	Rdg. Bd./Prch. Bm.	3	EA
1/2" CDX 5 Ply Plywd.	Beam Spacer	1	EA
7/16" OSB (Ply.)	Roof Decking	6	EA
1x6 - 8' Std. & Btr.	Fascia	4	EA
1x8 - 12' Std. & Btr. S4S	Fascia	2	EA
3 -Tab Shingles 20 Yr.	Shingle	6	BN
15-lb. Asphalt Rfg. Felt	Roofing	1	RL
1x4 -10' Std. & Btr. (Rip-1x2)	Drip Edge	3	EA
5# 8d Ctd. Box Nails	General Framing	2	EA
5# 10d Bright Box Nails	General Framing	2	EA
5# 16d Galv. Nails	General Framing	1	EA
5# 1/2" Galv. Roofing Nails	Roofing Felt	1	EA
5# 1-1/4" Galv. Rfg. Nails	Shingle	2	EA
5# 6d Galv. Box Nails	General Framing	1	EA
5# 6d Galv. Finish Nails	Siding/Soffit	1	EA

EXTERIOR TRIM & ACCESSORIES

Item	Location	Qty	UM
1x6 - 10' Ship Lap Siding	Siding	65	EA
2x4 - 10' Std. & Btr.	Corner Trim	4	EA
1x4 - 8' Std. & Btr.	Window Trim	9	EA
1/4" Plywood (Sanded)	Soffit Material	3	EA
1x4 - 10' Std. & Btr. (Rip-1x2)	Soffit Trim	2	EA
1x6 - 8' Std. & Btr.	Post Trim	2	EA
14x6 Metal Soffit Vent	Soffit	4	EA
4x4 - 10' Treated	Porch Post	4	EA
2x4 - 12' Treated	Railing	6	EA
1-3/8"x1-3/8" - 3' Baluster	Railing	20	EA
36"x80" Exterior LH Door	Exterior Door	1	EA
2030 SH Window	Window	4	EA
Lockset/Deadbolt Set	Exterior Door	1	EA
5# 6d Galv. Finish Nails	Siding/Soffit	4	EA
5# 8d Galv. Finish Nails	Window/Door	1	EA
10 oz. - Paintable Caulk	Siding/Trim	6	TB
1-1/4"x2" Brickmold	Exterior Door	3	EA
4" - 10' "Z" Flashing	Window/Door	2	EA

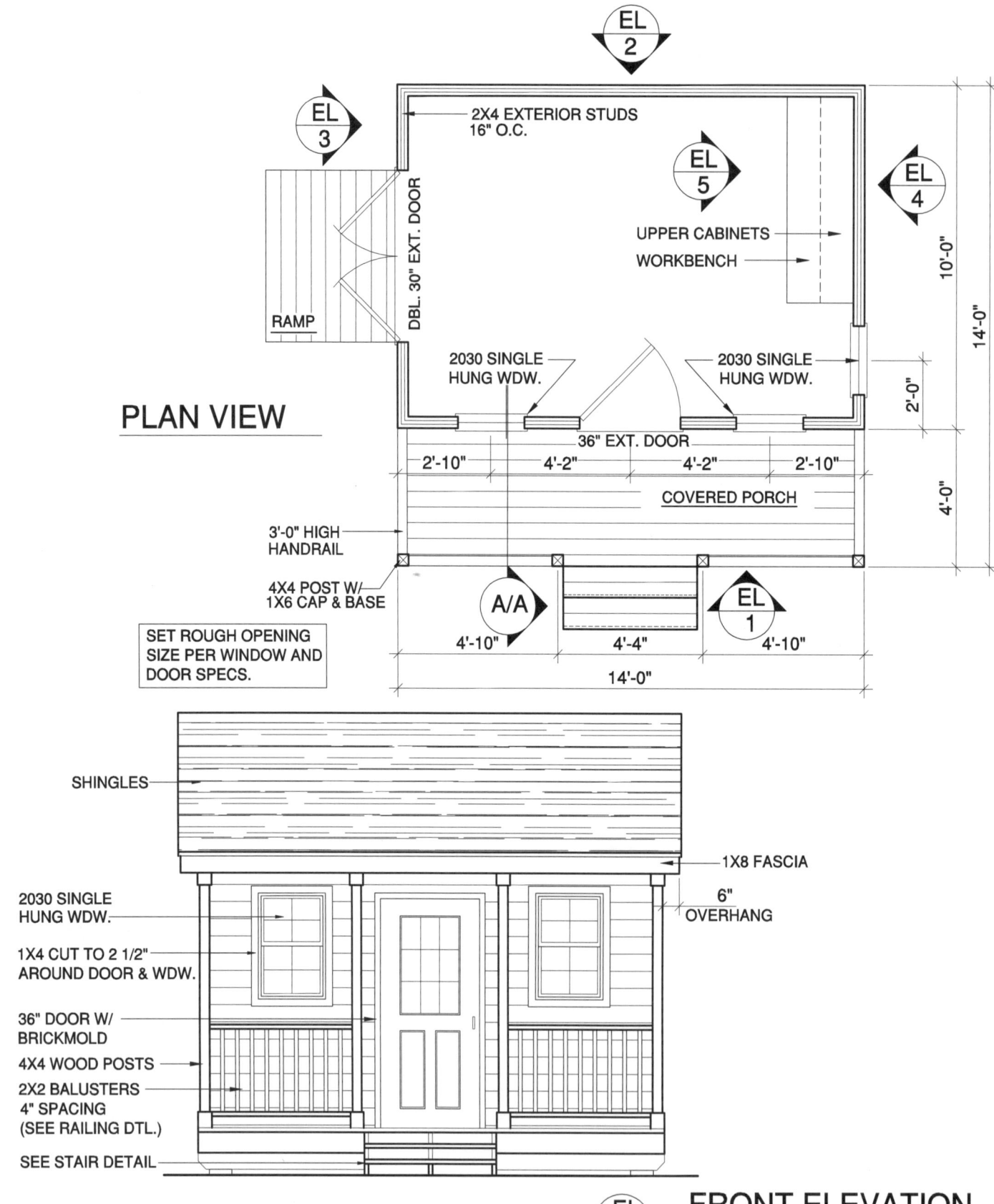

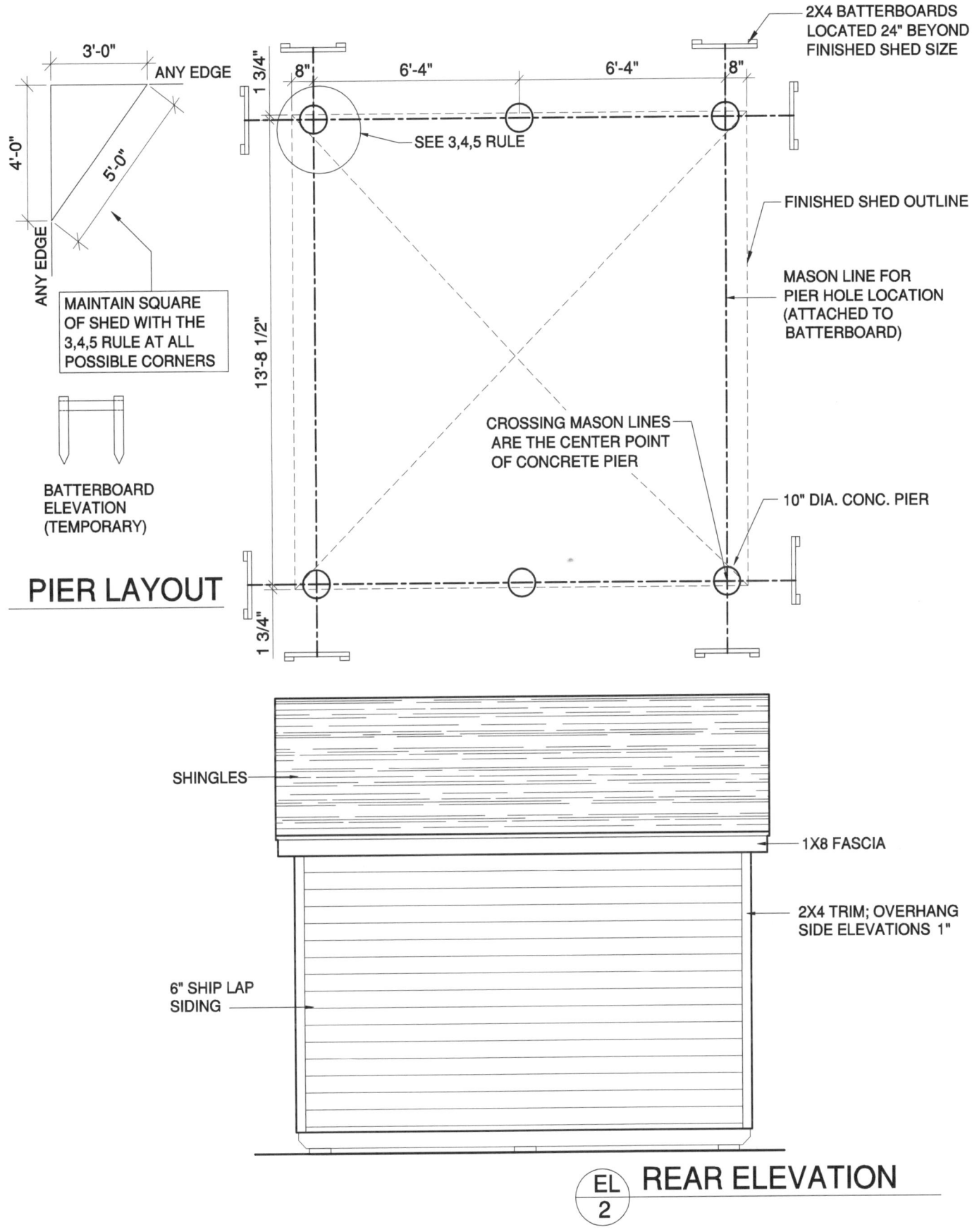

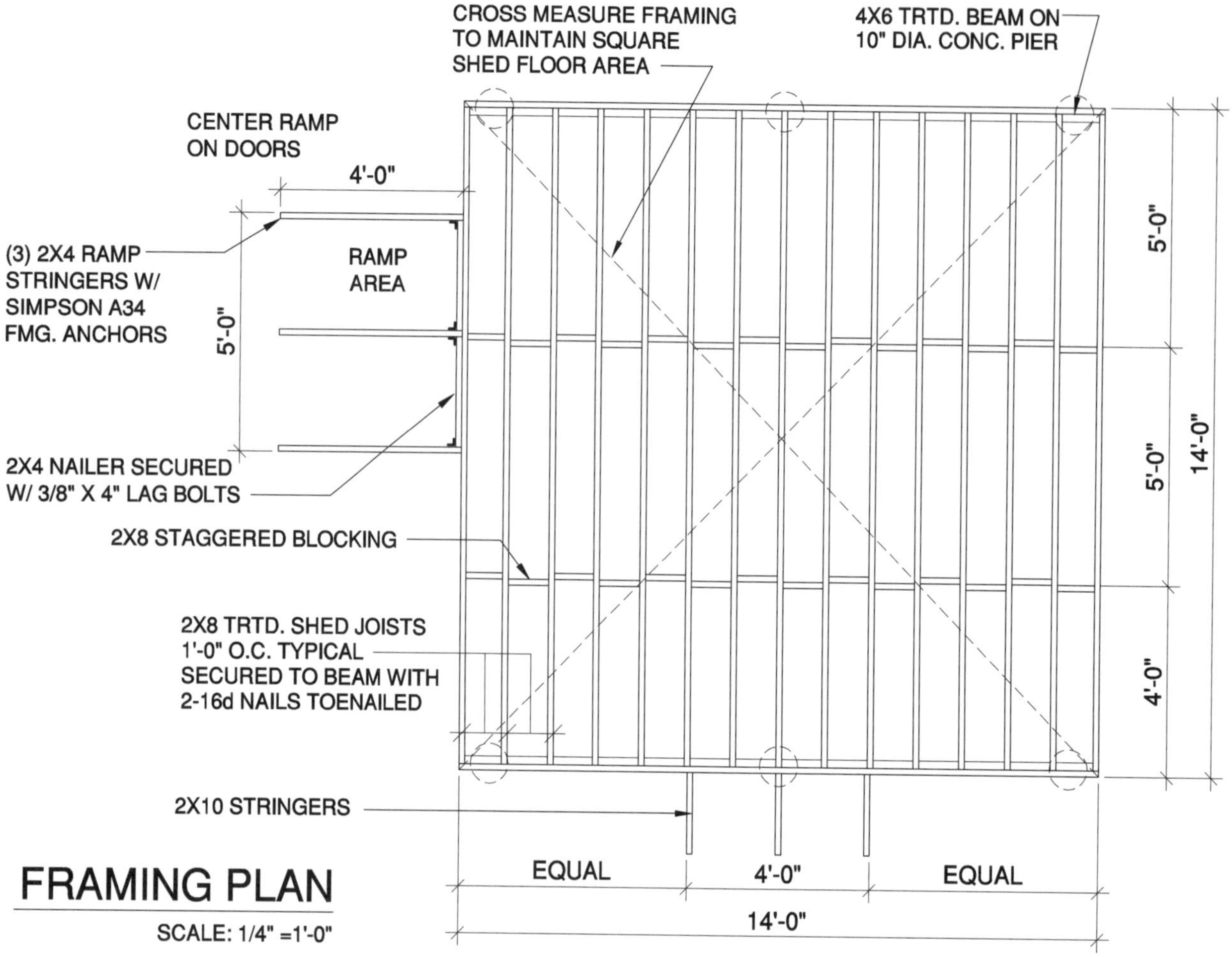

JACKSON — Framing Plan and Details

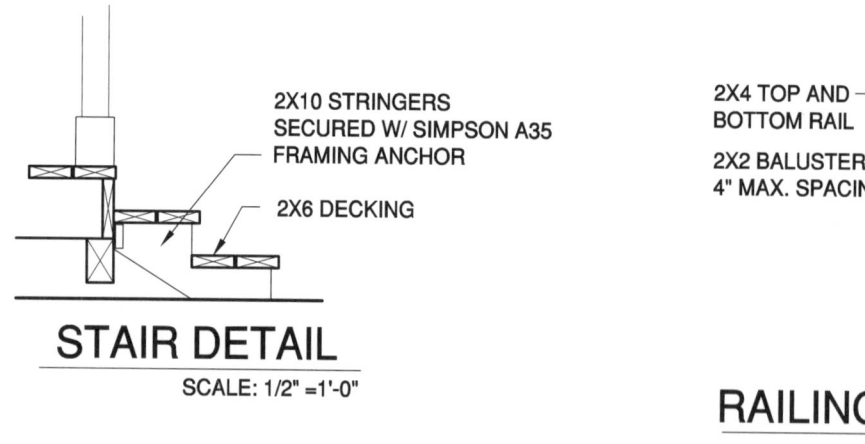

FRAMING PLAN
SCALE: 1/4" = 1'-0"

Labels:
- CROSS MEASURE FRAMING TO MAINTAIN SQUARE SHED FLOOR AREA
- 4X6 TRTD. BEAM ON 10" DIA. CONC. PIER
- CENTER RAMP ON DOORS
- (3) 2X4 RAMP STRINGERS W/ SIMPSON A34 FMG. ANCHORS
- RAMP AREA
- 2X4 NAILER SECURED W/ 3/8" X 4" LAG BOLTS
- 2X8 STAGGERED BLOCKING
- 2X8 TRTD. SHED JOISTS 1'-0" O.C. TYPICAL SECURED TO BEAM WITH 2-16d NAILS TOENAILED
- 2X10 STRINGERS

Dimensions: 4'-0"; 5'-0"; 5'-0", 5'-0", 4'-0" (14'-0"); EQUAL, 4'-0", EQUAL (14'-0")

STAIR DETAIL
SCALE: 1/2" = 1'-0"

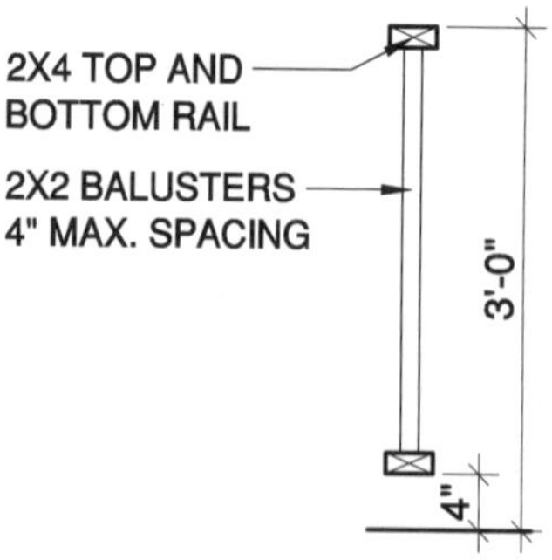

- 2X10 STRINGERS SECURED W/ SIMPSON A35 FRAMING ANCHOR
- 2X6 DECKING

RAILING DETAIL
SCALE: 1/2" = 1'-0"

- 2X4 TOP AND BOTTOM RAIL
- 2X2 BALUSTERS 4" MAX. SPACING
- 3'-0"
- 4"

JACKSON — Elevations

Scale: 1/4" = 1'-0"

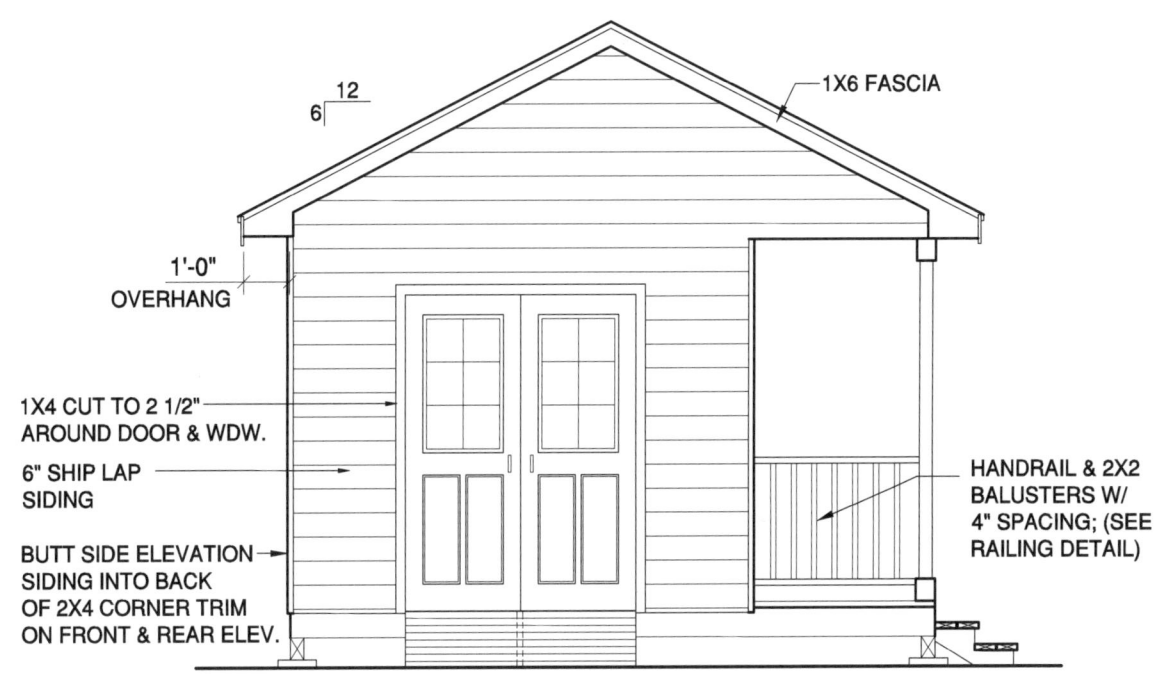

LEFT ELEVATION (EL/3)

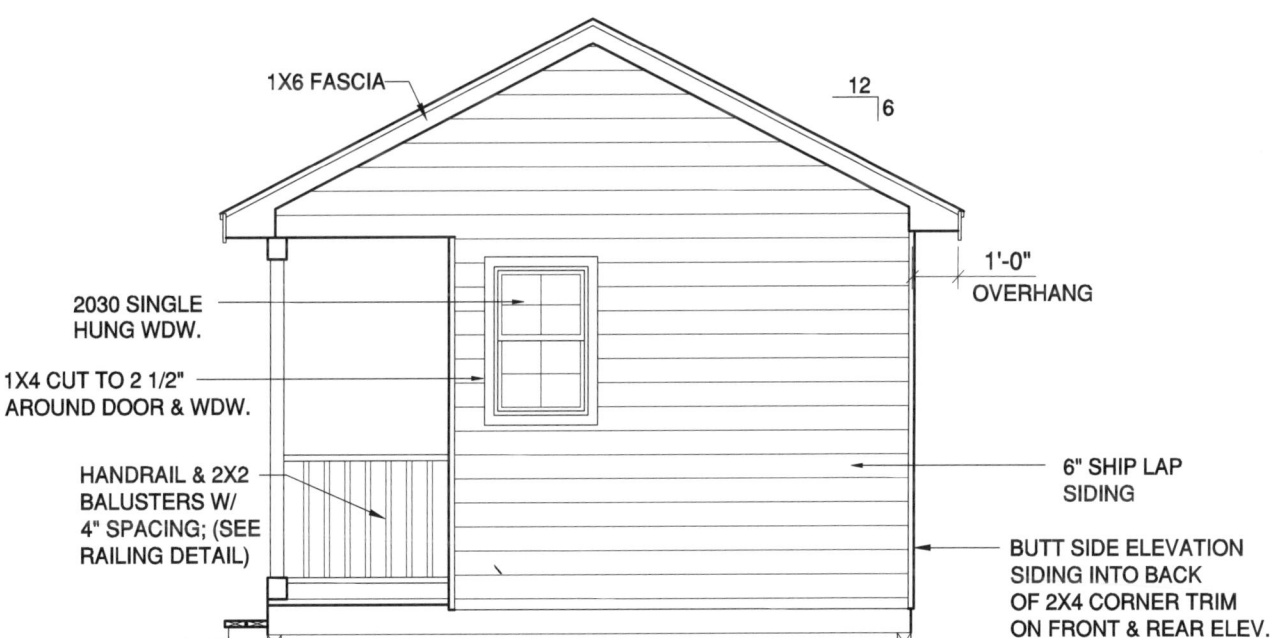

RIGHT ELEVATION (EL/4)

RAMP SECTION

SCALE: 1/2" =1'-0"

RAMP STRINGER

SCALE: 1/2" =1'-0"

A-A CROSS SECTION

SCALE: 1/4" =1'-0"

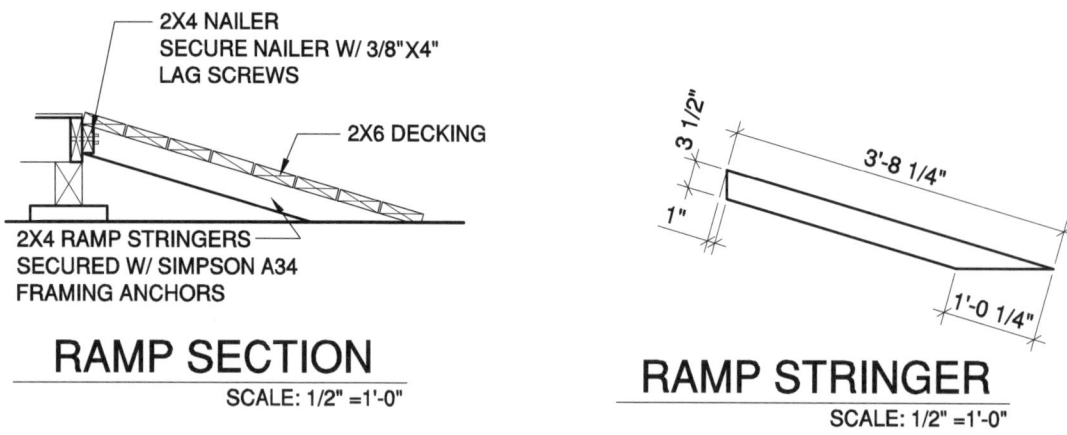

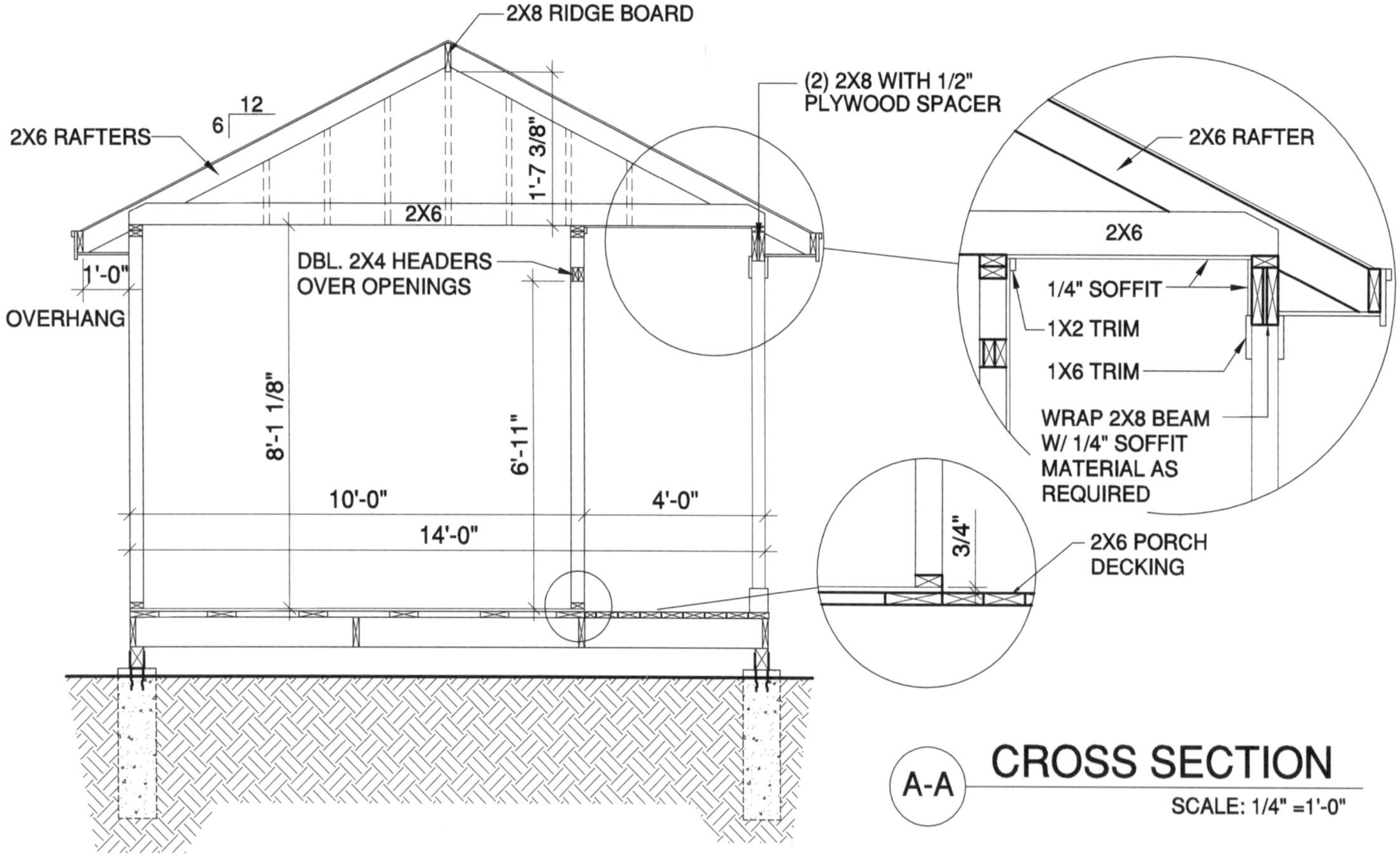

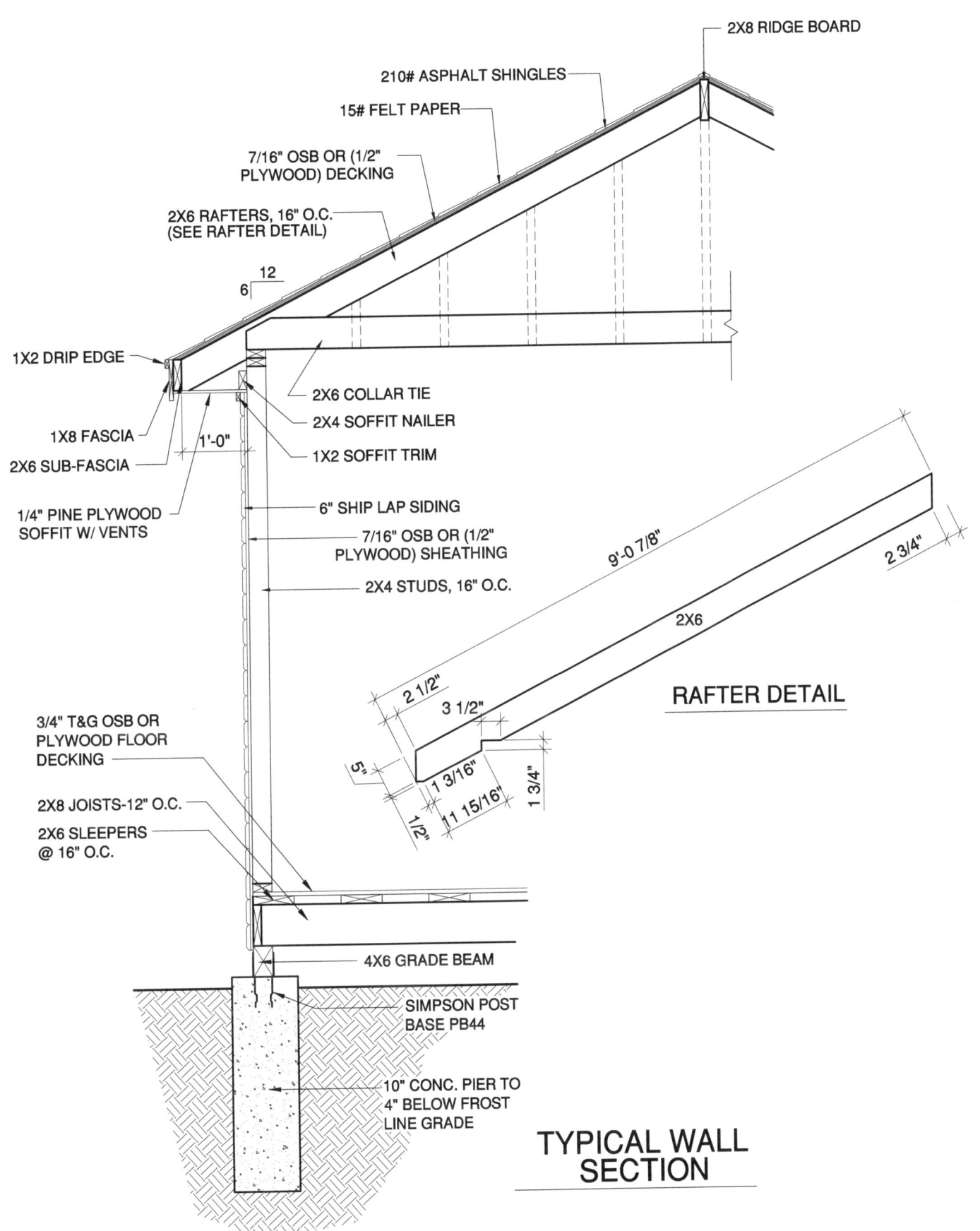

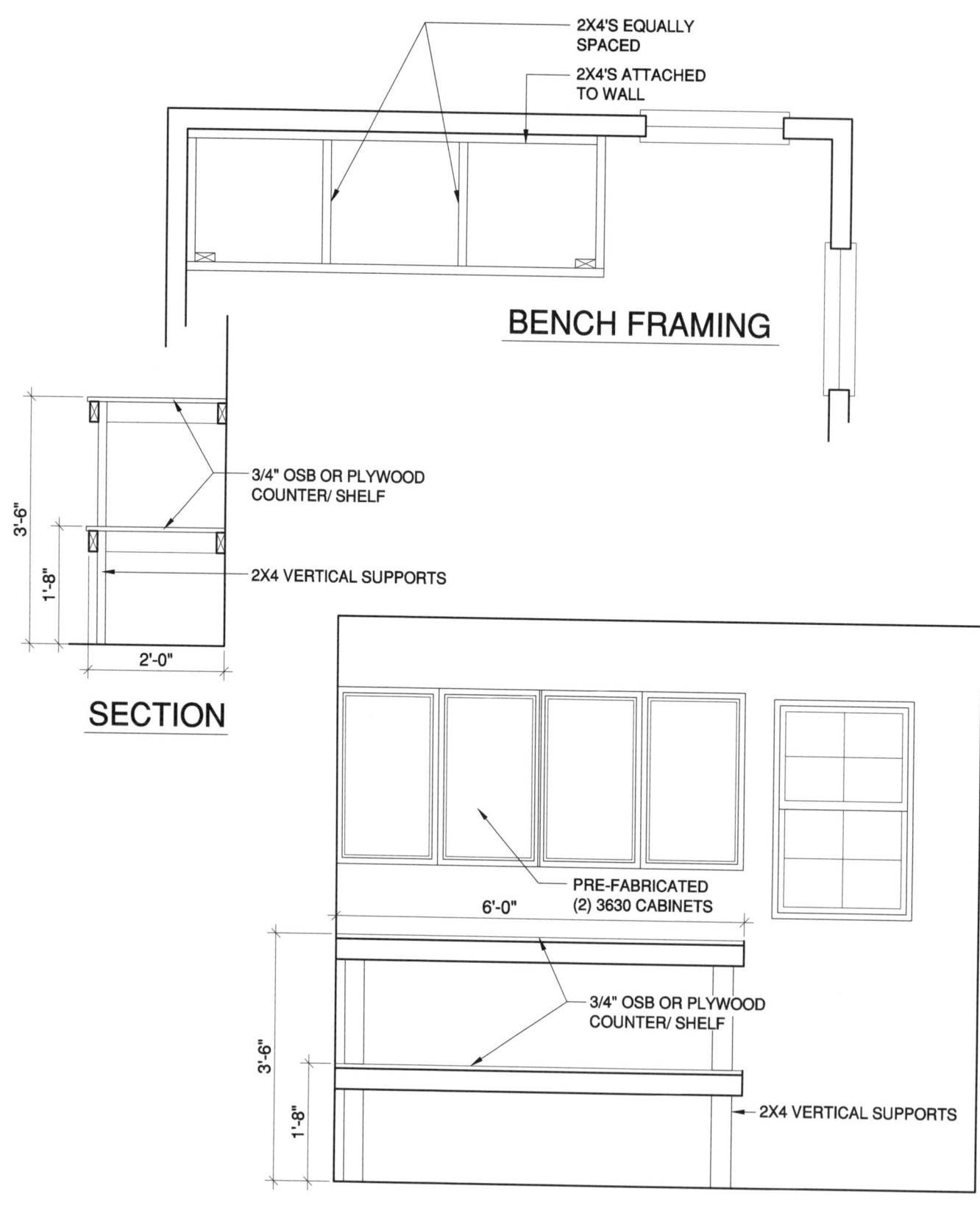

JACKSON — Material List

FOUNDATION

Item	Location	Qty	UM
60# Concrete Mix	Pier	30	BG
10"x 48" Fiber Tube	Pier	6	EA
2x4 - 10' Std. & Btr.	Batterboard	5	EA
Post Base (PB 44)	Pier	6	EA
1/2" Hex. Hd. Nut	Post Base	12	EA
1/2"x4-1/2" Bolt	Post Base	12	EA
1/2" Washer	Post Base	24	EA
Crushed Gravel	Pier	12	BG

FLOOR

Item	Location	Qty	UM
4x6 - 8' Treated	Beam	4	EA
2x8 - 14' Treated	Floor Jst./End Jst.	10	EA
2x8 - 14' Treated	Header Jst./Blkg.	9	EA
2x10 - 8' Treated	Stringer	1	EA
Framing Anchor (A34)	Stringer/Hdr. Joist	12	EA
2x6 - 8' Treated	Stair Tread	2	EA
2x4 - 8' Treated	Nailer/Stringer	3	EA
2x6 - 10' Treated	Decking	4	EA
2x6 - 16' Treated	Decking/Sleeper	18	EA
3/4" OSB (Ply.)	Floor Decking	5	EA
3/8"x4" Lag Screws	Nailer	4	EA
3/8"x1-1/2" Washer	Nailer	4	EA
5# 16d Galv. Nails	General Framing	1	EA
5# 8d Ctd. Box Nails	General Framing	1	EA
1# 2-1/2" Ctd. Ext. Screws	General Framing	1	EA
Construction Adhesive	Floor Decking	2	TB

WALL FRAMING

Item	Location	Qty	UM
2x4 - 10' Treated	Bottom Plate	2	EA
2x4 - 16' Treated	Bottom Plate	2	EA
2x4 - 96" Stud Grade	Stud/Crpl./Gable	58	EA
2x4 - 96" Stud Grade	Hdr./Sill/Blkg.	12	EA
2x4 - 14' Std. & Btr.	Top/Cap Plate	4	EA
2x4 - 10' Std. & Btr.	Top/Cap Plate	4	EA
7/16" OSB (Ply.)	Wall Shtg./Shim	15	EA
1x6 - 10' Std. & Btr.	Bracing	6	EA
40"x 97' Building Paper	Wall Covering	2	RL
5# 16d Galv. Nails	General Framing	2	EA
5# 8d Ctd. Box Nails	General Framing	2	EA
5# 1/2" Roofing Nails	Wall Covering	1	EA

CEILING/ROOF

Item	Location	Qty	UM
2x6 - 14' Std. & Btr.	Collar Tie	12	EA
2x6 - 10' Std. & Btr.	Rafter	24	EA
2x6 - 16' Std. & Btr.	Sub-Fascia	2	EA
2x4 - 10' Std. & Btr.	Rake	9	EA
2x4 - 14' Std. & Btr.	Bm. Plate/Soffit Nlr.	3	EA
2x8 - 16' Std. & Btr.	Rdg. Bd./Prch. Bm.	3	EA
1/2" CDX 5-Ply. Plywd.	Beam Spacer	1	EA
7/16" OSB (Ply.)	Roof Decking	9	EA
1x6 - 10' Std. & Btr. S4S	Fascia	4	EA
1x8 - 6' Std. & Btr. S4S	Fascia	1	EA
1x8 - 12' Std. & Btr. S4S	Fascia	2	EA
3 -Tab Shingles 20 Yr.	Shingle	10	BN
15-lb. Asphalt Rfg. Felt	Roofing	2	RL
Galv. Drip Edge	Roof Edge	7	EA
5# 8d Ctd. Box Nails	General Framing	2	EA
5# 10d Bright Box Nails	General Framing	2	EA
5# 16d Galv. Nails	General Framing	1	EA
5# 1/2" Roofing Nails	Roofing Felt	1	EA
5# 1-1/4" Roofing Nails	Shingle	2	EA
5# 6d Galv. Box Nails	General Framing	1	EA
5# 6d Galv. Finish Nails	Siding/Soffit	1	EA

EXTERIOR TRIM & ACCESSORIES

Item	Location	Qty	UM
1X6 - 10' Ship Lap Siding	Siding	100	EA
2x4 - 10' Std. & Btr.	Corner Trim	4	EA
1x4 - 8' Std. & Btr.	Window Trim	10	EA
1/4" Plywood (Sanded)	Soffit Material	4	EA
1x4 - 10' Std. & Btr. (Rip-1x2)	Soffit/Fascia Trim	5	EA
1x6 - 8' Std. & Btr.	Post Trim	2	EA
14x6 Metal Soffit Vent	Soffit	4	EA
4x4 - 10' Treated	Porch	4	EA
2x4 - 10' Treated	Railing	4	EA
1-3/8"x1-3/8" - 3' Baluster	Railing	60	EA
36"x80" Exterior LH Door	Exterior Door	1	EA
(2) 30"x80" Exterior Door	Exterior Door	1	EA
2030 Single Hung Window	Window	3	EA
Lockset/Deadbolt	Exterior Door	1	EA
Lockset/Deadbolt/Pin	Exterior Door	1	EA
2x4 - 10' Std. & Btr.	Bench	2	EA
2x4 - 12' Std. & Btr.	Bench	2	EA
36"x30" White Wall Cabinet	Over Bench	2	EA
White Door Package 'H'	Wall Cabinet	4	EA
3/4" OSB Sq. Edge (Ply.)	Bench	1	EA
5# 6d Galv. Finish Nail	Siding/Soffit	4	EA
5# 8d Galv. Finish Nail	Window/Door	1	EA
10 oz. - Paintable Caulk	Siding/Trim	6	TB
1-1/4"x2" Brickmold	Exterior Door	6	EA
4" - 10' "Z" Flashing	Window/Door	2	EA

CHAPTER 4

THE CHARLESTON   HPM-1401
Dimensions for this shed are 10' X 8'. 80 sq. ft.

THE CHARLESTON & VICEROY

Keystone trim accents and decorative flower boxes dress up these gingerbread-inspired sheds. Oversized landscaping and recreational equipment can be easily accessed and removed through the sheds' handy double doors. In addition to the storage space, there's room for the gardener or the do-it-yourselfer to entertain hobbies. Windows on three sides allow in plenty of light. The larger shed (Viceroy) has two front windows.

THE VICEROY   HPM-1301
Dimensions for this shed are 14' X 10'. 140 sq. ft.

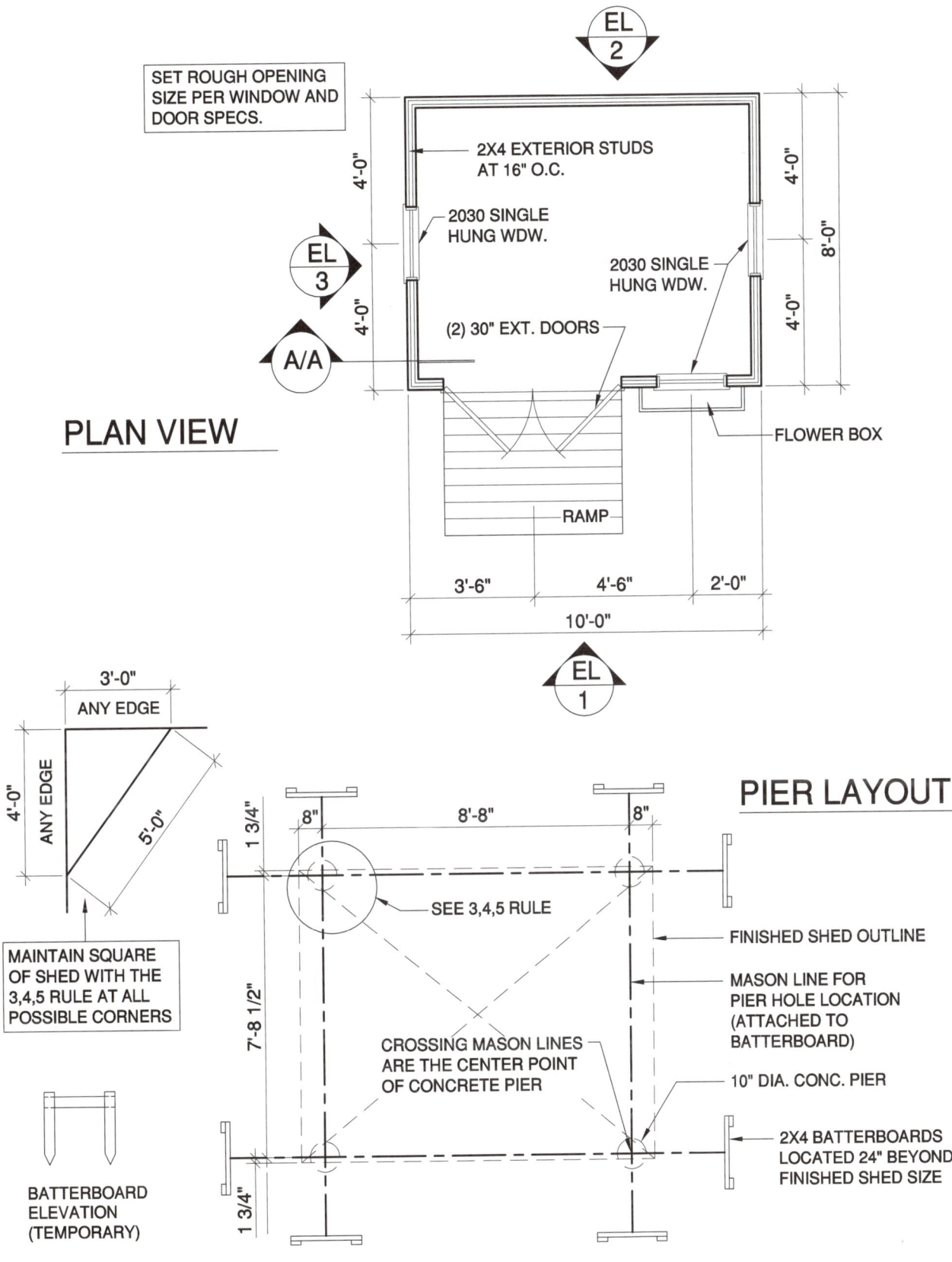

CHARLESTON Framing Plan and Section

Scale: 1/4" = 1'-0"

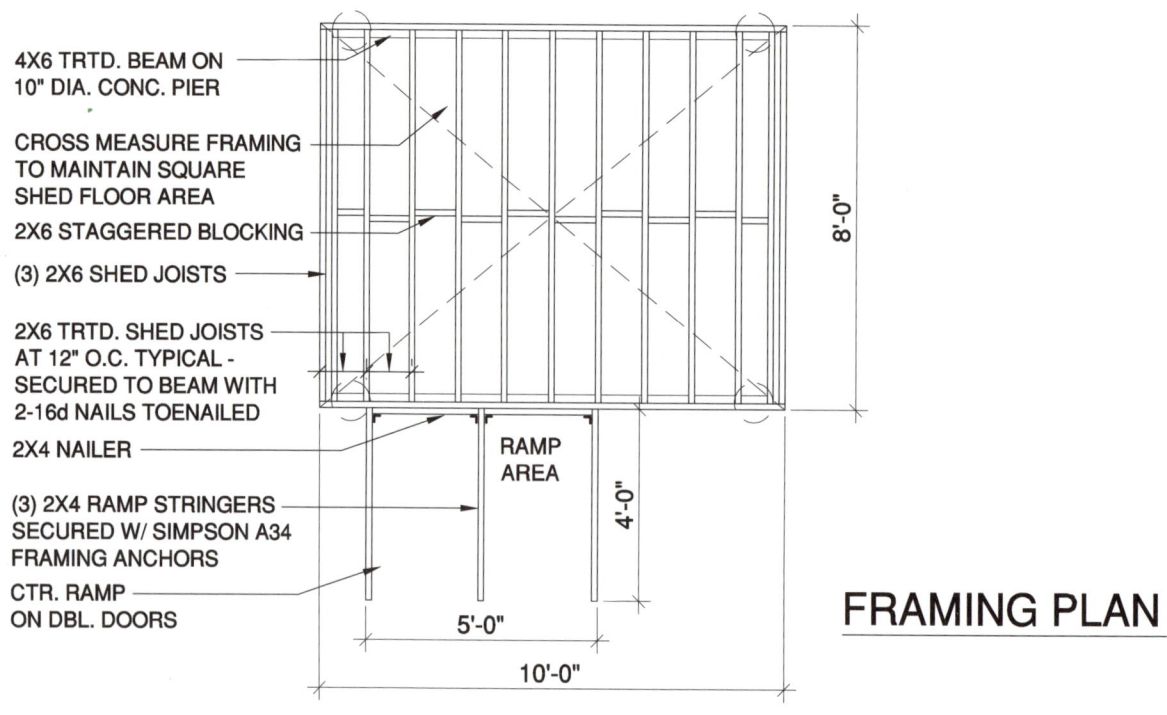

FRAMING PLAN

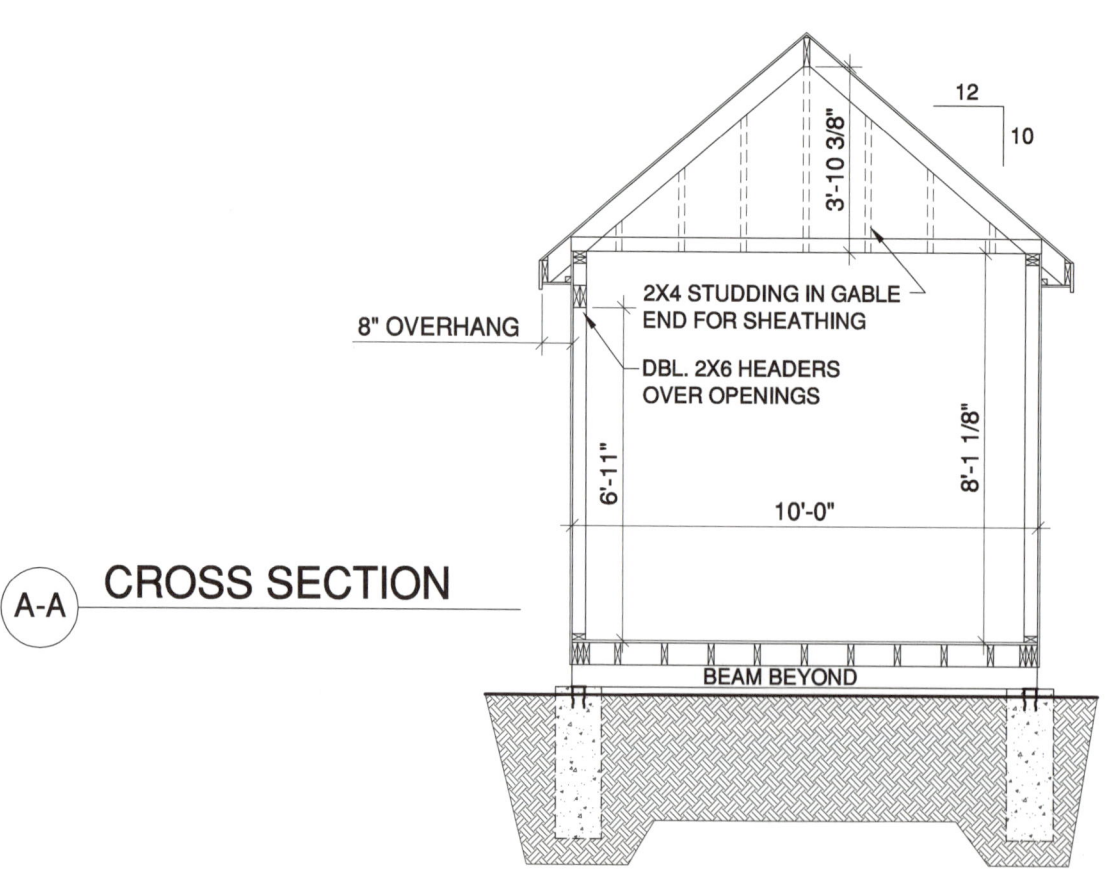

CROSS SECTION A-A

Charleston — Elevation and Details

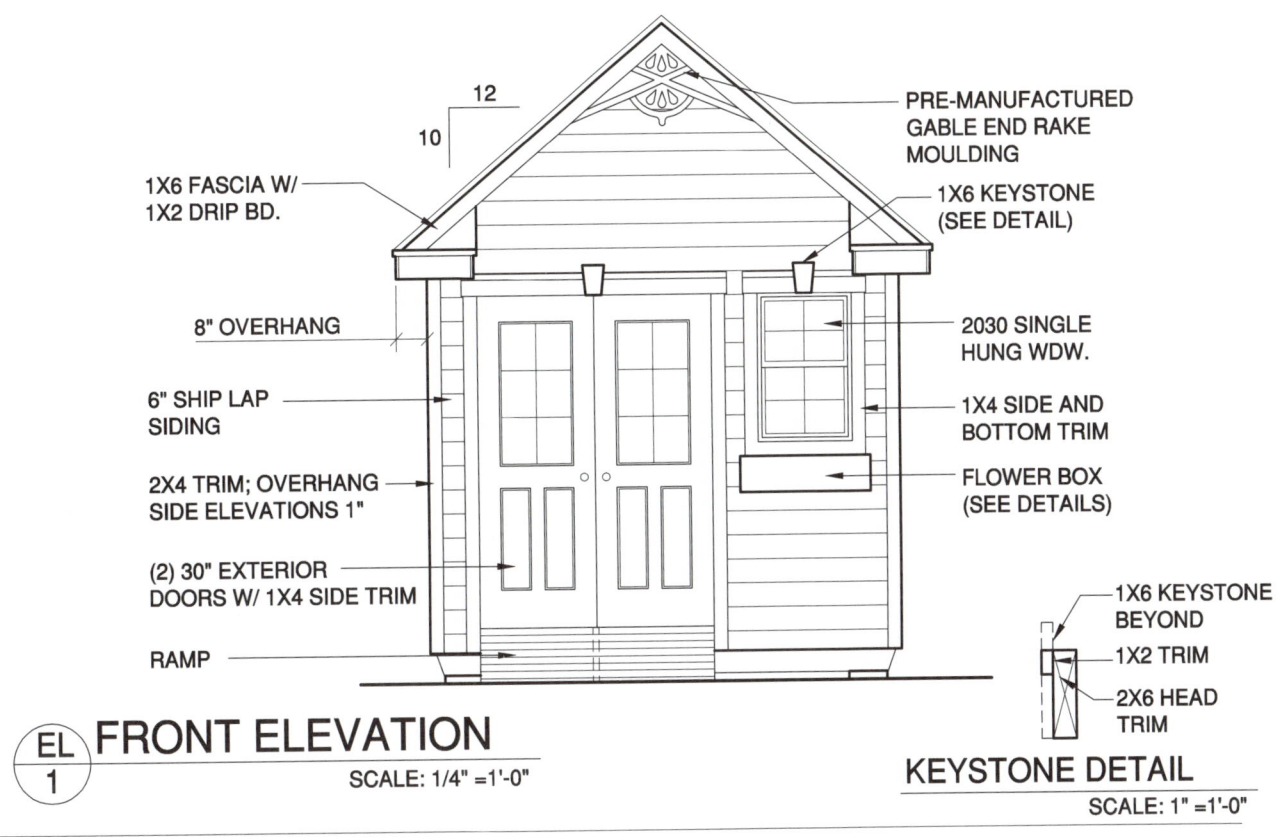

FRONT ELEVATION
SCALE: 1/4" =1'-0"
EL/1

KEYSTONE DETAIL
SCALE: 1" =1'-0"

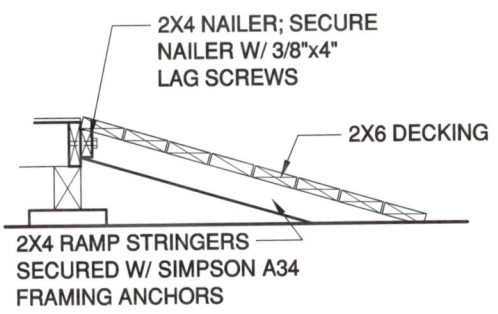

RAMP SECTION
SCALE: 1/2" =1'-0"

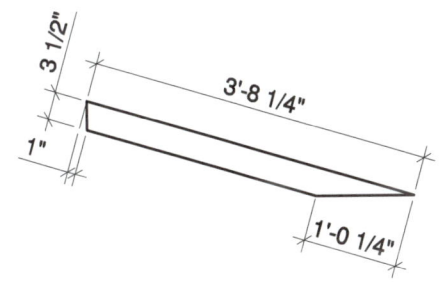

RAMP STRINGER
SCALE: 1/2" =1'-0"

FLOWER BOX DETAILS

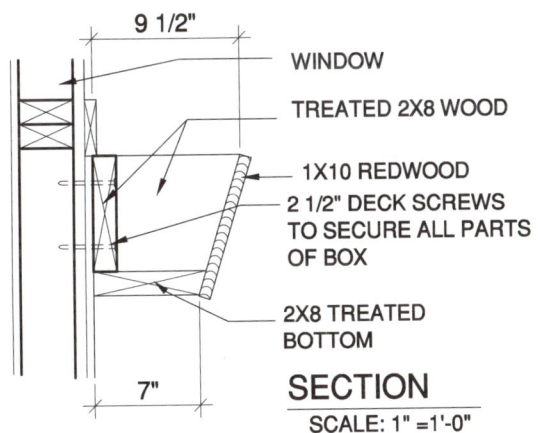

SECTION
SCALE: 1" =1'-0"

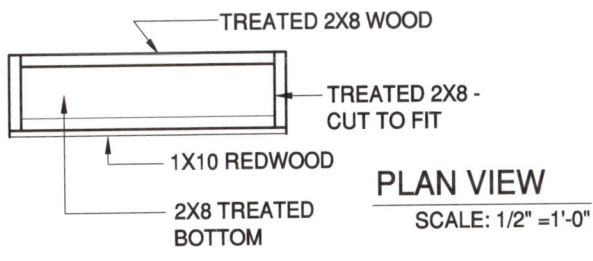

PLAN VIEW
SCALE: 1/2" =1'-0"

www.homedepot.com

CHARLESTON Elevations

Scale: 1/4" = 1'-0"

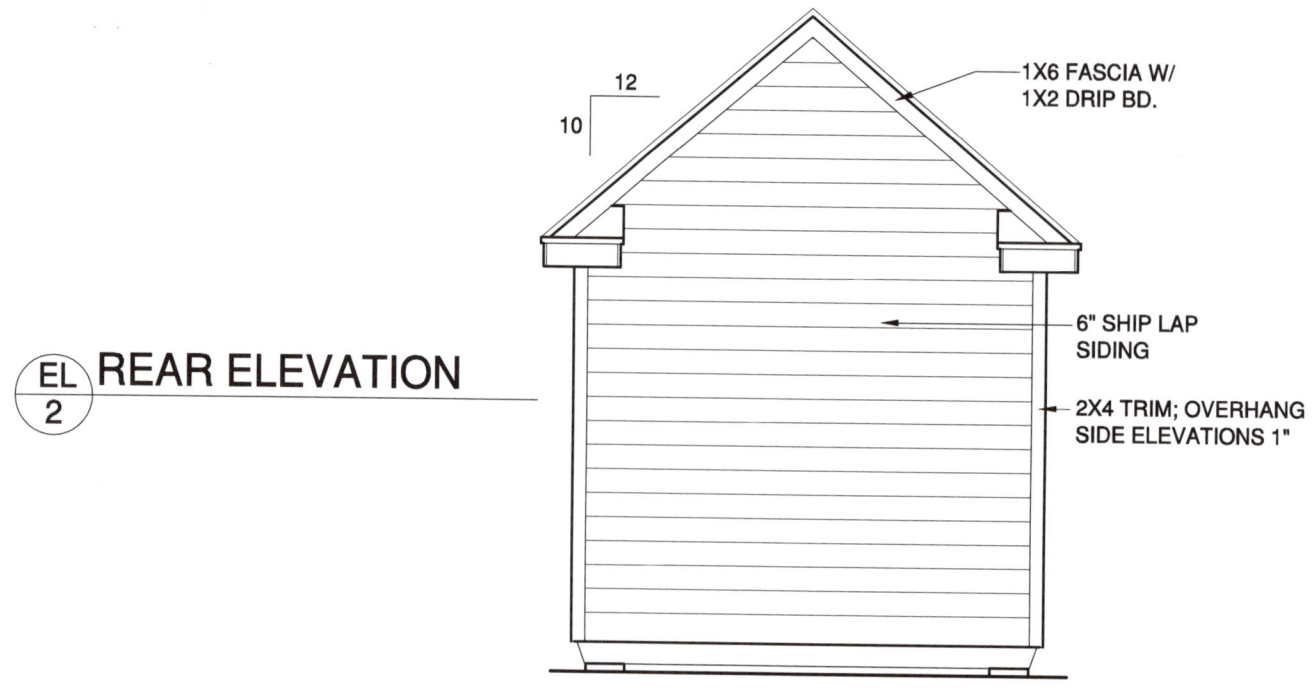

EL 2 REAR ELEVATION

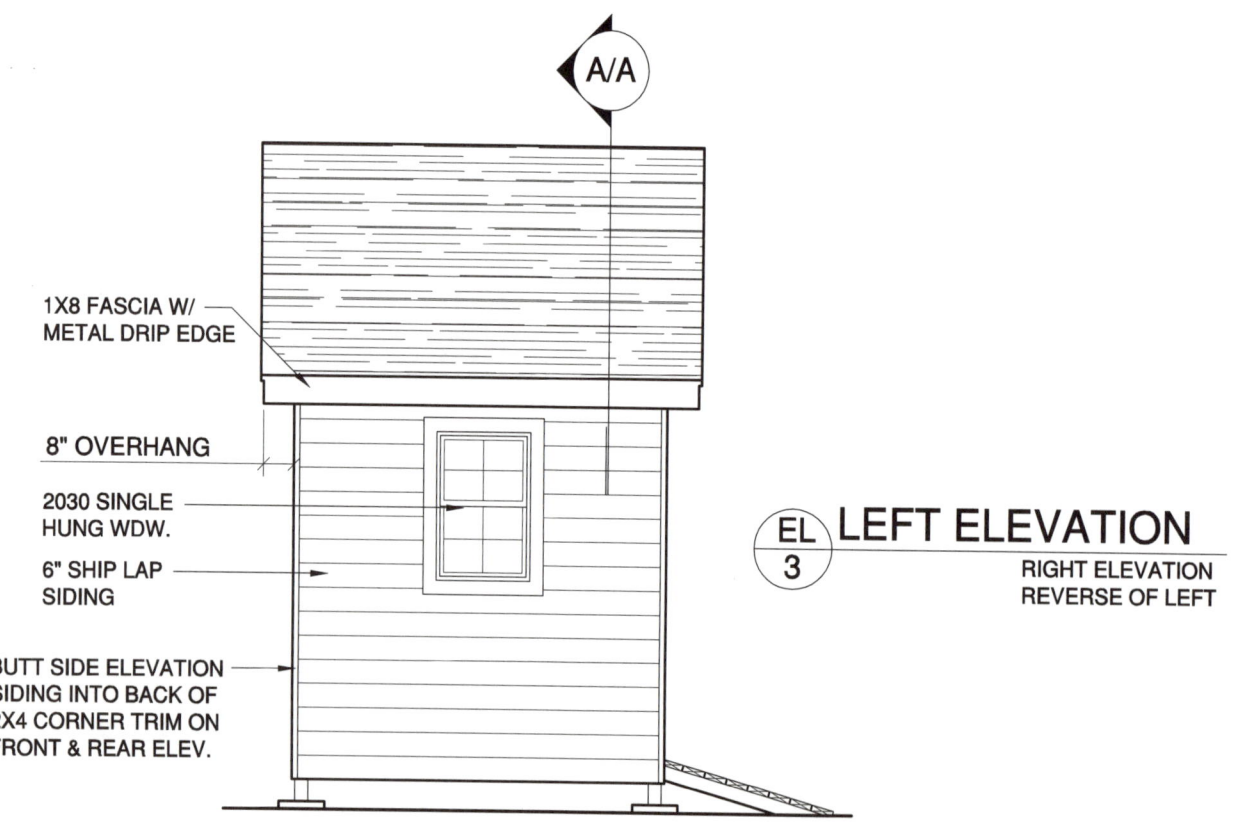

EL 3 LEFT ELEVATION
RIGHT ELEVATION REVERSE OF LEFT

Charleston Details

Scale: 1/2" = 1'-0"

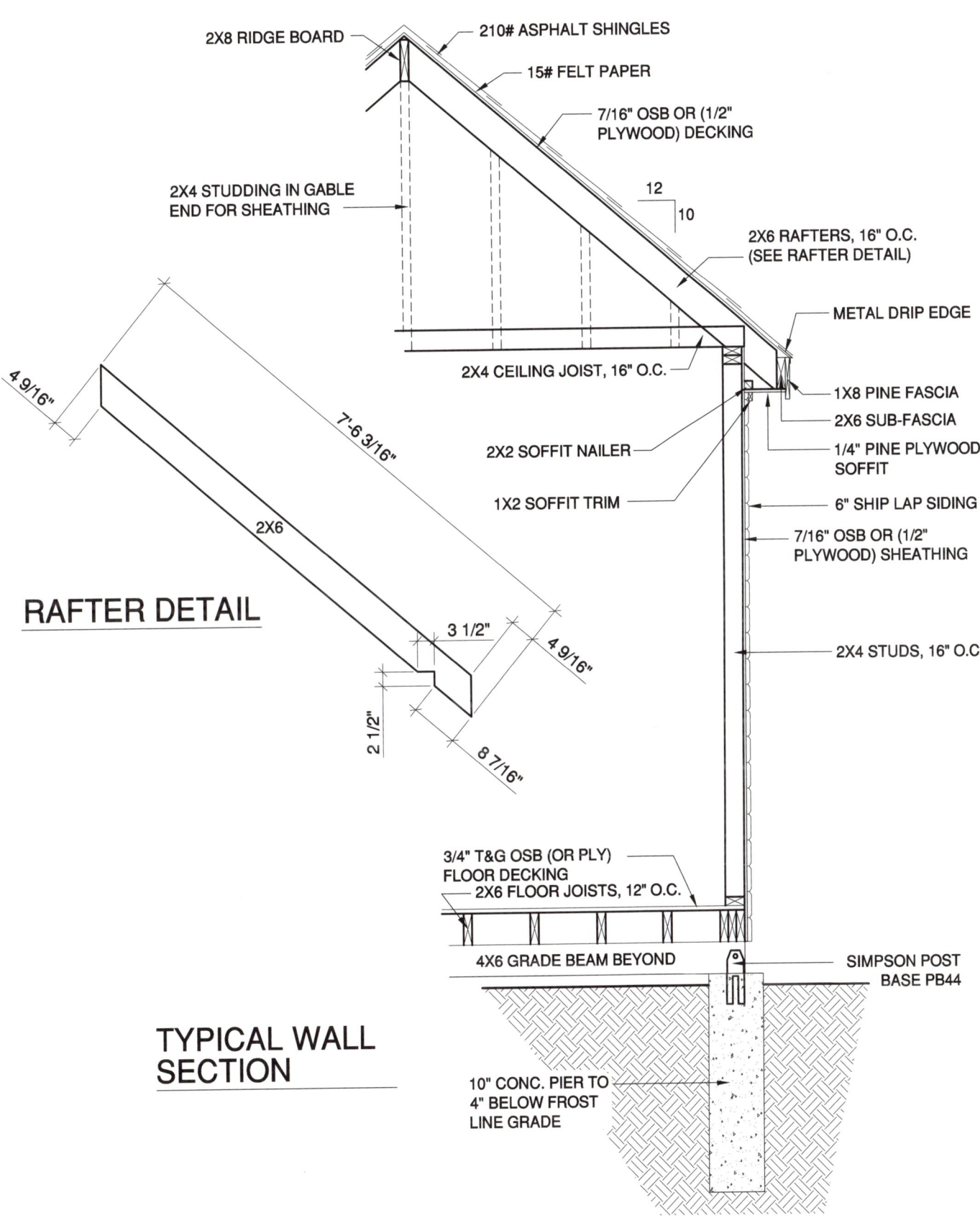

RAFTER DETAIL

TYPICAL WALL SECTION

- 2X8 RIDGE BOARD
- 210# ASPHALT SHINGLES
- 15# FELT PAPER
- 7/16" OSB OR (1/2" PLYWOOD) DECKING
- 2X4 STUDDING IN GABLE END FOR SHEATHING
- 12 / 10
- 2X6 RAFTERS, 16" O.C. (SEE RAFTER DETAIL)
- METAL DRIP EDGE
- 2X4 CEILING JOIST, 16" O.C.
- 1X8 PINE FASCIA
- 2X6 SUB-FASCIA
- 2X2 SOFFIT NAILER
- 1/4" PINE PLYWOOD SOFFIT
- 1X2 SOFFIT TRIM
- 6" SHIP LAP SIDING
- 7/16" OSB OR (1/2" PLYWOOD) SHEATHING
- 2X4 STUDS, 16" O.C.
- 3/4" T&G OSB (OR PLY) FLOOR DECKING
- 2X6 FLOOR JOISTS, 12" O.C.
- 4X6 GRADE BEAM BEYOND
- SIMPSON POST BASE PB44
- 10" CONC. PIER TO 4" BELOW FROST LINE GRADE

Rafter dimensions: 4 9/16", 7'-6 3/16", 2X6, 3 1/2", 4 9/16", 2 1/2", 8 7/16"

CHARLESTON Material List

FOUNDATION

Item	Location	Qty	UM
60# Concrete Mix	Pier	20	BG
10"x 8" Fiber Tube	Pier	4	EA
2x4 - 10' Std. & Btr.	Batterboard	5	EA
Post Base (PB44)	Pier	4	EA
1/2" Hex. Hd. Nut	Post Base	8	EA
1/2"x4-1/2" Bolt	Post Base	8	EA
1/2" Washer	Post Base	16	EA
Crushed Gravel	Pier	8	BG

FLOOR

Item	Location	Qty	UM
4x6 - 12' Treated	Beam	2	EA
2x6 - 8' Treated	Floor Joist	15	EA
2x6 - 10' Treated	Header Jst./Blkg.	3	EA
3/4" T & G OSB (Ply.)	Floor Decking	3	EA
Framing Anchor (A34)	Floor Framing	8	EA
2x4 - 8' Treated	Nailer/Stringer	3	EA
2x6 - 10' Treated	Ramp Decking	4	EA
3/8"x4" Lag Screws	Ramp Nailer	4	EA
3/8"x1-1/2" Washer	Ramp Nailer	4	EA
5# 16d Galv. Nails	General Framing	1	EA
5# 8d Ctd. Box Nails	General Framing	1	EA
1# 2-1/2" Ctd. Ext. Screws	General Framing	1	EA
Construction Adhesive	Floor Decking	2	TB

WALL FRAMING

Item	Location	Qty	UM
2x4 - 8' Treated	Bottom Plate	2	EA
2x4 - 10' Treated	Bottom Plate	2	EA
2x4 - 96" Stud Grade	Stud/Gable	46	EA
2x4 - 96" Stud Grade	Crpl./Sill/Blkg.	7	EA
2x4 - 8' Std. & Btr.	Top/Cap Plate	4	EA
2x4 - 10' Std. & Btr.	Top/Cap Plate	4	EA
2x6 - 8' Std. & Btr.	Header	4	EA
7/16" OSB (Ply.)	Wall Sheathing	11	EA
5# 16d Galv. Nails	General Framing	2	EA
5# 8d Ctd. Box Nails	General Framing	2	EA
1x6 - 10' Std. & Btr.	Bracing	6	EA
40"x 97' Building Paper	Wall Covering	2	RL
5# 1/2" Roofing Nails	Wall Covering	1	EA

CEILING/ROOF

Item	Location	Qty	UM
2x4 - 10' Std. & Btr.	Ceiling Joist	9	EA
2x6 - 8' Std. & Btr.	Rafter	18	EA
2x6 - 12' Std. & Btr.	Sub-Fascia	3	EA
2x4 - 8' Std. & Btr.	Rake/Boxed Rake	10	EA
2x2 - 8' #2 & Btr. S4S	Soffit Nailer	3	EA
2x8 - 12' Std. & Btr.	Ridge Board	1	EA
1x6 - 10' Std. & Btr.	Fascia/Keystone	4	EA
1x8 - 6' #2 & Btr. S4S	Fascia	1	EA
1x8 - 12' #2 & Btr. S4S	Fascia	2	EA
7/16" OSB (Ply.)	Roof Decking	5	EA
3 - Tab Shingle Tan 20 Yr.	Shingle	6	BN
15-lb. Asphalt Rfg. Felt	Roofing	1	RL
Galv. Drip Edge	Roof Edge	6	EA
5# 8d Ctd. Box Nails	General Framing	2	EA
5# 10d Bright Box Nails	General Framing	2	EA
5# 16d Galv. Nails	General Framing	1	EA
5# 1/2" Roofing Nails	Roofing Felt	1	EA
5# 1-1/4" Roofing Nails	Shingle	2	EA
5# 6d Galv. Box Nails	General Framing	1	EA
5# 6d Galv. Finish Nails	Siding/Soffit	1	EA

EXTERIOR TRIM & ACCESSORIES

Item	Location	Qty	UM
1X6 - 10' Ship Lap Siding	Siding	70	EA
2x4 - 10' Std. & Btr.	Corner Trim	4	EA
1x4 - 8' Std. & Btr.	Window Trim	7	EA
1x2 - 10' Trim Board	Soffit/Fascia	10	EA
1/4" Plywood (Sanded)	Soffit Material	3	EA
14x6 Metal Soffit Vent	Soffit	4	EA
(2) 30"x80" Exterior Door	Exterior Door	1	EA
2030 SH Window	Window	3	EA
Lockset/Deadbolt/Pin	Exterior Door	1	EA
2x8 - 12' Treated	Flower Box	1	EA
1x10 -4' Redwood	Flower Box	1	EA
2x6 - 8' Std. & Btr.	Keystone	1	EA
1x2 - 8' Trim Board	Keystone	1	EA
Gable End Moulding	Gable	1	EA
5# 6d Galv. Finish Nails	Siding/Soffit	4	EA
5# 8d Galv. Finish Nails	Window/Door	1	EA
10 oz. - Paintable Caulk	Siding/Trim	6	TB
4" - 10' "Z" Flashing	Window/Door	2	EA

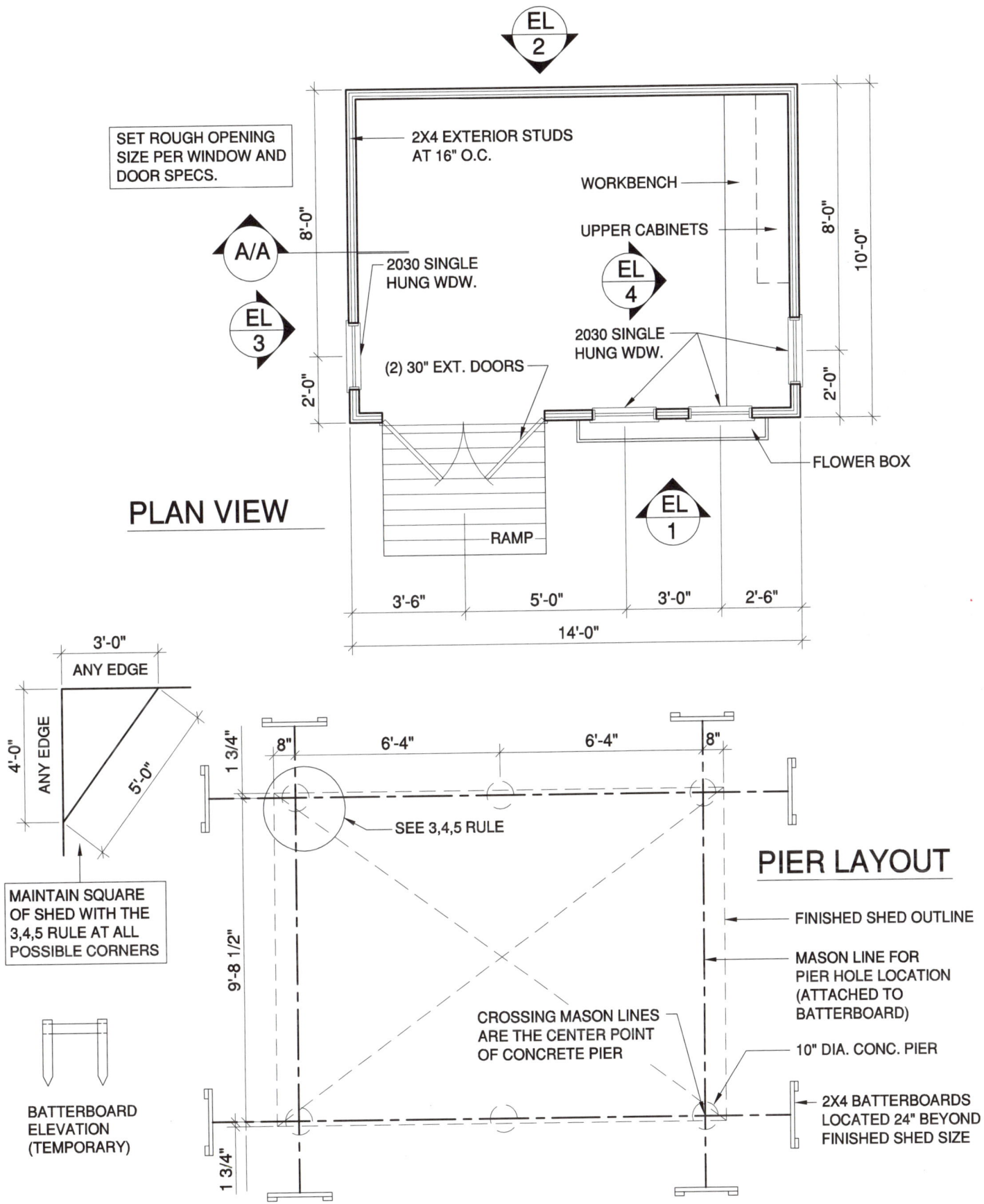

VICEROY
Framing Plan and Details

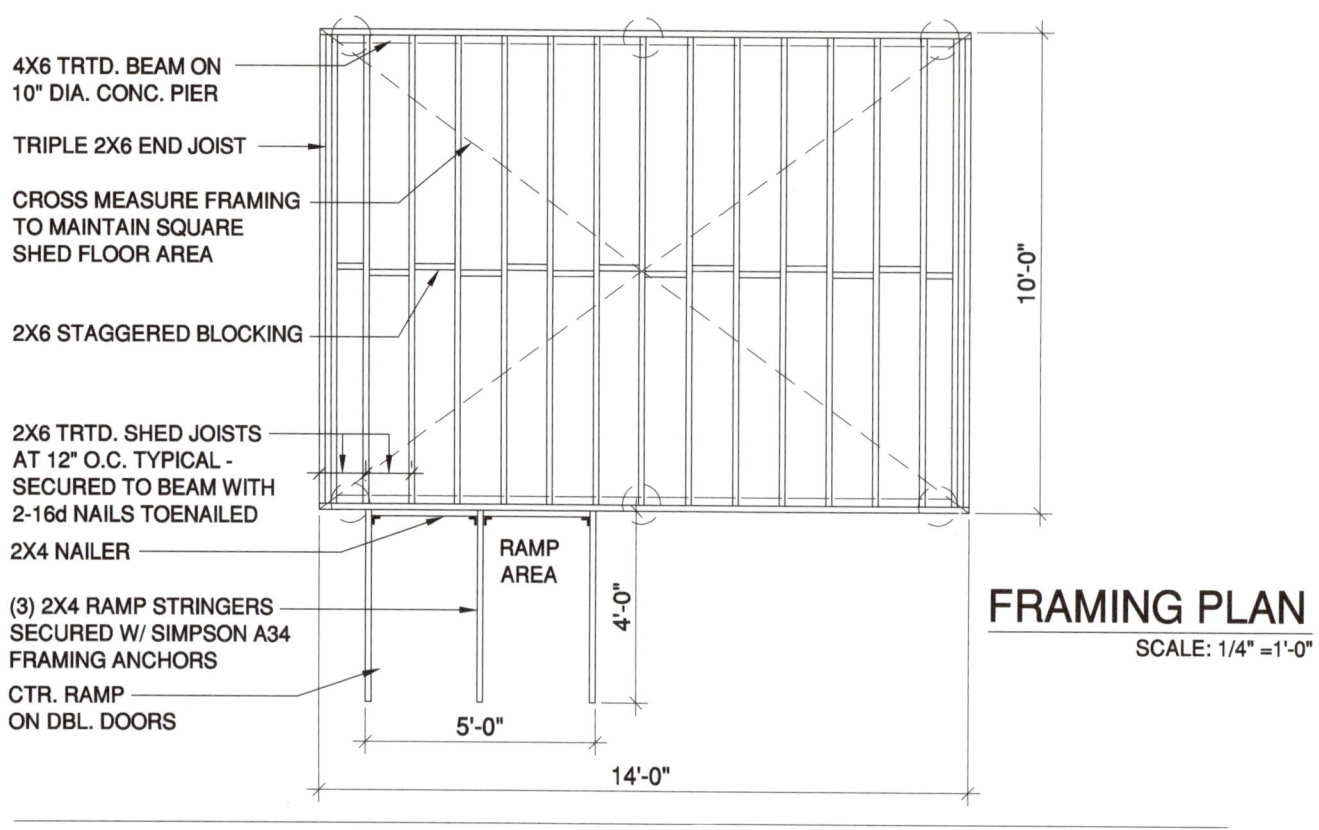

FRAMING PLAN
SCALE: 1/4" =1'-0"

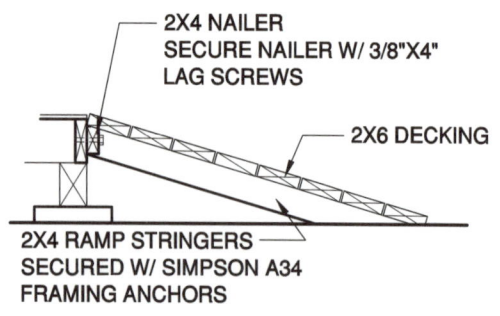

RAMP SECTION
SCALE: 1/2" =1'-0"

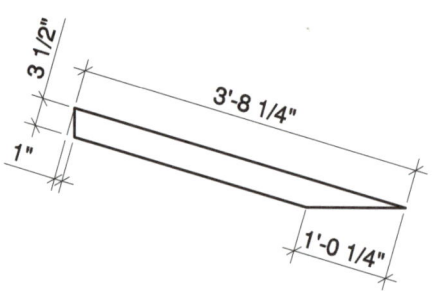

RAMP STRINGER
SCALE: 1/2" =1'-0"

FLOWER BOX DETAILS

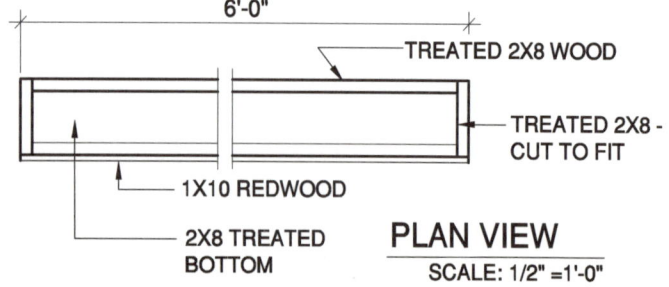

PLAN VIEW
SCALE: 1/2" =1'-0"

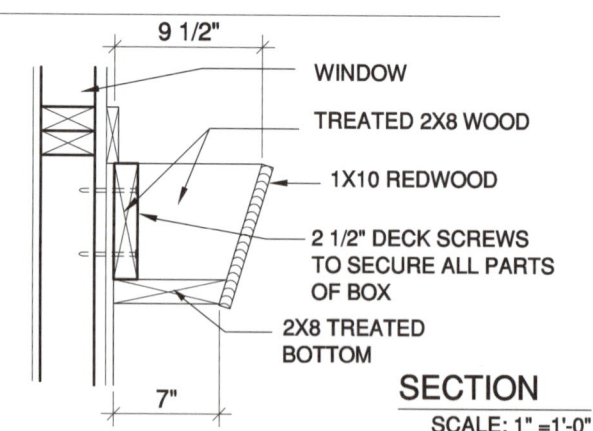

SECTION
SCALE: 1" =1'-0"

VICEROY — Elevations

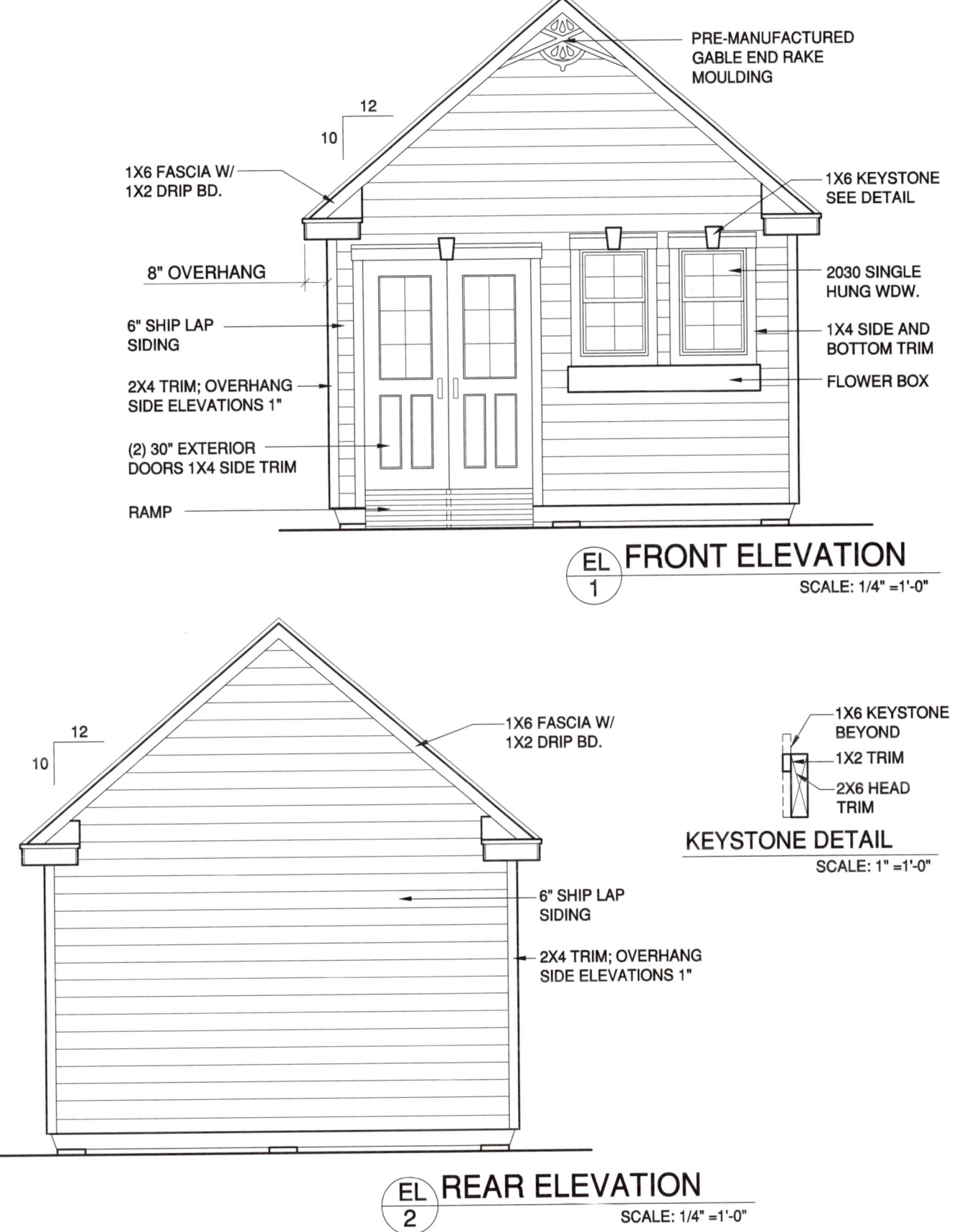

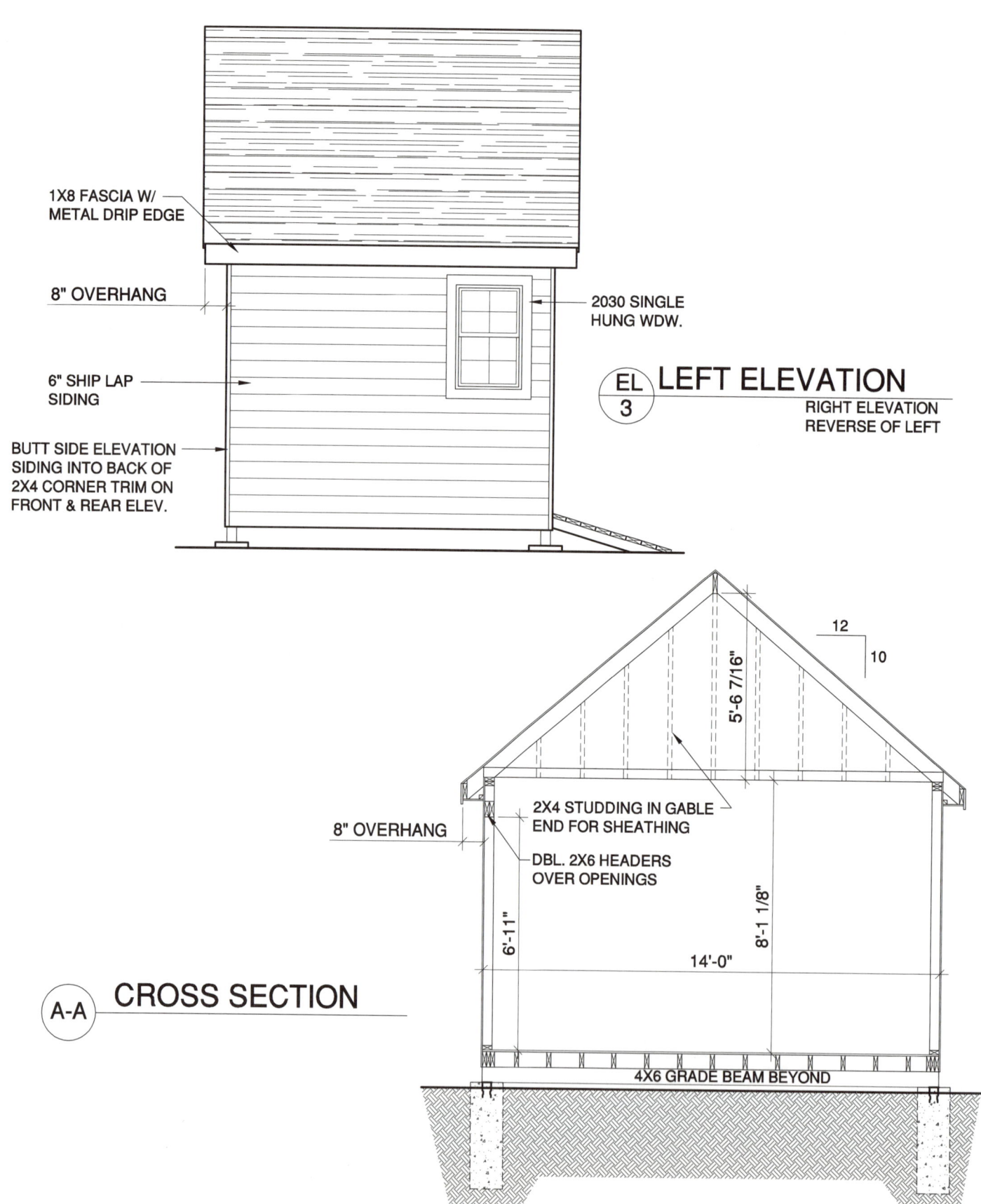

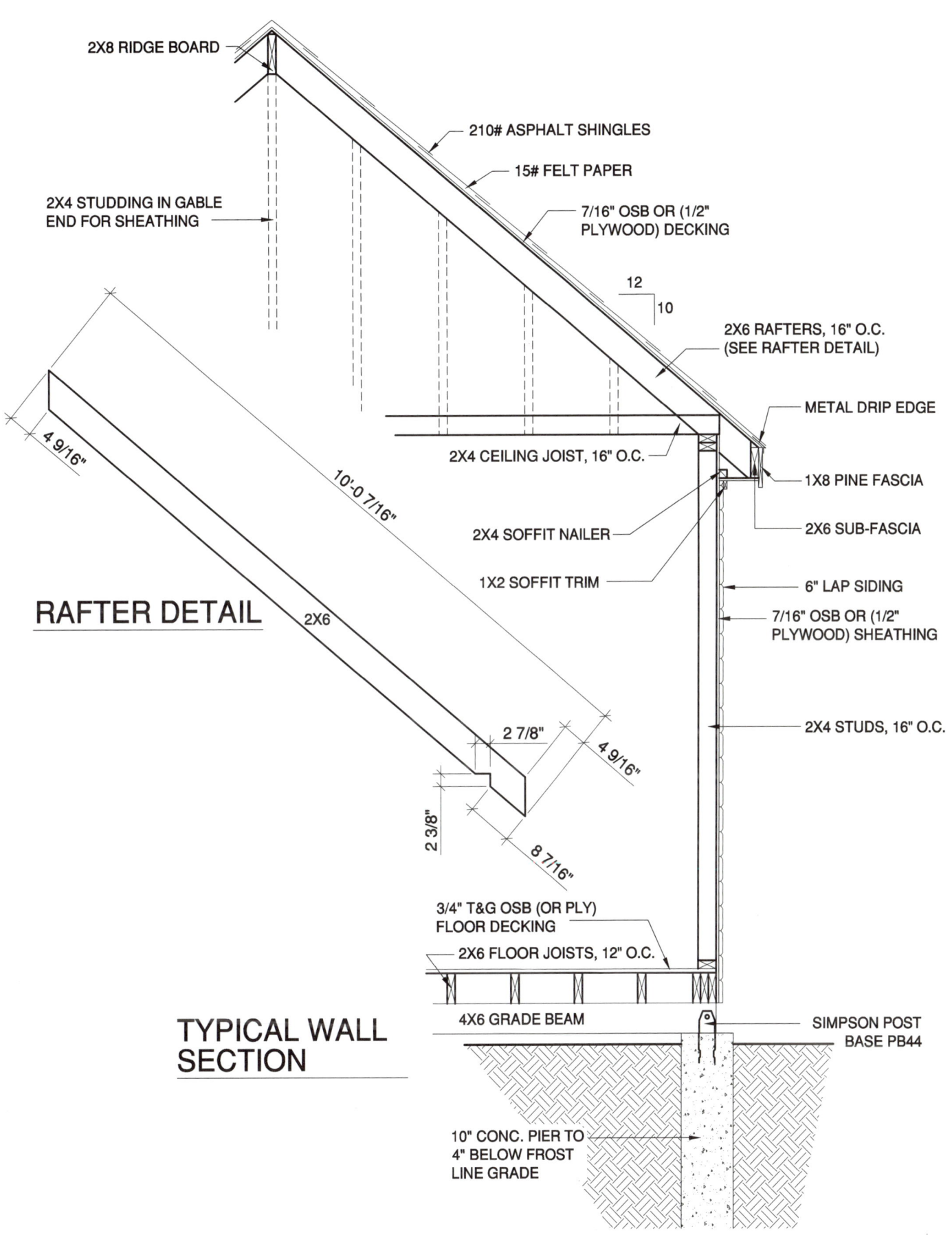

VICEROY Workbench Layout

Scale: 1/2" = 1'-0"

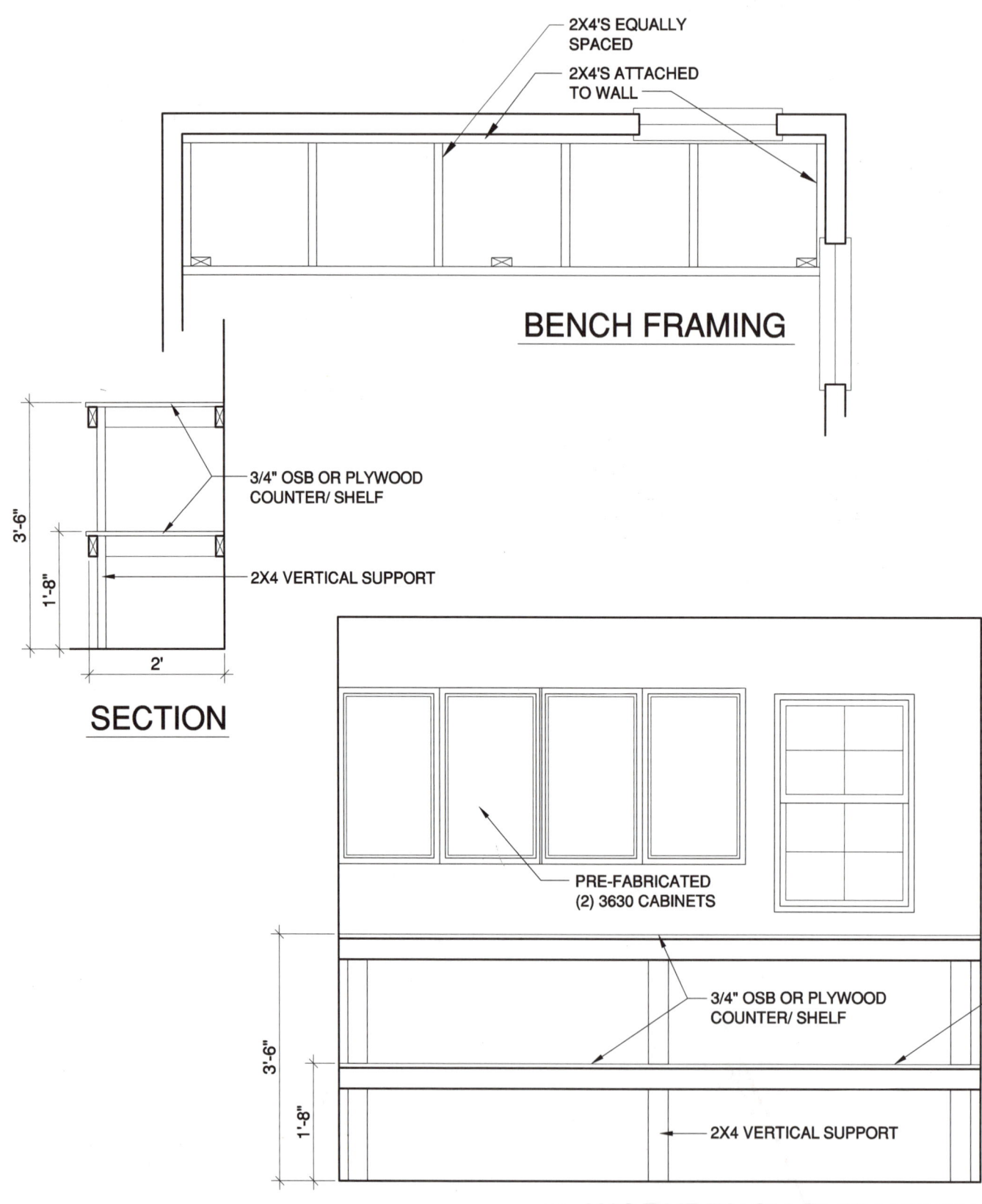

88 www.DreamIt-BuildIt.com

VICEROY — Material List

FOUNDATION

Item	Location	Qty	UM
60# Concrete Mix	Pier	30	BG
10"x 48" Fiber Tube	Pier	6	EA
2x4 - 10' Std. & Btr.	Batterboard	5	EA
Post Base (PB44)	Pier	6	EA
1/2" Hex. Hd. Nut	Post Base	12	EA
1/2"x 4-1/2" Bolt	Post Base	12	EA
1/2" Washer	Post Base	24	EA
Crushed Gravel	Pier	12	BG

FLOOR

Item	Location	Qty	UM
4x6 - 8' Treated	Beam	4	EA
2x6 - 10' Treated	Floor Joist	13	EA
2x6 - 16' Treated	Header Jst./Blkg.	3	EA
3/4" T & G OSB (Ply.)	Floor Decking	5	EA
Framing Anchor (A34)	Floor Framing	8	EA
2x4 - 8' Treated	Nailer/Stringer	3	EA
2x6 - 10' Treated	Decking	4	EA
3/8"x4" Lag Screws	Ramp Nailer	4	EA
3/8"x1-1/2" Washer	Ramp Nailer	4	EA
5# 16d Hot Galv. Nails	General Framing	1	EA
5# 8d Ctd. Box Nails	General Framing	1	EA
1# 2-1/2" Ctd. Ext. Screws	General Framing	1	EA
Construction Adhesive	Floor Decking	2	TB

WALL FRAMING

Item	Location	Qty	UM
2x4 - 10' Treated	Bottom Plate	2	EA
2x4 - 16' Treated	Bottom Plate	2	EA
2x4 - 96" Stud Grade	Stud/Gable	52	EA
2x4 - 96" Stud Grade	Crpl./Sill/Blkg.	12	EA
2x4 - 10' Std. & Btr.	Top/Cap Plate	4	EA
2x4 - 14' Std. & Btr.	Top/Cap Plate	4	EA
7/16" OSB (Ply.)	Wall Sheathing	15	EA
5# 16d Galv, Nails	General Framing	2	EA
5# 8d Ctd. Box Nails	General Framing	2	EA
1x6 - 10' Std. & Btr.	Bracing	6	EA
40"x 97' Building Paper	Wall Covering	2	RL
5# 1/2" Galv. Roofing Nails	Wall Covering	1	EA

CEILING/ROOF

Item	Location	Qty	UM
2x4 - 14' Std. & Btr.	Ceiling Joist	12	EA
2x6 - 10' Std. & Btr.	Rafter/Boxed Rake	25	EA
2x6 - 12' Std. & Btr.	Sub-Fascia	2	EA
2x4 - 12' Std. & Btr.	Rake/Boxed Rake	8	EA
2x2 - 8' #2 & Btr. S4S	Soffit Nailer	3	EA
2x8 - 12' Std. & Btr.	Ridge Board	1	EA
1x6 - 12' Std. & Btr.	Fascia	4	EA
1x8 - 12' #2 & Btr. S4S	Fascia	3	EA
7/16" OSB (Ply.)	Roof Decking	8	EA
3 -Tab Shingle 20 Yr.	Shingle	9	BN
15-lb. Asphalt Rfg. Felt	Roofing	2	RL
Galv. Drip Edge	Roof Edge	2	EA
5# 8d Ctd. Box Nails	General Framing	2	EA
5# 10d Bright Box Nail	General Framing	2	EA
5# 16d Galv. Nails	General Framing	1	EA
5# 1/2" Galv. Roofing Nails	Roofing Felt	1	EA
5# 1-1/4" Roofing Nails	Shingle	2	EA
5# 6d Galv. Box Nails	General Framing	1	EA
5# 6d Galv. Finish Nails	Siding/Soffit	1	EA

EXTERIOR TRIM & ACCESSORIES

Item	Location	Qty	UM
1X6 - 10' Ship Lap Siding	Siding	100	EA
2x4 - 10' Std. & Btr.	Corner Trim	4	EA
1x4 - 8' Std. & Btr.	Window Trim	9	EA
1x2 - 10' Trim Board	Soffit/Fascia	8	EA
1/4" Plywood (Sanded)	Soffit Material	2	EA
14x6 Metal Soffit Vent	Soffit	4	EA
(2) 30"x80" Exterior Door	Exterior Door	1	EA
2030 SH Window	Window	4	EA
Lockset/Deadbolt/Pin	Exterior Door	1	EA
2x8 - 12' Treated	Flower Box	1	EA
1x10 - 10' Redwood	Flower Box	1	EA
2x6 - 12' Std. & Btr.	Keystone	1	EA
1x2 - 8' Trim Board	Keystone	2	EA
Gable End Moulding	Gable	1	EA
2x4 - 10' Std. & Btr.	Bench	4	EA
2x4 - 8' Std. & Btr.	Bench	4	EA
36"x30" White Wall Cabinet	Over Bench	2	EA
White Door Package 'H'	Cabinet	4	EA
3/4" OSB Sq. Edge (Ply.)	Bench	2	EA
5# 6d Galv. Finish Nails	Siding/Soffit	4	EA
5# 8d Galv. Finish Nails	Window/Door	1	EA
10 oz. - Paintable Caulk	Siding/Trim	6	TB
4" - 10' "Z" Flashing	Window/Door	2	EA

CHAPTER 4

THE CEDARVILLE   HPM-1402
Dimensions for this shed are 10' X 8'. 80 sq. ft.

THE CEDARVILLE & SPRINGFIELD

Cute as a button and functional too, these terrific sheds house your wheelbarrow, lawn mower and other cumbersome outdoor equipment. Double doors and a ramp ensure that you can move your equipment in and out with ease. Decorative flower boxes and windows are featured in both sheds; the larger shed (Springfield) has one more window on its wider front elevation.

THE SPRINGFIELD   HPM-1302
Dimensions for this shed are 14' X 10'. 140 sq. ft.

CEDARVILLE
Plan View and Pier Layout
Scale: 1/4" = 1'-0"

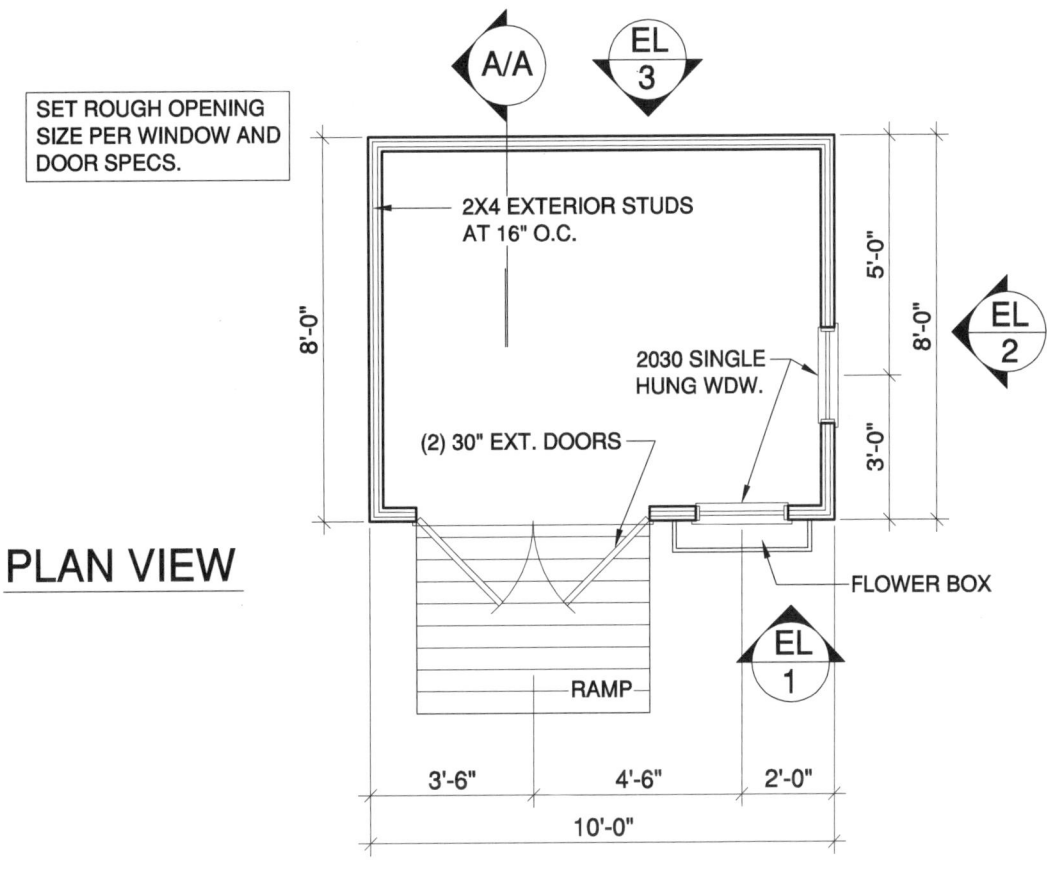

PLAN VIEW

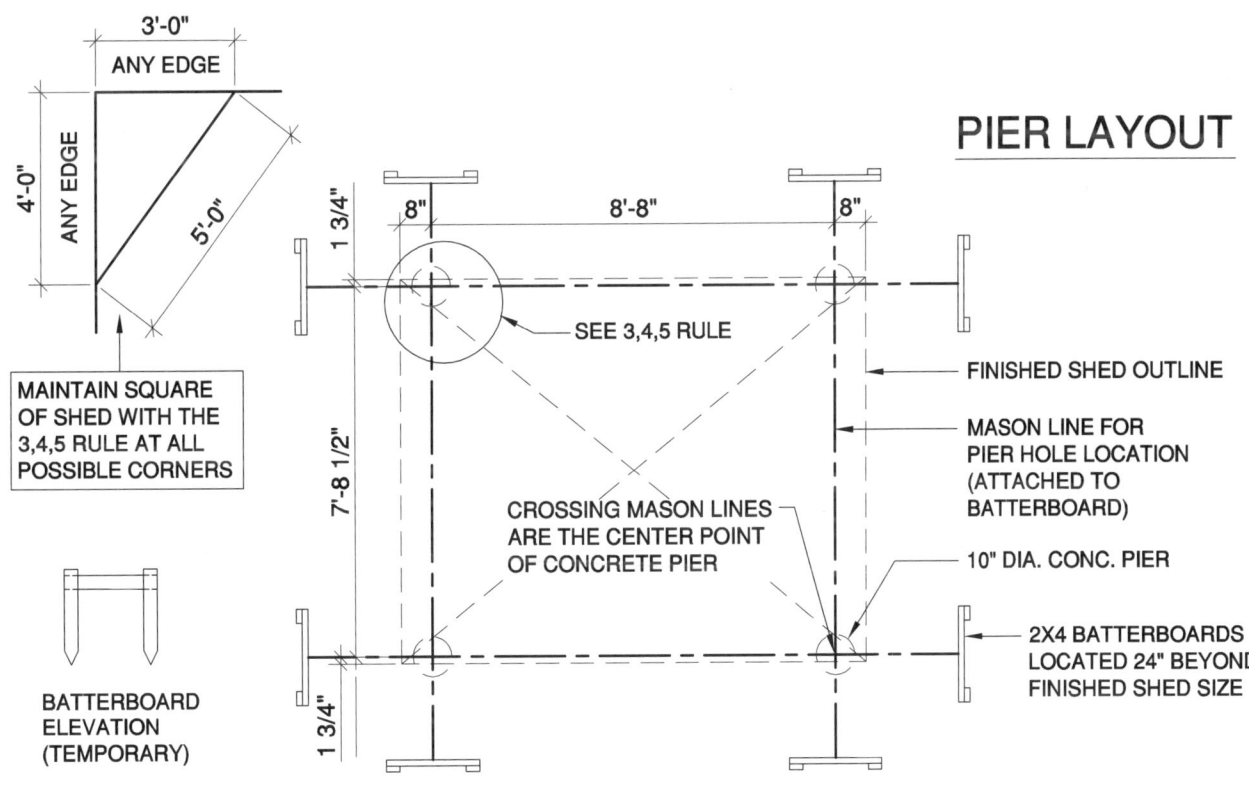

PIER LAYOUT

www.homedepot.com

Cedarville — Framing Plan and Details

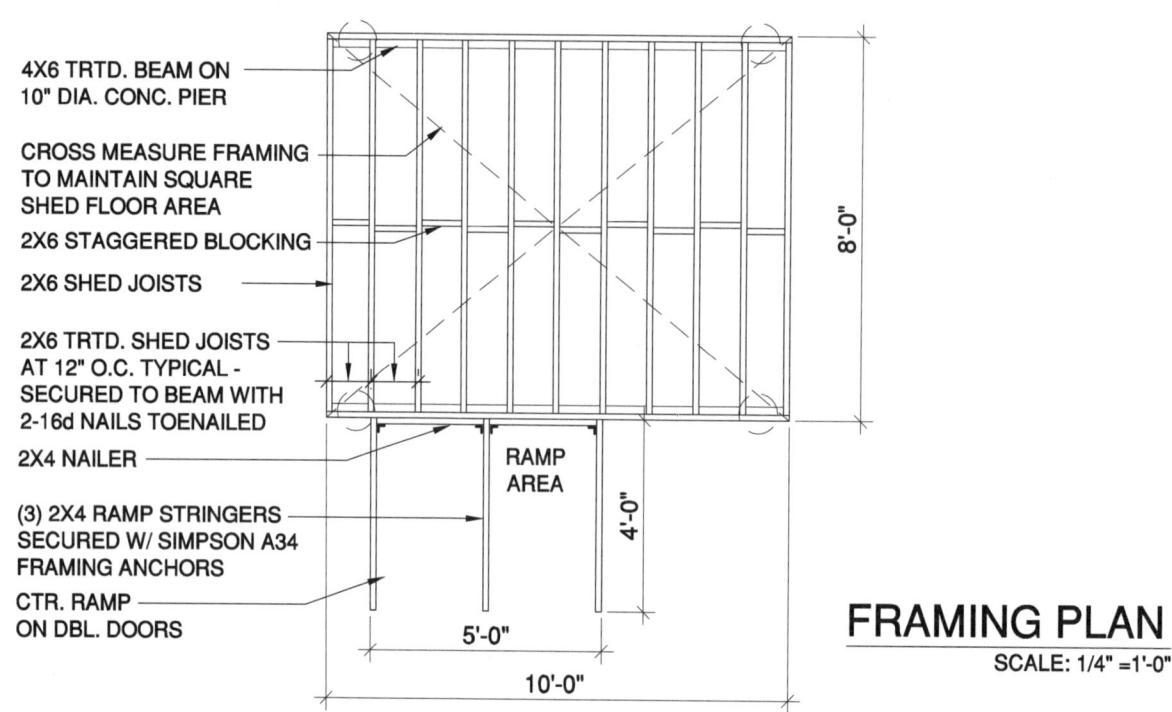

FRAMING PLAN
SCALE: 1/4" = 1'-0"

- 4X6 TRTD. BEAM ON 10" DIA. CONC. PIER
- CROSS MEASURE FRAMING TO MAINTAIN SQUARE SHED FLOOR AREA
- 2X6 STAGGERED BLOCKING
- 2X6 SHED JOISTS
- 2X6 TRTD. SHED JOISTS AT 12" O.C. TYPICAL - SECURED TO BEAM WITH 2-16d NAILS TOENAILED
- 2X4 NAILER
- (3) 2X4 RAMP STRINGERS SECURED W/ SIMPSON A34 FRAMING ANCHORS
- CTR. RAMP ON DBL. DOORS

RAMP AREA — 5'-0" / 10'-0" / 4'-0" / 8'-0"

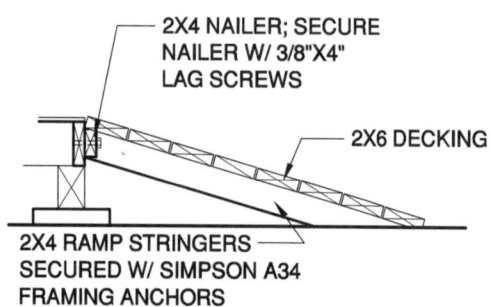

RAMP SECTION
SCALE: 1/2" = 1'-0"

- 2X4 NAILER; SECURE NAILER W/ 3/8"X4" LAG SCREWS
- 2X6 DECKING
- 2X4 RAMP STRINGERS SECURED W/ SIMPSON A34 FRAMING ANCHORS

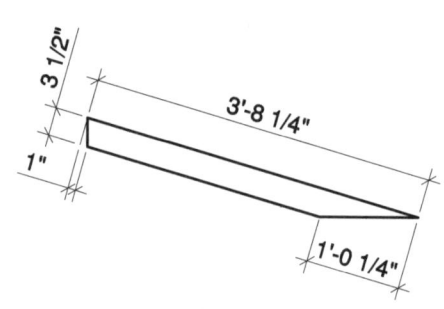

RAMP STRINGER
SCALE: 1/2" = 1'-0"

3 1/2" / 3'-8 1/4" / 1" / 1'-0 1/4"

CEDARVILLE — Elevations and Details

FRONT ELEVATION
SCALE: 1/4" = 1'-0"
EL 1

Labels:
- 1X8 FASCIA W/ 1X2 DRIP BD.
- 8" OVERHANG
- 6" SHIP LAP SIDING
- 2X4 TRIM; OVERHANG SIDE ELEVATIONS 1"
- (2) 30" EXTERIOR DOORS W/ 1X4 TRIM
- RAMP
- 2030 SINGLE HUNG WDW.
- 1X4 SIDE, TOP AND BOTTOM TRIM
- FLOWER BOX (SEE DETAILS)

FLOWER BOX DETAILS

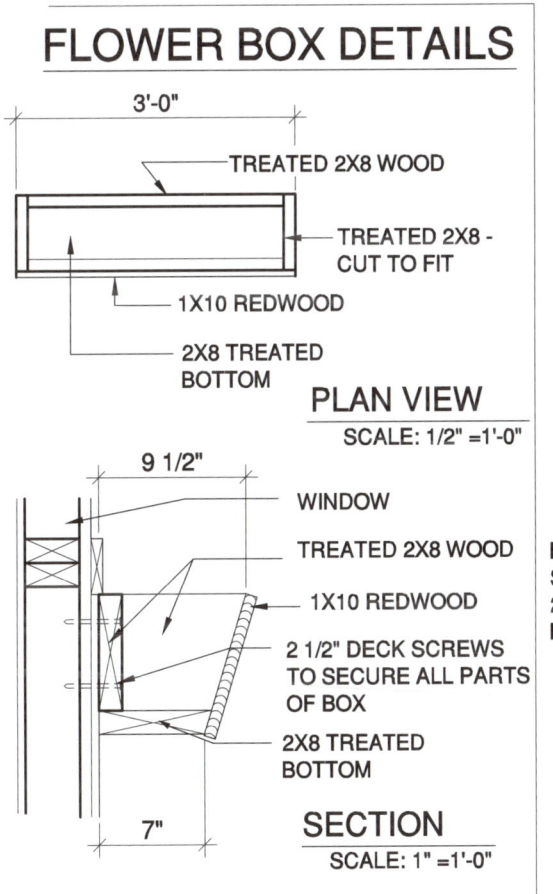

PLAN VIEW — SCALE: 1/2" = 1'-0"

Labels:
- 3'-0"
- TREATED 2X8 WOOD
- TREATED 2X8 - CUT TO FIT
- 1X10 REDWOOD
- 2X8 TREATED BOTTOM

SECTION — SCALE: 1" = 1'-0"

Labels:
- 9 1/2"
- WINDOW
- TREATED 2X8 WOOD
- 1X10 REDWOOD
- 2 1/2" DECK SCREWS TO SECURE ALL PARTS OF BOX
- 2X8 TREATED BOTTOM
- 7"

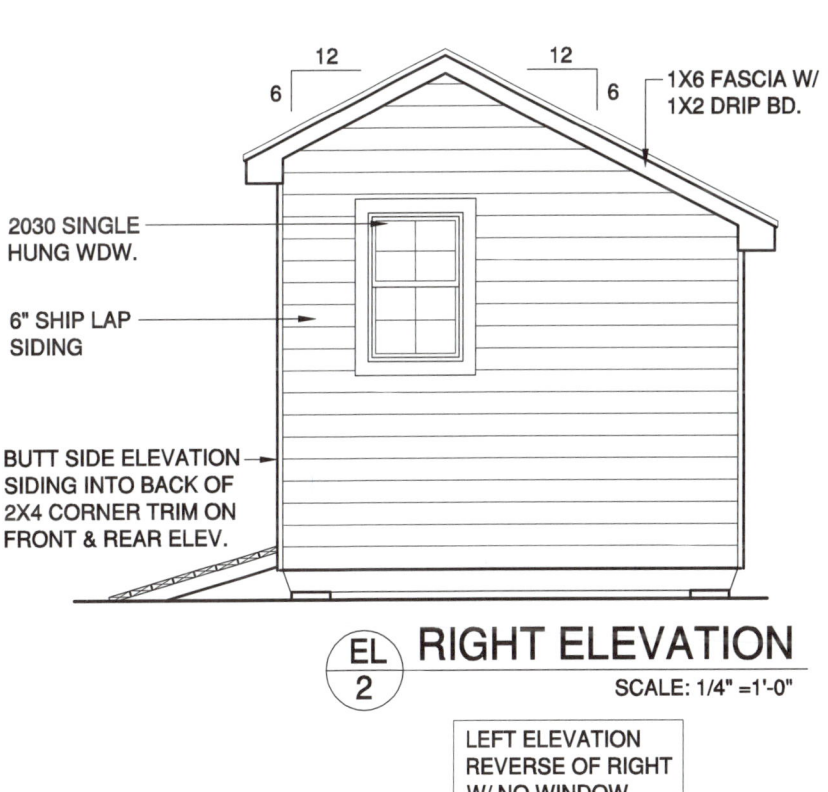

RIGHT ELEVATION
SCALE: 1/4" = 1'-0"
EL 2

Labels:
- 12 / 6 (roof pitch, both sides)
- 1X6 FASCIA W/ 1X2 DRIP BD.
- 2030 SINGLE HUNG WDW.
- 6" SHIP LAP SIDING
- BUTT SIDE ELEVATION SIDING INTO BACK OF 2X4 CORNER TRIM ON FRONT & REAR ELEV.

LEFT ELEVATION REVERSE OF RIGHT W/ NO WINDOW

CEDARVILLE — Elevation Details

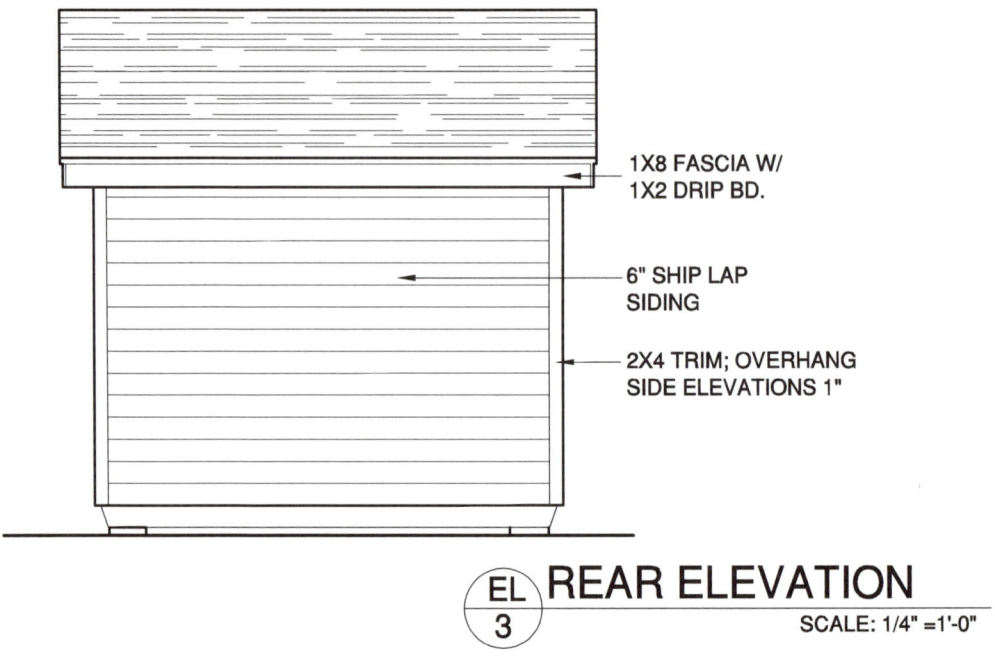

REAR ELEVATION
SCALE: 1/4" = 1'-0"
EL 3

- 1X8 FASCIA W/ 1X2 DRIP BD.
- 6" SHIP LAP SIDING
- 2X4 TRIM; OVERHANG SIDE ELEVATIONS 1"

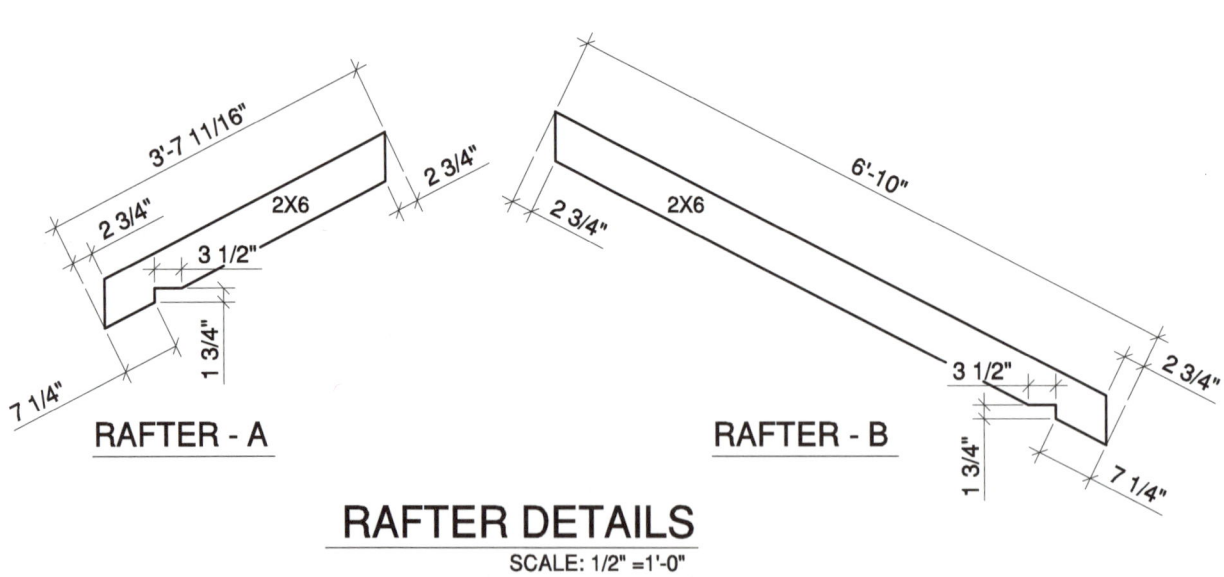

RAFTER - A

RAFTER - B

RAFTER DETAILS
SCALE: 1/2" = 1'-0"

CEDARVILLE — Cross Section

Scale: 1/2" = 1'-0"

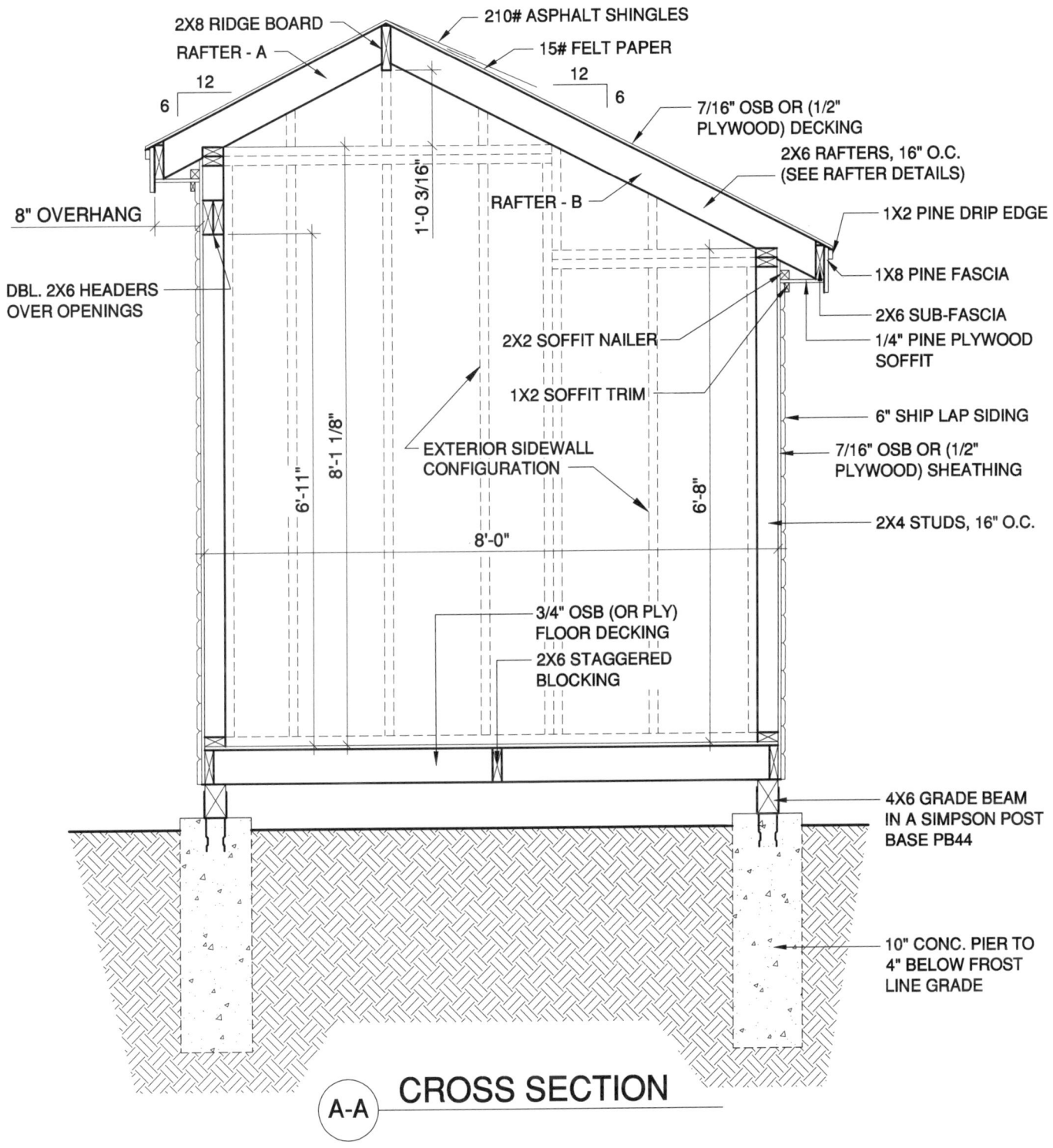

CROSS SECTION A-A

CEDARVILLE Material List

FOUNDATION

Item	Location	Qty	UM
60# Concrete Mix	Pier	20	BG
10"x 48" Fiber Tube	Pier	4	EA
2x4 - 10' Std. & Btr.	Batterboard	5	EA
Post Base (PB44)	Pier	4	EA
1/2" Hex. Hd. Nut	Post Base	8	EA
1/2"x4-1/2" Bolt	Post Base	8	EA
1/2" Washer	Post Base	16	EA
Crushed Gravel	Pier	8	BG

FLOOR

Item	Location	Qty	UM
4x6 - 12' Treated	Beam	2	EA
2x6 - 8' Treated	Floor Joist	11	EA
2x6 - 10' Treated	Header Jst./Blkg.	3	EA
3/4" T & G OSB (Ply.)	Floor Decking	3	EA
Framing Anchor (A34)	Floor Framing	8	EA
2x4 - 8' Treated	Nailer/Stringer	3	EA
2x6 - 10' Treated	Decking	4	EA
3/8"x4" Lag Screws	Ramp Nailer	4	EA
3/8"x1-1/2" Washer	Ramp Nailer	4	EA
5# 16d Galv. Nails	General Framing	1	EA
5# 8d Ctd. Box Nails	General Framing	1	EA
1# 2-1/2" Ctd. Ext. Screws	General Framing	1	EA
Construction Adhesive	Floor Decking	2	TB

WALL FRAMING

Item	Location	Qty	UM
2x4 - 8' Treated	Bottom Plate	2	EA
2x4 - 10' Treated	Bottom Plate	2	EA
2x4 - 96" Stud Grade	Stud/Gable	40	EA
2x4 - 96" Stud Grade	Crpl./Sill/Blkg.	6	EA
2x4 - 8' Std. & Btr.	Top & Cap Plate	4	EA
2x4 - 10' Std. & Btr.	Top & Cap Plate	4	EA
2x6 - 8' Std. & Btr.	Header	4	EA
7/16" OSB (Ply.)	Wall Sheathing	10	EA
5# 16d Galv. Nails	General Framing	2	EA
5# 8d Ctd. Box Nails	General Framing	2	EA
1x6 - 10' Std. & Btr.	Bracing	6	EA
40"x 97' Building Paper	Wall Covering	2	RL
5# 1/2" Roofing Nails	Wall Covering	1	EA

CEILING/ROOF

Item	Location	Qty	UM
2x6 - 8' Std. & Btr.	Rafter	14	EA
2x6 - 12' Std. & Btr.	Sub-Fascia	2	EA
2x4 - 12' Std. & Btr.	Rake	5	EA
2x2 - 8' #2 & Btr. S4S	Soffit Nailer	3	EA
2x8 - 12' Std. & Btr.	Ridge Board	1	EA
1x6 - 12' Std. & Btr.	Fascia	2	EA
1x8 - 12' #2 & Btr. S4S	Fascia	2	EA
7/16" OSB (Ply.)	Roof Decking	4	EA
3 - Tab Shingle 20 Yr.	Shingle	5	BN
15-lb. Asphalt Rfg. Felt	Roofing	1	RL
5# 8d Ctd. Box Nails	General Framing	2	EA
5# 10d Bright Box Nails	General Framing	2	EA
5# 16d Galv. Nails	General Framing	1	EA
5# 1/2" Roofing Nails	Roofing Felt	1	EA
5# 1-1/4" Roofing Nails	Shingle	2	EA
5# 6d Galv. Box Nails	General Framing	1	EA
5# 6d Galv. Finish Nails	Siding/Soffit	1	EA

EXTERIOR TRIM & ACCESSORIES

Item	Location	Qty	UM
1x6 - 10' Ship Lap Siding	Siding	70	EA
2x4 - 10' Std. & Btr.	Corner Trim	4	EA
1x4 - 8' Std. & Btr.	Window Trim	6	EA
1x2 - 10' Trim Board	Soffit/Fascia	7	EA
1/4" Plywood (Sanded)	Soffit Material	2	EA
14"x6" Metal Soffit Vent	Soffit	4	EA
(2) 30"x80" Exterior Door	Exterior Door	1	EA
2030 SH Window	Window	2	EA
Lockset/Deadbolt/Pin	Exterior Door	1	EA
2x8 - 12' Treated	Flower Box	1	EA
1x10 - 4' Redwood	Flower Box	1	EA
5# 6d Galv. Finish Nail	Siding/Soffit	4	EA
5# 8d Galv. Finish Nail	Window/Door	1	EA
10 oz. - Paintable Caulk	Siding/Trim	6	TB
4" - 10' "Z" Flashing	Window/Door	1	EA

SPRINGFIELD — Plan View and Pier Layout

Scale: 1/4" = 1'-0"

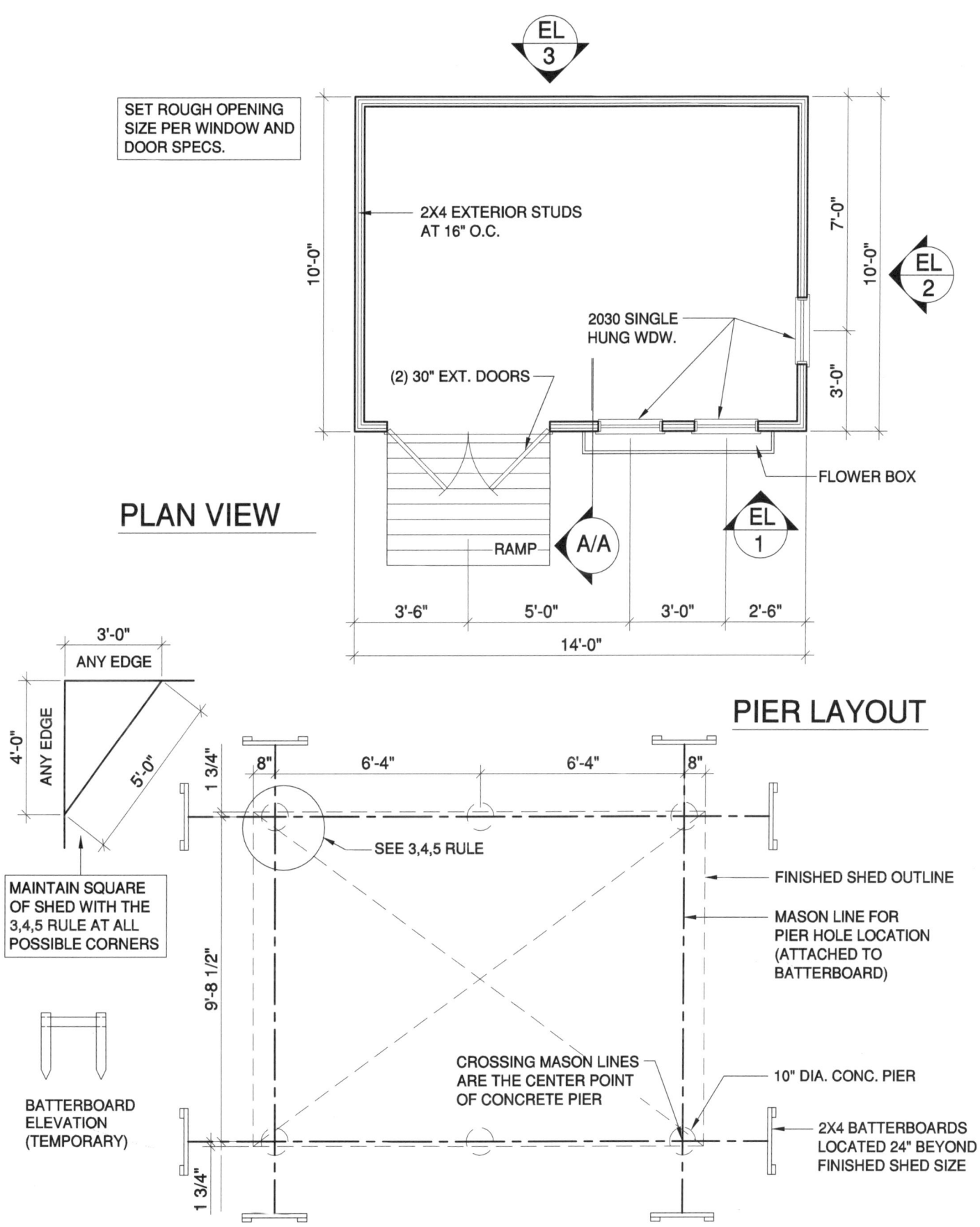

SPRINGFIELD — Framing Plan and Details

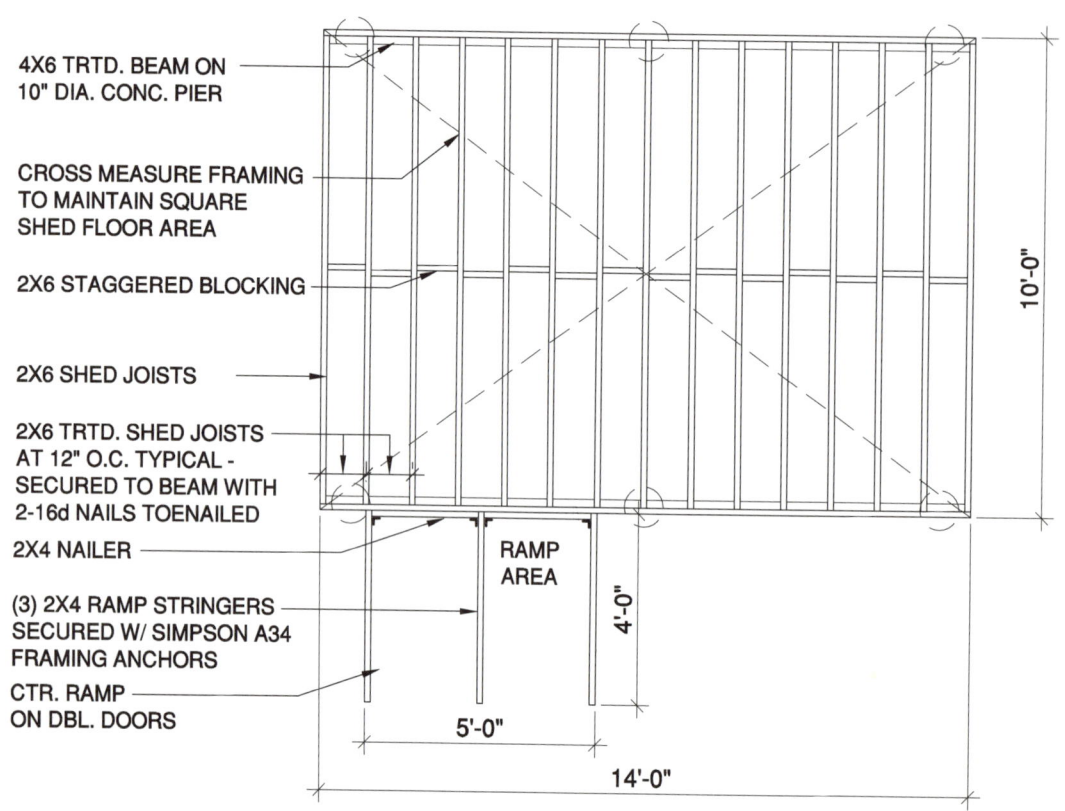

FRAMING PLAN
SCALE: 1/4" = 1'-0"

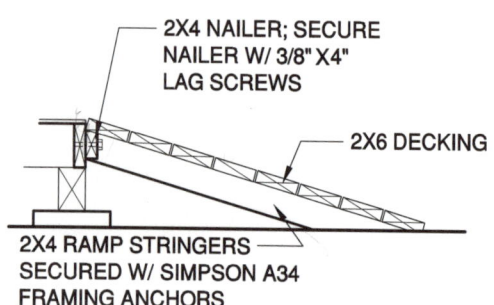

RAMP SECTION
SCALE: 1/2" = 1'-0"

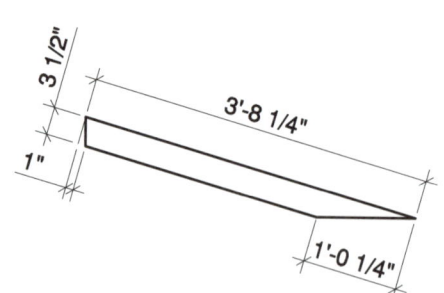

RAMP STRINGER
SCALE: 1/2" = 1'-0"

SPRINGFIELD — Elevations and Details

FRONT ELEVATION
SCALE: 1/4" = 1'-0"
EL 1

Labels:
- 1X8 FASCIA W/ 1X2 DRIP BD.
- 8" OVERHANG
- 6" SHIP LAP SIDING
- 2X4 TRIM; OVERHANG SIDE ELEVATIONS 1"
- (2) 30" EXTERIOR DOORS W/ 1X4 TRIM
- RAMP
- 2030 SINGLE HUNG WDW.
- 1X4 SIDE, TOP AND BOTTOM TRIM
- FLOWER BOX (SEE DETAILS)

FLOWER BOX DETAILS

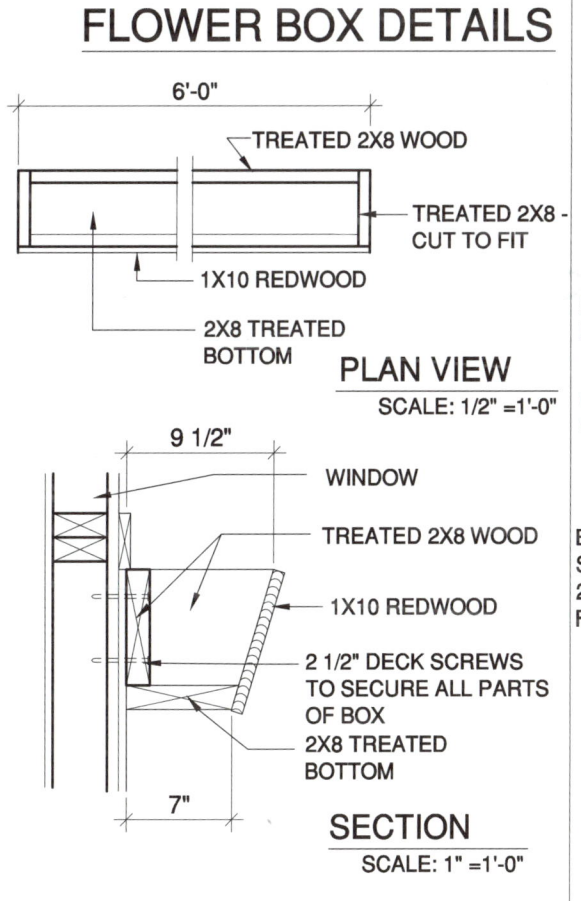

- 6'-0"
- TREATED 2X8 WOOD
- TREATED 2X8 - CUT TO FIT
- 1X10 REDWOOD
- 2X8 TREATED BOTTOM

PLAN VIEW
SCALE: 1/2" = 1'-0"

- 9 1/2"
- WINDOW
- TREATED 2X8 WOOD
- 1X10 REDWOOD
- 2 1/2" DECK SCREWS TO SECURE ALL PARTS OF BOX
- 2X8 TREATED BOTTOM
- 7"

SECTION
SCALE: 1" = 1'-0"

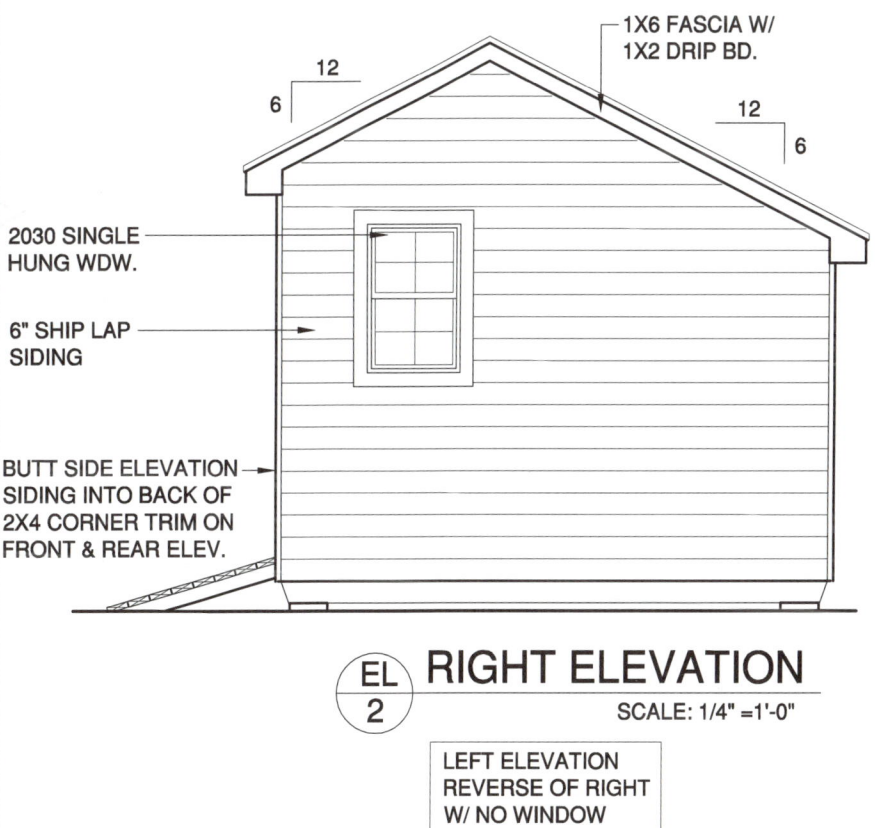

Labels:
- 1X6 FASCIA W/ 1X2 DRIP BD.
- 12 / 6 (roof pitch, both sides)
- 2030 SINGLE HUNG WDW.
- 6" SHIP LAP SIDING
- BUTT SIDE ELEVATION SIDING INTO BACK OF 2X4 CORNER TRIM ON FRONT & REAR ELEV.

RIGHT ELEVATION
SCALE: 1/4" = 1'-0"
EL 2

LEFT ELEVATION REVERSE OF RIGHT W/ NO WINDOW

www.homedepot.com 99

SPRINGFIELD — Elevation and Details

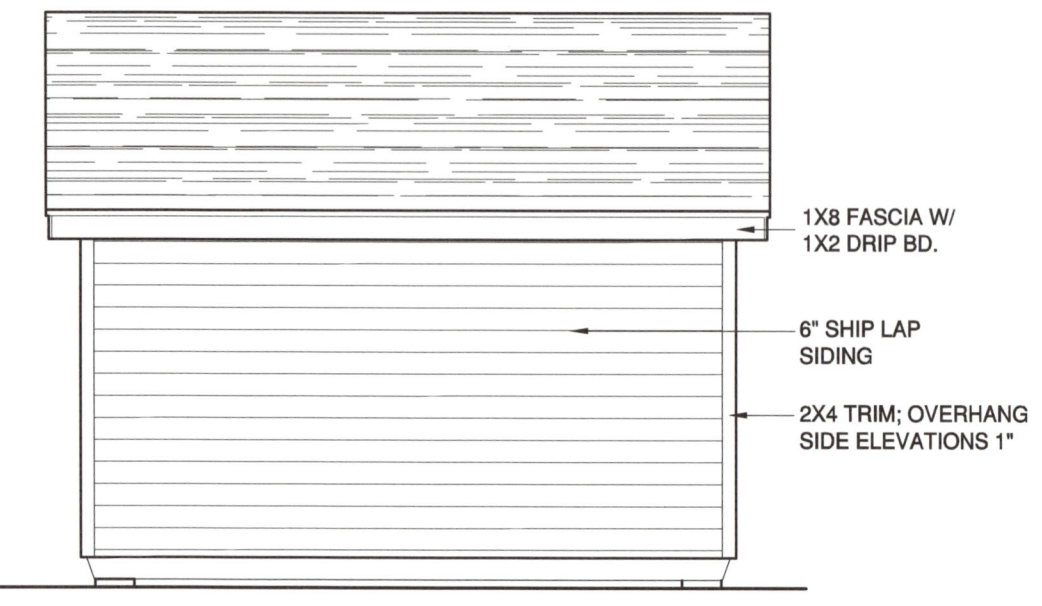

REAR ELEVATION
SCALE: 1/4" = 1'-0"
EL/3

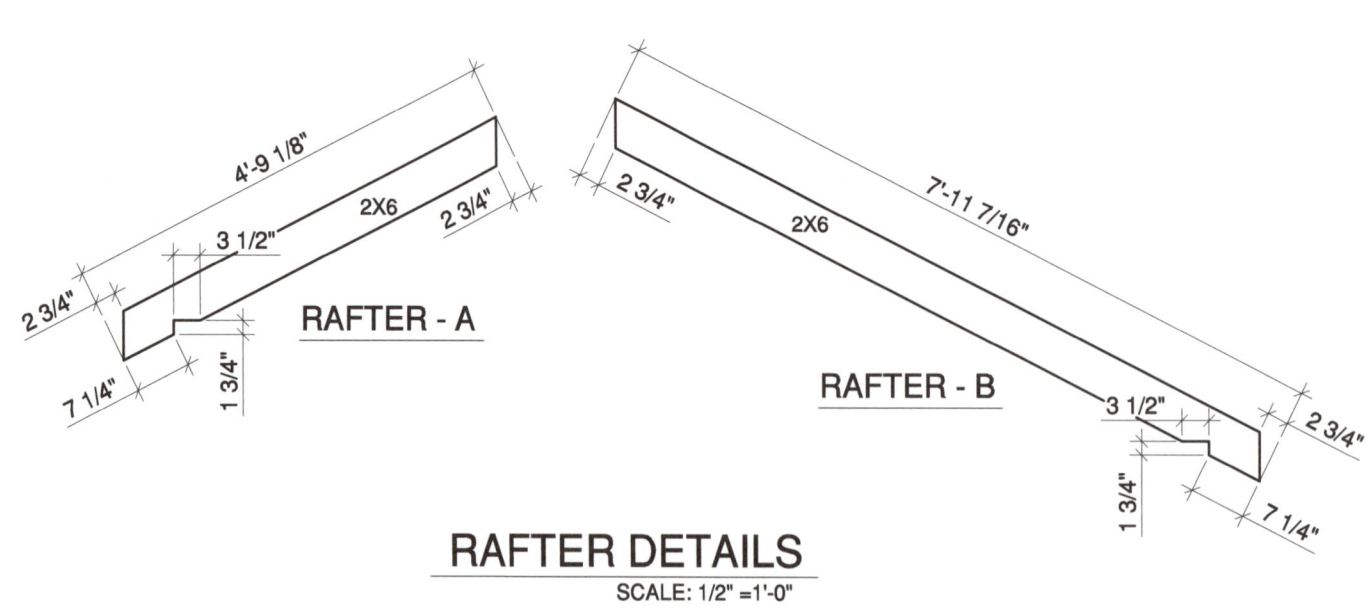

RAFTER DETAILS
SCALE: 1/2" = 1'-0"

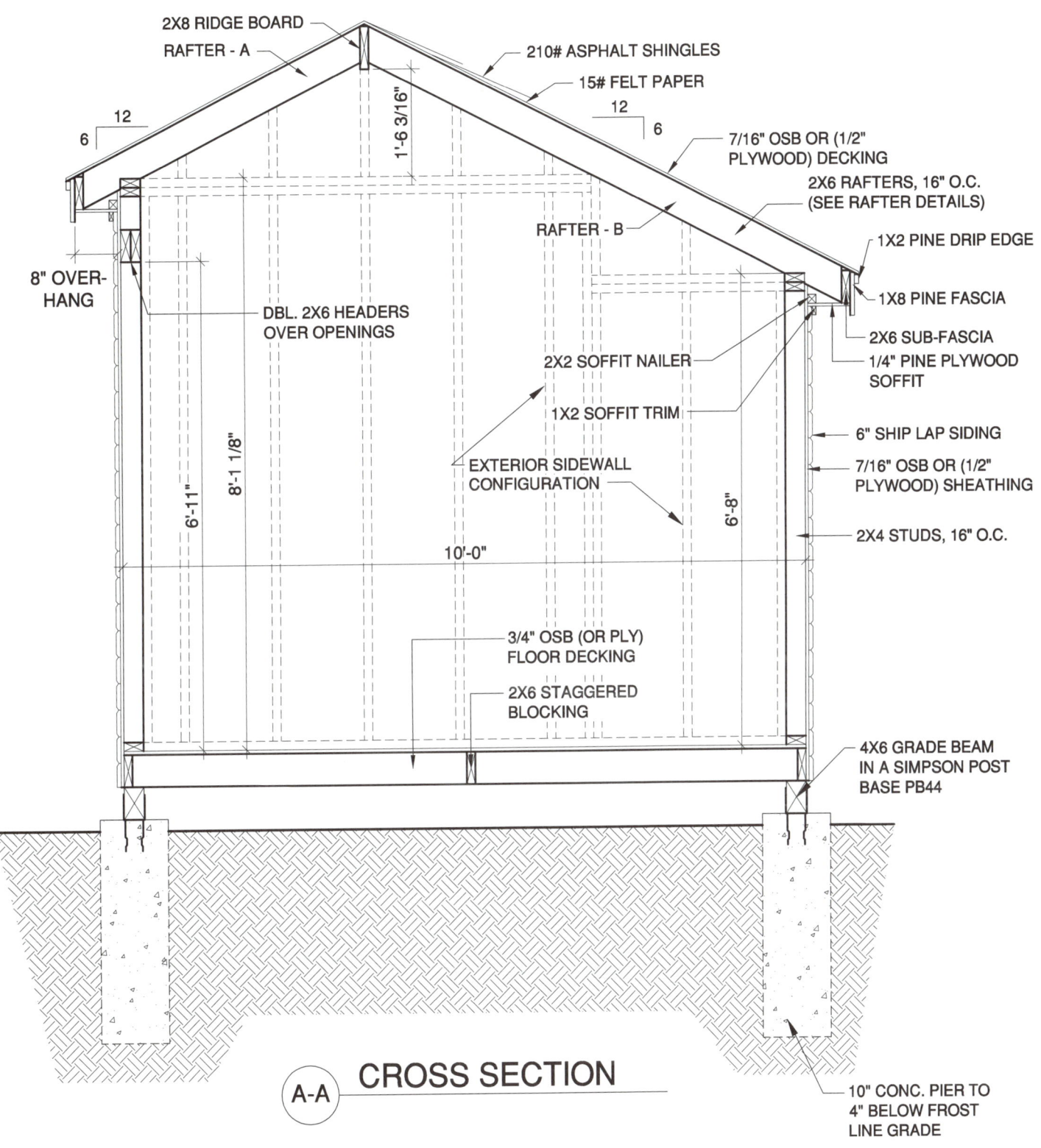

CROSS SECTION A-A

SPRINGFIELD Material List

FOUNDATION

Item	Location	Qty	UM
60# Concrete Mix	Pier	30	BG
10"x 48" Fiber Tube	Pier	6	EA
2x4 - 10' Std. & Btr.	Batterboard	5	EA
Post Base (PB44)	Pier	6	EA
1/2" Hex. Hd. Nut	Post Base	12	EA
1/2"x4-1/2" Bolt	Post Base	12	EA
1/2" Washer	Post Base	24	EA
Crushed Gravel	Pier	12	BG

FLOOR

Item	Location	Qty	UM
4x6 - 8' Treated	Beam	4	EA
2x6 - 10' Treated	Floor Joist	15	EA
2x6 - 16' Treated	Hdr. Jst./Blkg.	3	EA
3/4" T & G OSB (Ply.)	Floor Decking	5	EA
Framing Anchor (A34)	Floor Framing	8	EA
2x4 - 8' Treated	Nailer/Stringer	3	EA
2x6 - 10' Treated	Decking	4	EA
3/8"x4" Lag Screws	Ramp Nailer	4	EA
3/8"x1-1/2" Washer	Ramp Nailer	4	EA
5# 16d Galv. Nails	General Framing	1	EA
5# 8d Ctd. Box Nails	General Framing	1	EA
1# 2-1/2" Ctd. Ext. Screws	General Framing	1	EA
Construction Adhesive	Floor Decking	2	TB

WALL FRAMING

Item	Location	Qty	UM
2x4 - 10' Treated	Bottom Plate	2	EA
2x4 - 16' Treated	Bottom Plate	2	EA
2x4 - 96" Stud Grade	Stud/Gable	52	EA
2x4 - 96" Stud Grade	Crpl./Sill/Blkg.	10	EA
2x4 - 10' Std. & Btr	Top/Cap Plate	4	EA
2x4 - 14' Std. & Btr.	Top/Cap Plate	4	EA
2x6 - 8' Std. & Btr.	Header	5	EA
7/16" OSB (Ply.)	Wall Sheathing	13	EA
5# 16d Galv. Nails	General Framing	2	EA
5# 8d Ctd. Box Nails	General Framing	2	EA
1x6 - 10' Std. & Btr.	Bracing	6	EA
40"x 97' Building Paper	Wall Covering	2	RL
5# 1/2" Galv. Roofing Nails	Wall Covering	1	EA

CEILING/ROOF

Item	Location	Qty	UM
2x6 - 8' Std. & Btr.	Rafter	12	EA
2x6 - 10' Std. & Btr.	Rafter	6	EA
2x6 - 16' Std. & Btr.	Sub-Fascia	2	EA
2x4 - 8' Std. & Btr.	Rake	5	EA
2x4 - 10' Std. & Btr.	Rake	2	EA
2x2 - 8' #2 & Btr. S4S	Soffit Nailer	4	EA
2x8 - 16' Std. & Btr.	Ridge Board	1	EA
1x6 - 8' Std. & Btr.	Fascia	4	EA
1x6 - 10' Std. & Btr.	Fascia	1	EA
1x8 - 12' #2 & Btr. S4S	Fascia	3	EA
7/16" OSB (Ply.)	Roof Decking	7	EA
3 -Tab Shingle 20 Yr.	Shingle	7	BN
15-lb. Asphalt Rfg. Felt	Roofing	1	RL
5# 8d Ctd. Box Nails	General Framing	2	EA
5# 10d Bright Box Nails	General Framing	2	EA
5# 16d Galv. Nails	General Framing	1	EA
5# 1/2" Roofing Nails	Roofing Felt	1	EA
5# 1-1/4" Roofing Nails	Shingle	2	EA
5# 6d Galv. Box Nails	General Framing	1	EA
5# 6d Galv. Finish Nails	Siding/Soffit	1	EA

EXTERIOR TRIM & ACCESSORIES

Item	Location	Qty	UM
1x6 - 10' Ship Lap Siding	Siding	90	EA
2x4 - 10' Std. & Btr.	Corner Trim	4	EA
1x4 - 8' Std. & Btr.	Window Trim	7	EA
1x2 - 10' C & Btr. S4S	Soffit/Fascia	9	EA
1/4" Plywood (Sanded)	Soffit Material	2	EA
14"x6" Metal Soffit Vents	Soffit	4	EA
(2) 30"x80" Exterior Door	Exterior Door	1	EA
2030 SH Window	Window	3	EA
Lockset/Deadbolt/Pin	Exterior Door	1	EA
2x8 - 12' Treated	Flower Box	1	EA
1x10 - 8' Redwood	Flower Box	1	EA
5# 6d Galv. Finish Nails	Siding/Soffit	4	EA
5# 8d Galv. Finish Nails	Window/Door	1	EA
10 oz. - Paintable Caulk	Siding/Trim	6	TB
4" - 10' "Z" Flashing	Window/Door	2	EA

THE BOULDER

HPM-1303

This unique shed draws in plenty of sunshine and natural light through high clerestory windows. Three additional windows plus two in the double-door entry further open up the interior. With 140 square feet to use as work space or storage, this shed is a great functional addition to your home.

Dimensions for this shed are 14' X 10'. 140 sq. ft.

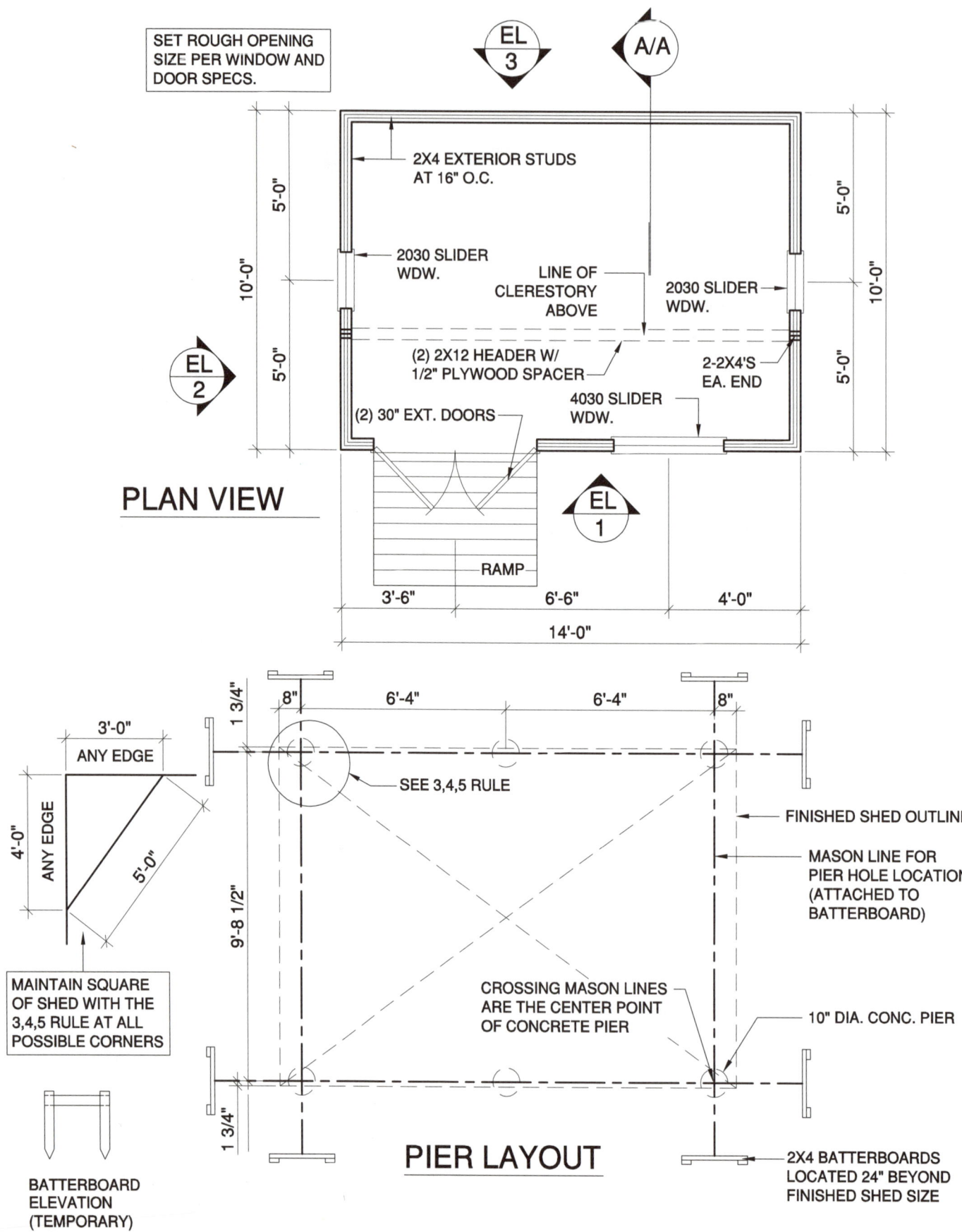

Boulder
Framing Plan and Elevation

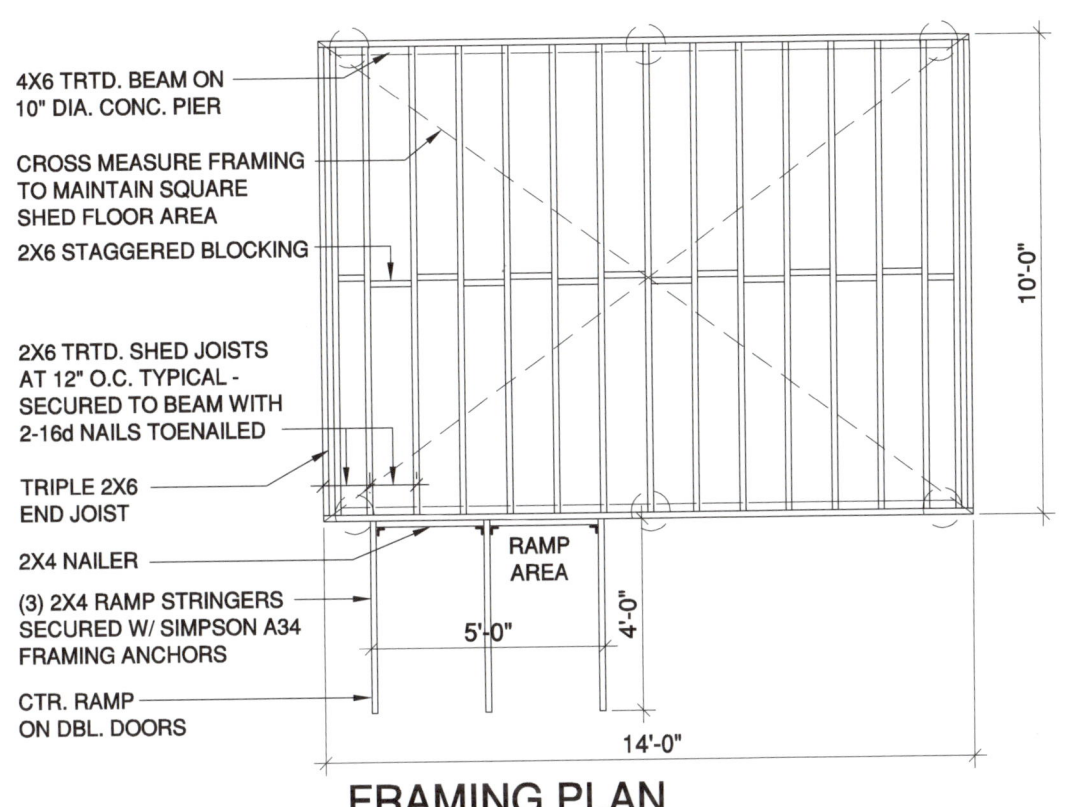

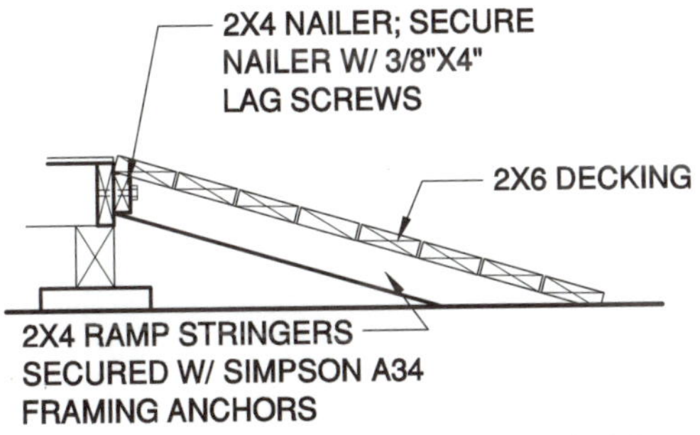

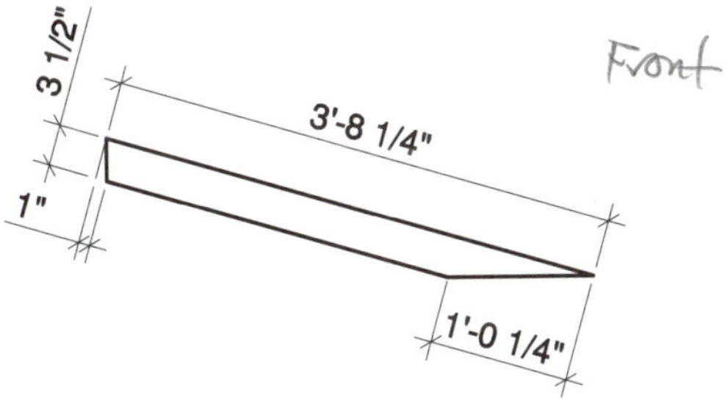

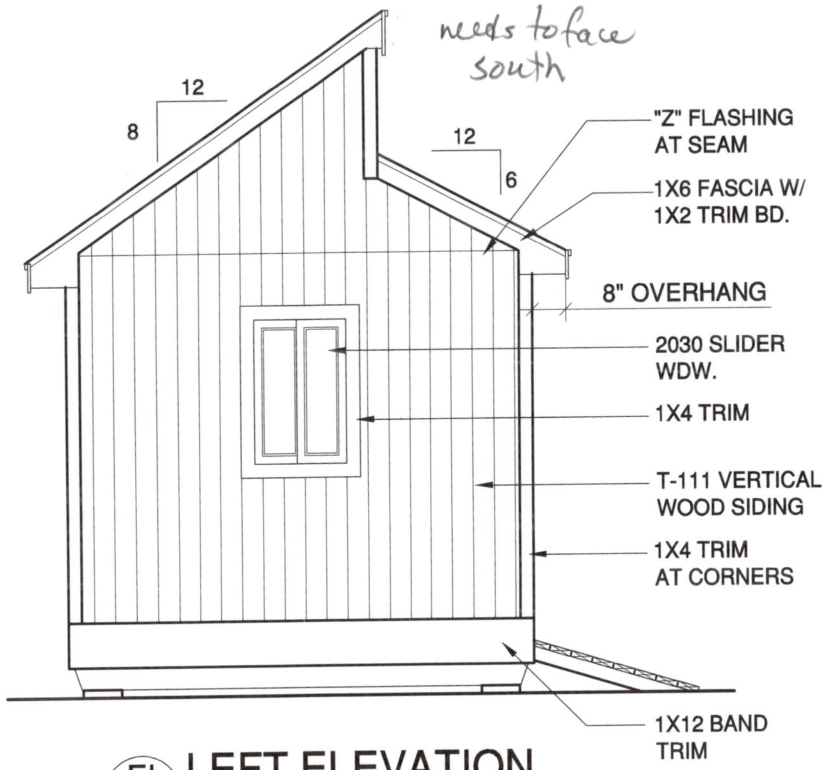

Boulder — Elevations and Details

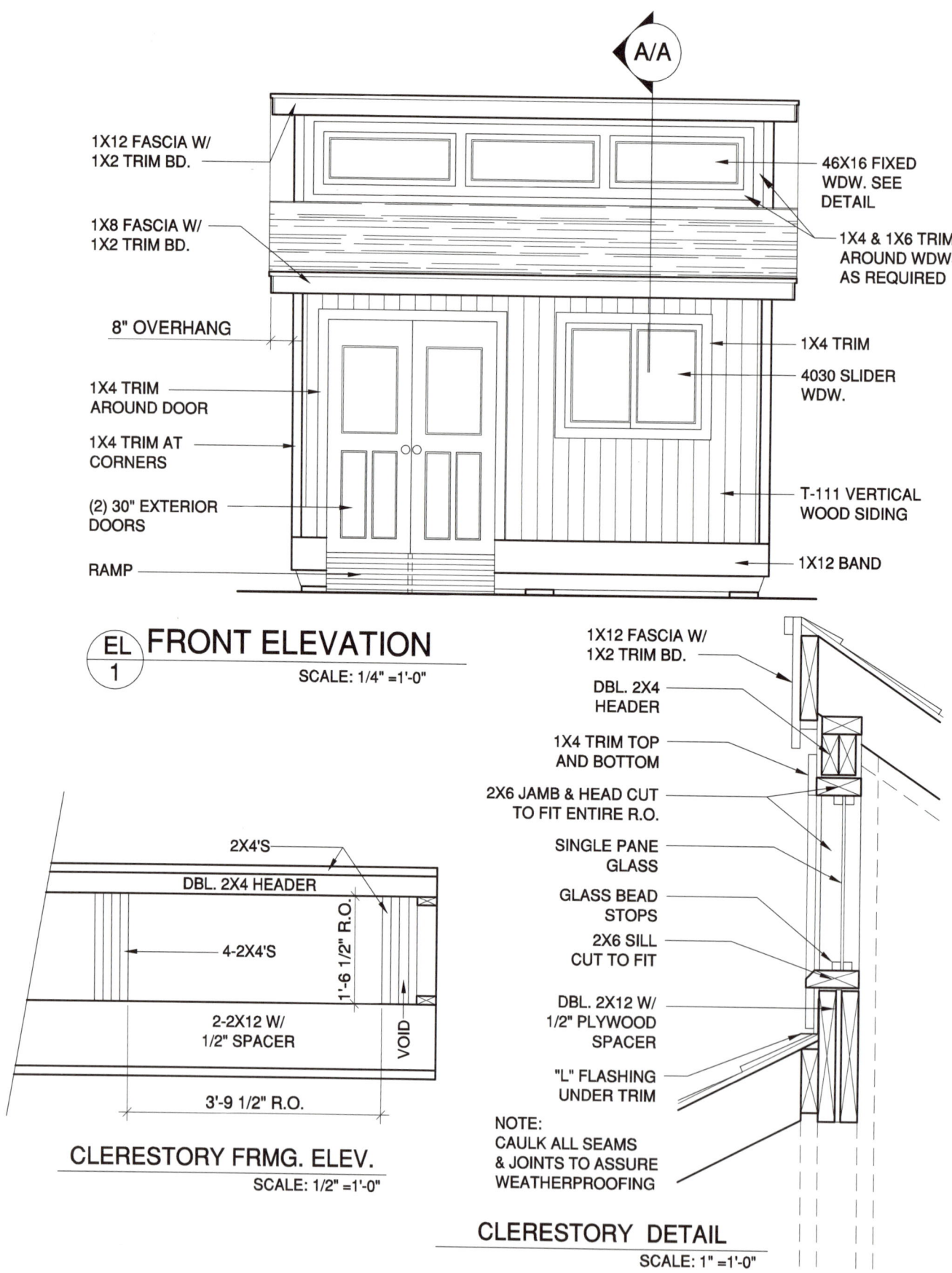

BOULDER — Elevation and Rafter Details

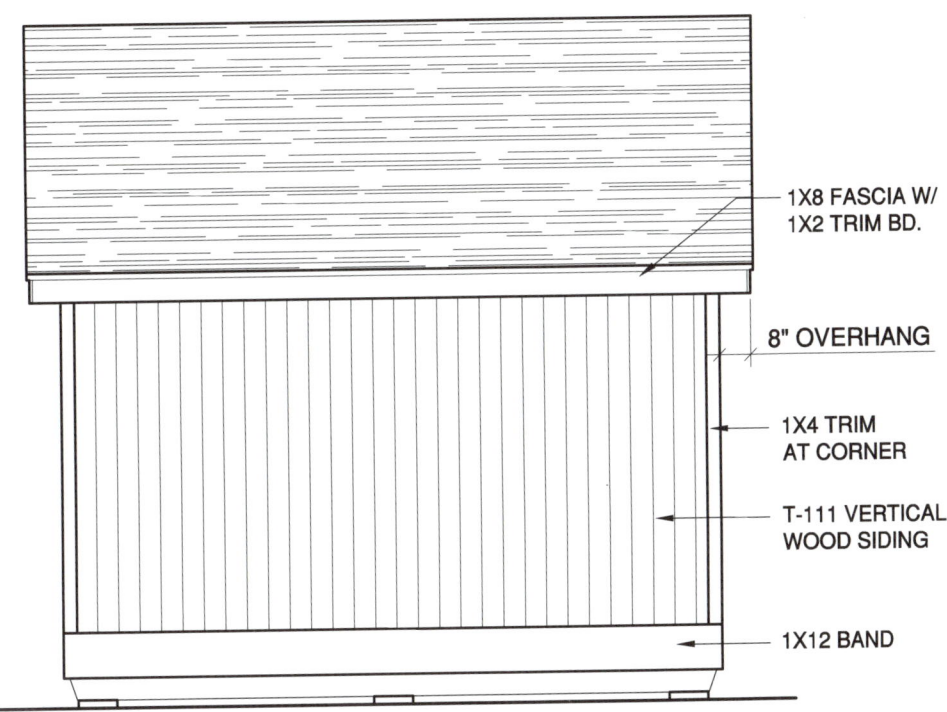

REAR ELEVATION — EL/3
SCALE: 1/4" = 1'-0"

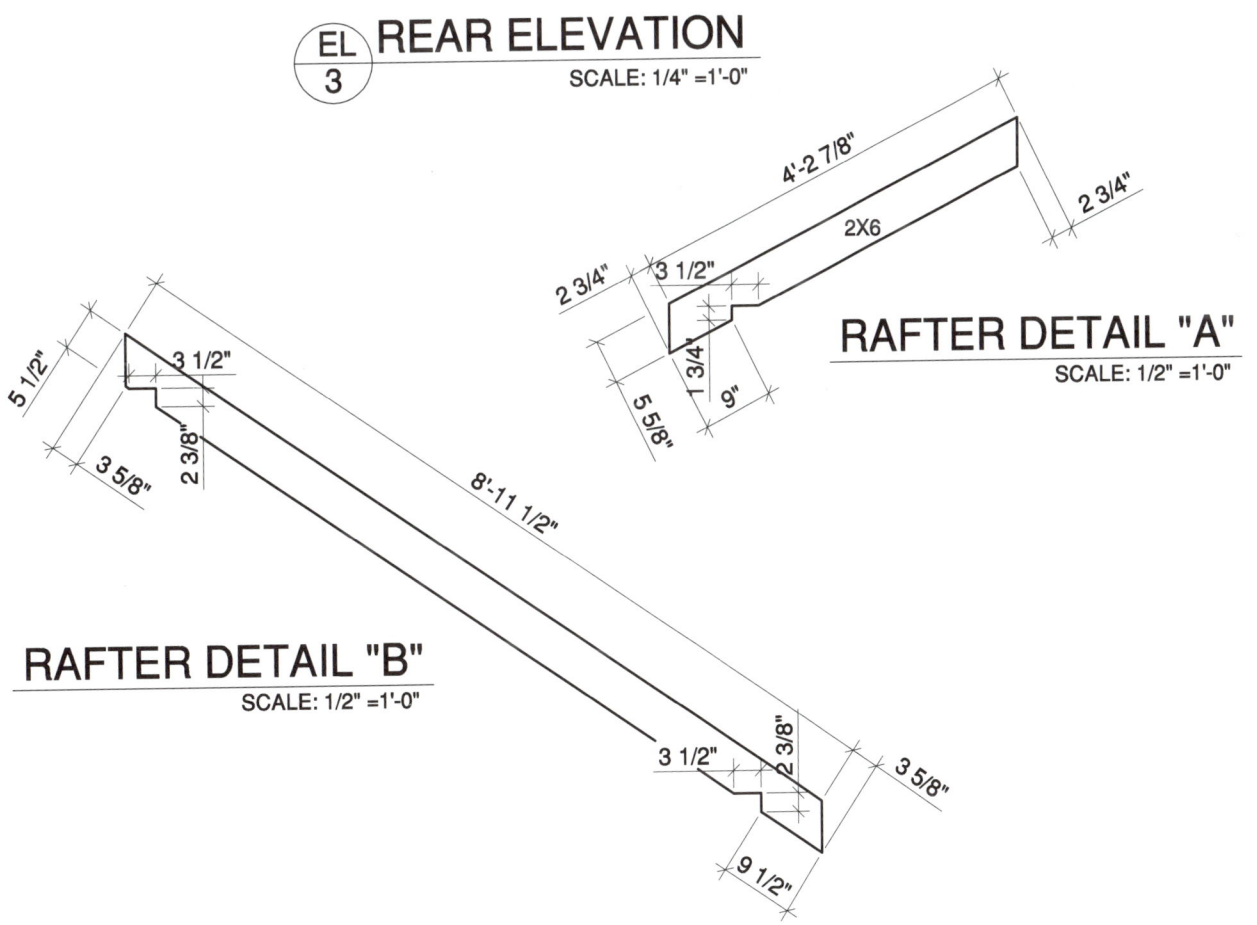

RAFTER DETAIL "A"
SCALE: 1/2" = 1'-0"

RAFTER DETAIL "B"
SCALE: 1/2" = 1'-0"

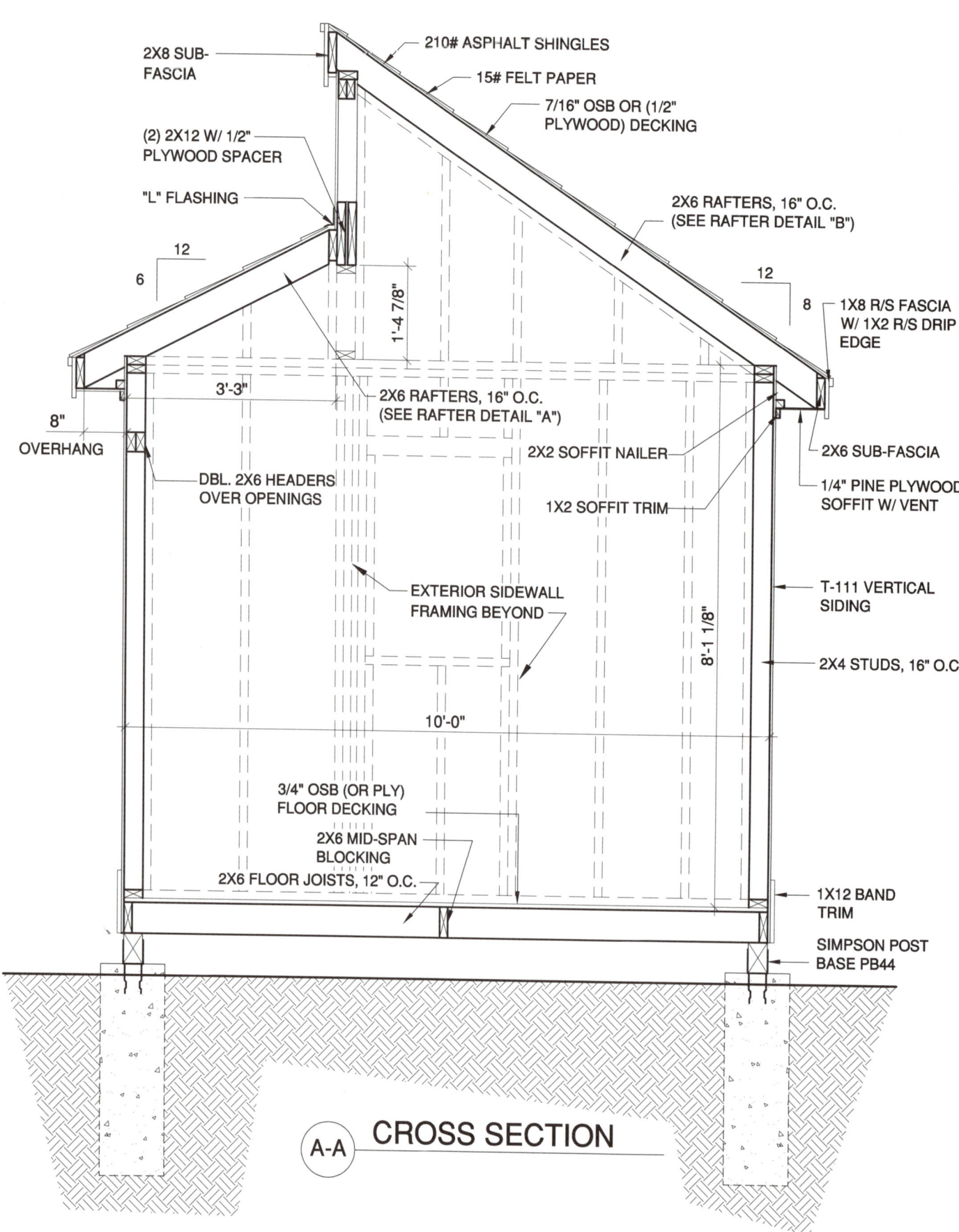

BOULDER Material List

FOUNDATION

Item	Location	Qty	UM
60# Concrete Mix	Pier	30	BG
10"x 48" Fiber Tube	Pier	6	EA
2x4 - 10' Std. & Btr.	Batterboard	5	EA
Post Base (PB44)	Pier	6	EA
1/2" Hex. Hd. Nut	Post Base	12	EA
1/2" x 4-1/2" Bolt	Post Base	12	EA
1/2" Washer	Post Base	24	EA
Crushed Gravel	Pier	12	BG

FLOOR

Item	Location	Qty	UM
4x6 - 8' Treated	Beam	4	EA
2x6 - 10' Treated	Floor Joist	19	EA
2x6 - 16' Treated	Header Jst./Blkg.	3	EA
3/4" OSB (Ply.)	Floor Decking	5	EA
Framing Anchor (A34)	Floor Framing	8	EA
2x4 - 8' Treated	Nailer/Stringer	3	EA
2x6 - 10' Treated	Decking	4	EA
3/8"x4" Lag Screws	Ramp Nailer	4	EA
3/8"x1-1/2" Washer	Ramp Nailer	4	EA
5# 16d Galv. Nail	General Framing	1	EA
5# 8d Ctd. Box Nail	General Framing	1	EA
1# 2-1/2" Ctd. Ext. Screws	General Framing	1	EA
Construction Adhesive	Floor Decking	2	TB

WALL FRAMING

Item	Location	Qty	UM
2x4 - 10' Treated	Bottom Plate	2	EA
2x4 - 16' Treated	Bottom Plate	2	EA
2x4 - 96" Stud Grade	Wall/Gable/Clerestory	57	EA
2x4 - 96" Stud Grade	Crpl./Sill/Blkg./Plate	7	EA
2x4 - 10' Std. & Btr.	Top/Cap Plate	4	EA
2x4 - 14' Std. & Btr.	Top/Cap Plate	7	EA
2x4 - 14' Std. & Btr.	Clerestory Hdr./Plate	7	EA
2x6 - 10' Std. & Btr.	Header	3	EA
2x6 - 12' Std. & Btr.	Header	1	EA
2x12 - 16' Std. & Btr.	Clerestory Hdr.	2	EA
1/2" CDX - 5 Ply. Plywood	Header	1	EA
7/16" OSB (Ply.)	Wall Sheathing	13	EA
5# 6d Galv. Nails	General Framing	2	EA
5# 8d Ctd. Box Nails	General Framing	2	EA
1x6 - 10' Std. & Btr.	Bracing	6	EA
40"x 97' Building Paper	Wall Covering	2	RL
5# 1/2" Roofing Nails	Wall Covering	1	EA

CEILING/ROOF

Item	Location	Qty	UM
2x6 - 10' Std. & Btr.	Rafter	18	EA
2x6 - 16' Std. & Btr.	Sub-Fascia/Ledger	3	EA
2x4 - 10' Std. & Btr.	Ladder Rake/Blk.	7	EA
2x2 - 8' #2 & Btr. S4S	Soffit Nailer	4	EA
2x8 - 16' Std. & Btr.	Sub-Fascia	4	EA
1x6 - 10' #2 & Btr. S4S	Fascia	2	EA
1x8 - 16' #2 & Btr. S4S	Fascia	3	EA
1x12 - 16' #2 & Btr. S4S	Fascia	3	EA
7/16" OSB (ply.)	Roof Decking	7	EA
3 - Tab Shingle 20 Yr.	Shingle	7	BN
15-lb. Asphalt Rfg. Felt	Roofing	1	RL
"L" Flashing - Roof To Wall	Clerestory	2	EA
5# 8d Ctd. Box Nails	General Framing	2	EA
5# 10d Bright Box Nails	General Framing	2	EA
5# 16d Galv. Nails	General Framing	1	EA
5# 1/2" Roofing Nails	Roofing Felt	1	EA
5# 1-1/4" Roofing Nails	Shingle	2	EA
5# 6d Galv. Box Nails	General Framing	1	EA
5# 6d Galv. Finish Nails	Siding/Soffit	1	EA

EXTERIOR TRIM & ACCESSORIES

Item	Location	Qty	UM
3/8" T1-11 Siding 8" O.C.	Siding	15	EA
2x4 - 10' Std. & Btr.	Corner Trim	5	EA
1x4 - 8' Std. & Btr.	Window Trim	12	EA
1x6 - 8' #2 & Btr.	Window Trim	4	EA
1x2 - 10' Trim Board	Soffit/Fascia	10	EA
1x2 - 10' Trim Bd. (Rip- 1x1)	Window Stop	2	EA
1x12 -12' #2 & Btr.	Trim Board	5	EA
1/4" Plywood (Sanded)	Soffit Material	2	EA
2x6 - 12' Std. & Btr.	Window Jamb	3	EA
14"x6" Metal Soffit Vent	Soffit	4	EA
Single Pane Glass (46"x16")	Window	3	EA
(2) 30"x80" Exterior Door	Exterior Door	1	EA
2030 Slider Window	Window	2	EA
4030 Slider Window	Window	1	EA
Lockset/Deadbolt/Pin	Exterior Door	2	EA
5# 6d Galv. Finish Nails	Siding/Soffit	4	EA
5# 8d Galv. Finish Nails	Window/Door	1	EA
10 oz. - Paintable Caulk	Siding/Trim	6	TB
3/8" - 10' "Z" - Bar Flashing	Horz. Siding Seam	2	EA
4" - 10' "Z" Flashing	Window/Door	4	EA

CHAPTER 4

THE EMERSON *see page 26 w/ garage door to one side*   HPM-1012

Simple, easy to build and adaptable to almost any style of home, this one-car garage has wide appeal. Along one wall, a door and a window offer side access and light; orient the opposite wall to face the street or neighbors. A low-pitched roof overhang at the front and back of the garage combines the look of a hip and gable roof while providing shelter from the elements.

Dimensions for this garage are 14' X 24'. 336 sq. ft.

EMERSON — Plan View

Scale: 1/4" = 1'-0"

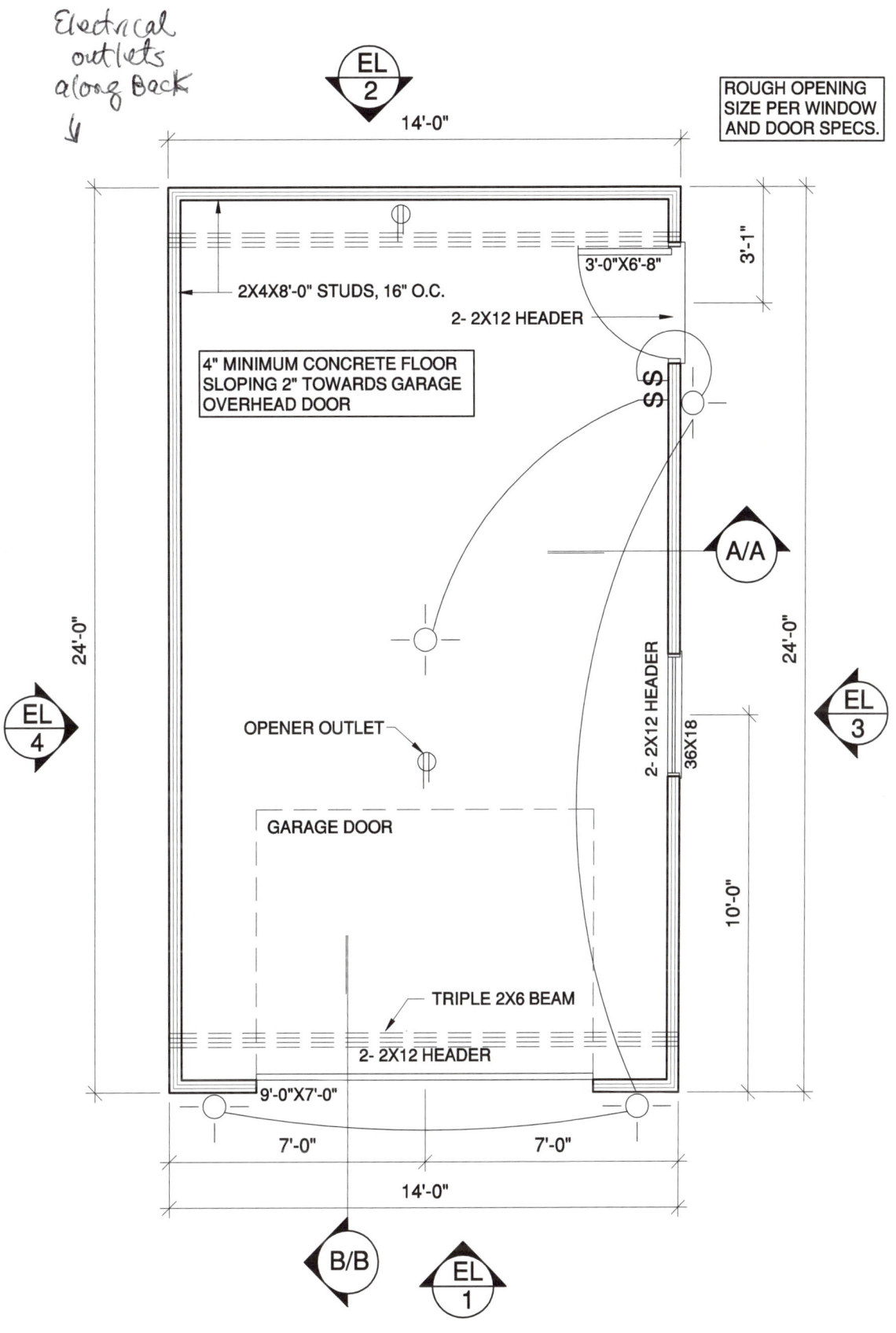

www.homedepot.com 111

EMERSON — Foundation Plan

Scale: 1/4" = 1'-0"

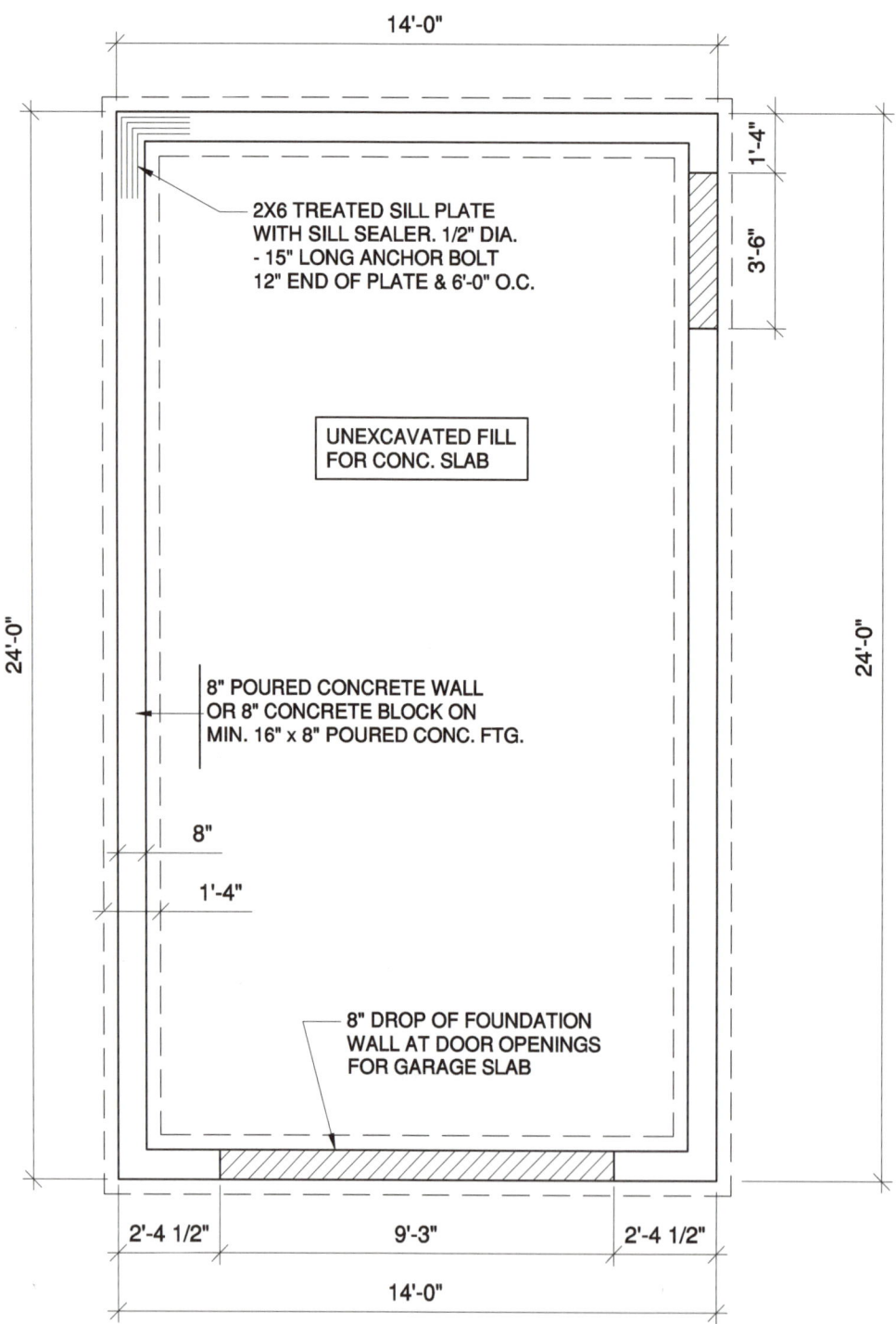

Emerson

Elevations

Scale: 1/4" = 1'-0"

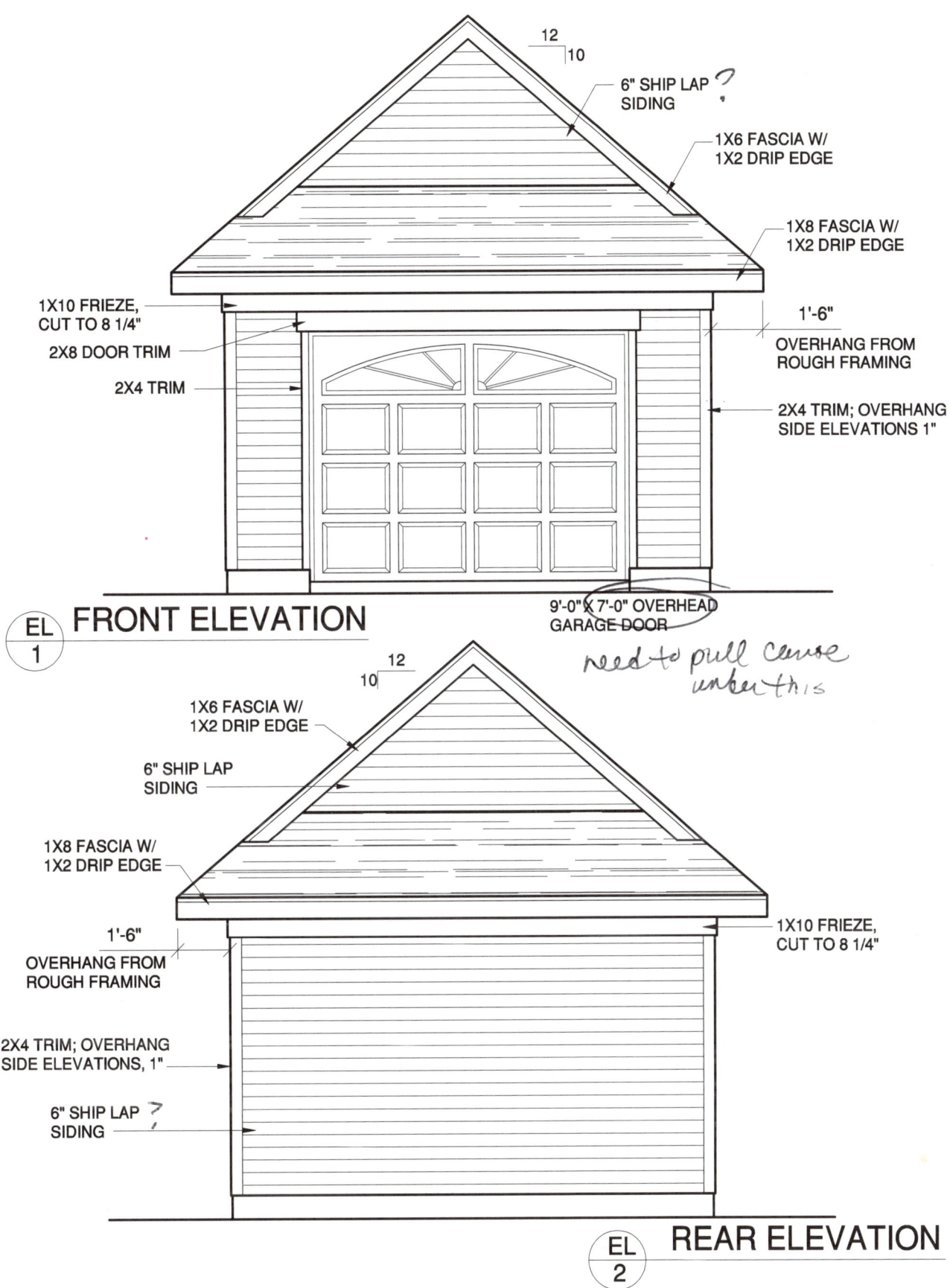

EMERSON — Elevations

Scale: 1/4" = 1'-0"

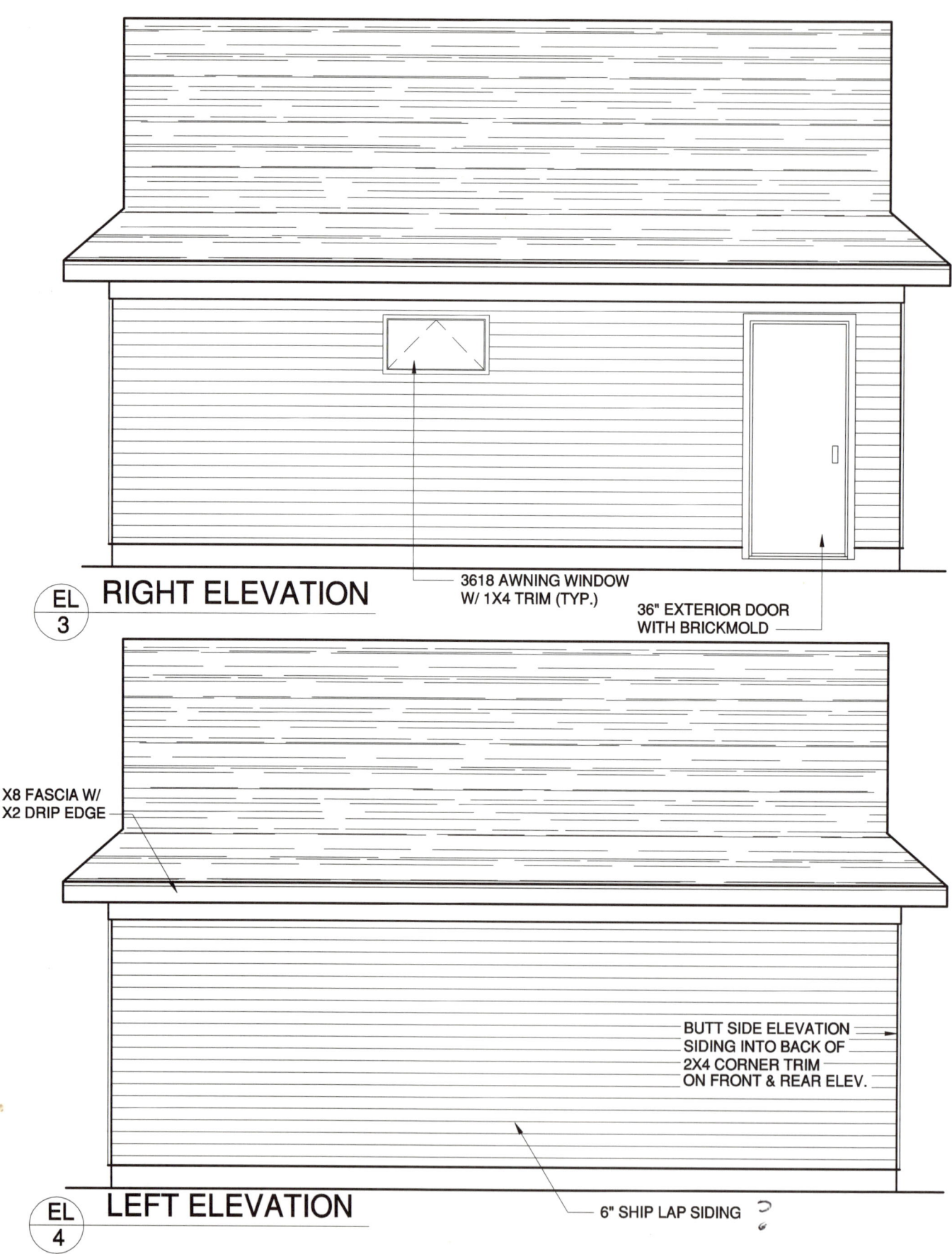

EL 3 — RIGHT ELEVATION

3618 AWNING WINDOW W/ 1X4 TRIM (TYP.)

36" EXTERIOR DOOR WITH BRICKMOLD

1X8 FASCIA W/ 1X2 DRIP EDGE

EL 4 — LEFT ELEVATION

BUTT SIDE ELEVATION SIDING INTO BACK OF 2X4 CORNER TRIM ON FRONT & REAR ELEV.

6" SHIP LAP SIDING

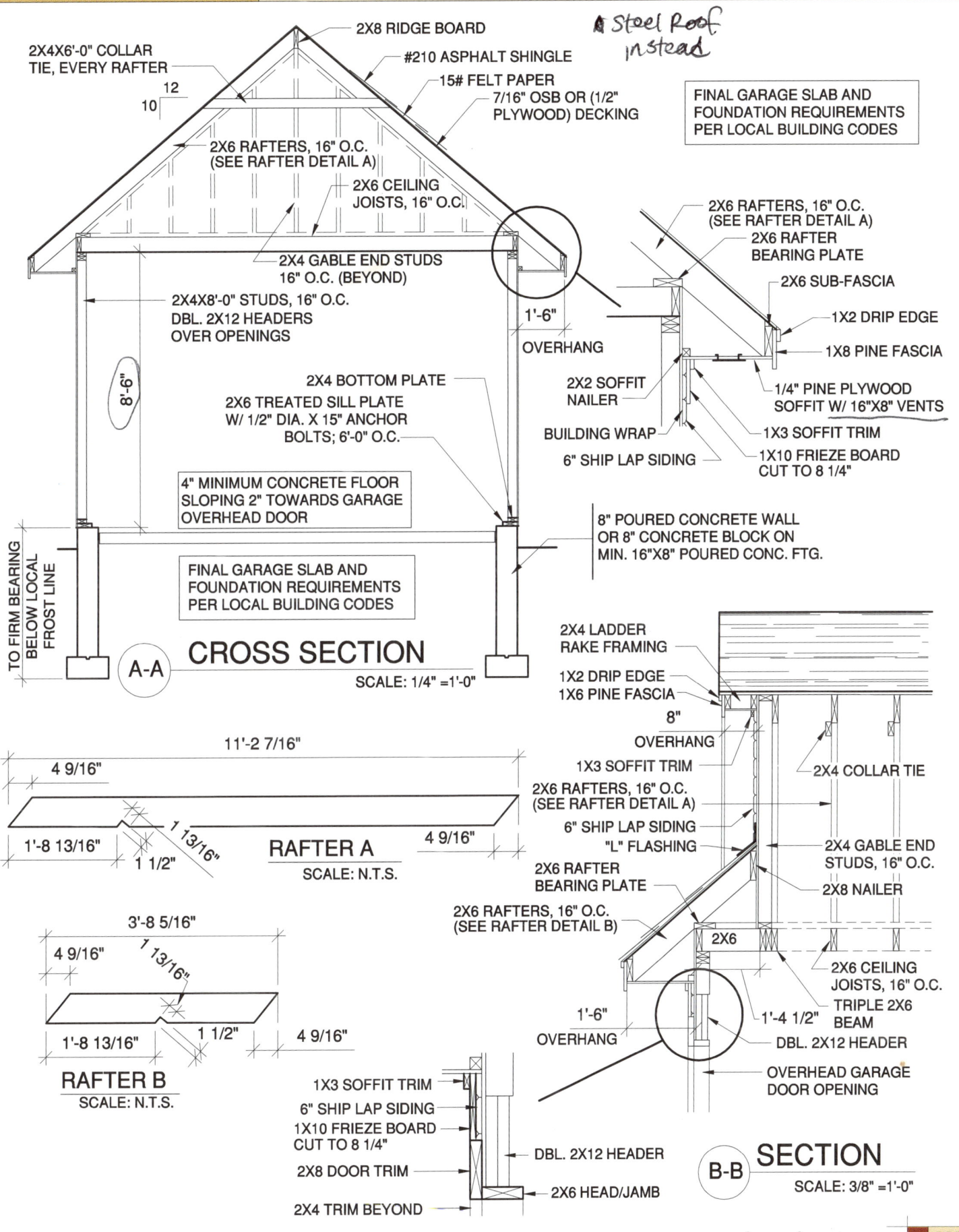

EMERSON Material List

ROOF

Item	Location	Qty	UM
2x8 - 12' # 2 & Btr.	Ridge Board	3	EA
2x8 - 12' # 2 & Btr.	Hip Rafter Nailer	3	EA
2x6 - 12' # 2 & Btr.	Rafter	42	EA
2x4 - 12' # 2 & Btr.	Collar Tie	9	EA
2x4 - 10' # 2 & Btr.	Rake/Block	9	EA
2x4 - 14' # 2 & Btr. (Rip-2x2)	Soffit Nailer	3	EA
2x6 - 16' # 2 & Btr.	Sub-Fascia	6	EA
2x6 - 16' # 2 & Btr.	Rafter Plate	5	EA
1x6 - 10' # 2 & Btr. S4S	Fascia	4	EA
1x8 - 12' # 2 & Btr. S4S	Fascia	8	EA
7/16" OSB (Ply.)	Roof Decking	20	EA
3 - Tab Shingles 20 Yr.	Shingle	23	BN
15-lb. Asphalt Rfg. Felt	Roofing Paper	3	RL
Galv. Drip Edge	Above Fascia	13	EA
"L" Flashing - 10' Roof to Wall	Roof	3	EA
5# 16d Galv. Nails	General Framing	3	EA
5# 8d Ctd. Box Nails	General Framing	3	EA
5# 10d Bright Box Nails	General Framing	3	EA
5# 6d Galv. Box Nails	General Framing	2	EA
5# 6d Galv. Finish Nails	General Finish Trim	1	EA
5# 8d Galv. Finish Nails	General Finish Trim	1	EA
5# 1-1/4" Roofing Nails	Shingle	3	EA
10 oz. - Paintable Caulk	Flashing	2	TB

GABLE END (RAKE WALLS)

Item	Location	Qty	UM
2x4 - 12' # 2 & Btr.	Gable/Wall Stud	6	EA
2x4 - 96" Stud Grade	Bracing	3	EA
2x4 - 10' # 2 & Btr.	Gable Top Plate	4	EA
5# 16d Galv. Nails	General Framing	2	EA
5# 10d Bright Box Nails	General Framing	1	EA
5# 8d Ctd. Box Nails	General Framing	3	EA

CEILING FRAMING

Item	Location	Qty	UM
2x6 - 12' #2 & Btr.	Rim Joist	6	EA
2x6 - 14' #2 & Btr.	Ceiling Jst./Beam	13	EA
2x6 - 14' #2 & Btr.	Stub Joist	13	EA
5# 16d Hot Dip Galv. Nails	General Framing	2	EA
5# 8d Ctd. Box Nails	General Framing	2	EA

WALL FRAMING

Item	Location	Qty	UM
2x4 - 8' Std. & Btr.	Stud	100	EA
2x4 - 12' Std. & Btr.	Plate	10	EA
2x4 - 16' Std. & Btr.	Plate	8	EA
2x6 - 16' Treated	Bottom Sill Plate	5	EA
3-1/2"x50'x1/4" Sill Sealer	Sill	2	RL
2x12 - 8' #2 & Btr.	Header	4	EA
2x12 - 10' #2 & Btr.	Header	2	EA
7/16" OSB (Ply.)	Wall Sheathing	23	EA
40"x 97' Building Paper	Wall	3	RL
5# 1/2" Roofing Nails	Building Paper	3	EA
5# 16d Galv. Nails	General Framing	4	EA
5# 8d Ctd. Box Nails	General Framing	2	EA
5# 10d Bright Box Nails	General Framing	3	EA

EXTERIOR TRIM & ACCESSORIES

Item	Location	Qty	UM
1x6 - 10' Ship Lap Siding	Siding	150	EA
2x4 - 10' Std. & Btr.	Corner Trim	4	EA
2x6 - 8' #2 & Btr.	Door Jamb	2	EA
2x6 - 10' #2 & Btr.	Door Head	1	EA
2x4 - 8' #2 & Btr.	Ovh. Gar. Dr. Trim	2	EA
2x8 - 12' #2 & Btr.	Ovh. Gar. Dr. Trim	1	EA
1x4 - 10' Std. & Btr.	Window Trim	1	EA
1x6 - 10' Std. & Btr. (Rip-1x3)	Soffit Trim	6	EA
1/4" Plywood (Sanded)	Soffit Material	4	EA
1x4 - 10 Std. & Btr. (Rip-1x2)	Soffit Trim	7	EA
1x10 - 12' #2 & Btr. S4S	Frieze Board	7	EA
14"x6" Metal Soffit Vent	Soffit	4	EA
5# 6d Galv. Finish Nails	General Finish Trim	5	EA
5# 8d Galv. Finish Nails	General Finish Trim	4	EA
10 oz. - Paintable Caulk	Ledger	4	TB
9'x7' Ovh. Gar. Dr. w/Hrdwr.	Garage Door	1	EA
36"x80" Exterior LH Door	Service Door	1	EA
3618 Awning Window	Window	1	EA
Lockset/Deadbolt Set	Service Door	1	EA
1-1/4"x2" Brickmold	Service Door	3	EA
4" - 10' "Z" Flashing	Door/Window	2	EA

CHAPTER 4

THE CARLTON

HPM-1006

A sheltered service door offers a second access to this oversized two-car garage. Inside, use the space alongside the car stalls as a workshop. This garage is ideal when more width is available than depth. A window lets in natural light.

Dimensions for this garage are 28' X 24'. 656 sq. ft.

CARLTON — Plan View

Scale: 3/16" = 1'-0"

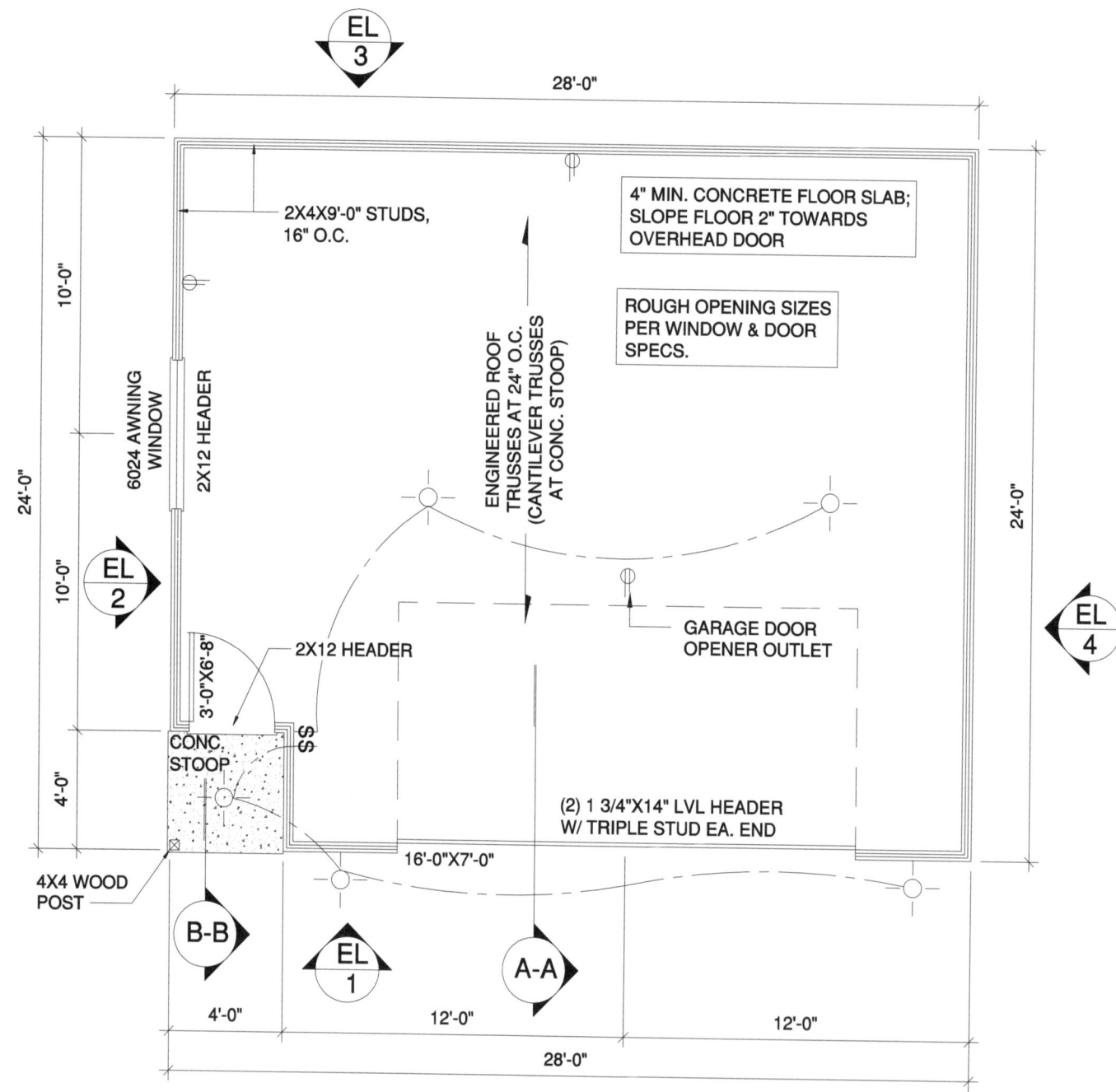

CARLTON — Foundation Plan

Scale: 3/16" = 1'-0"

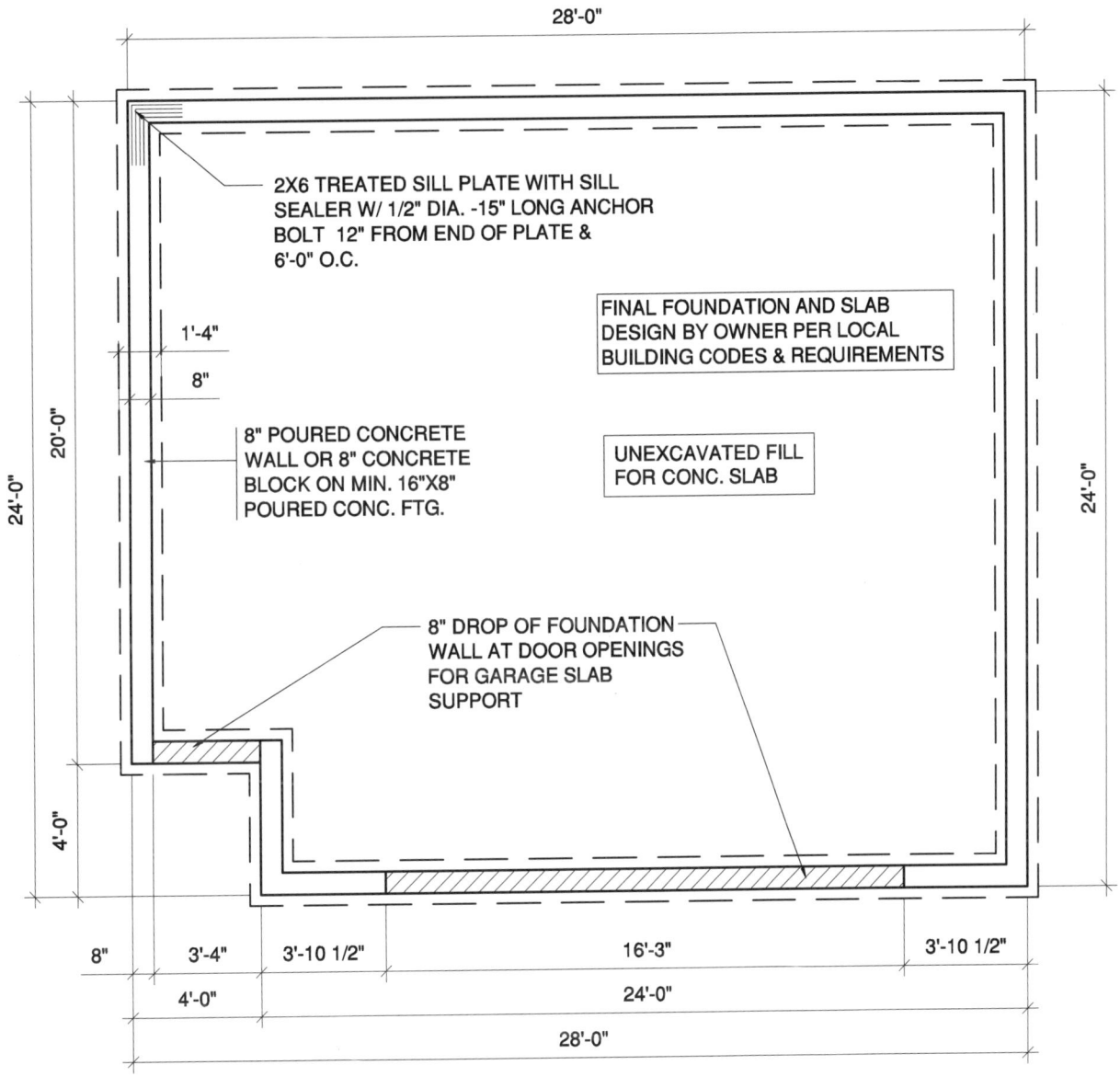

CARLTON — Elevations

Scale: 3/16" = 1'-0"

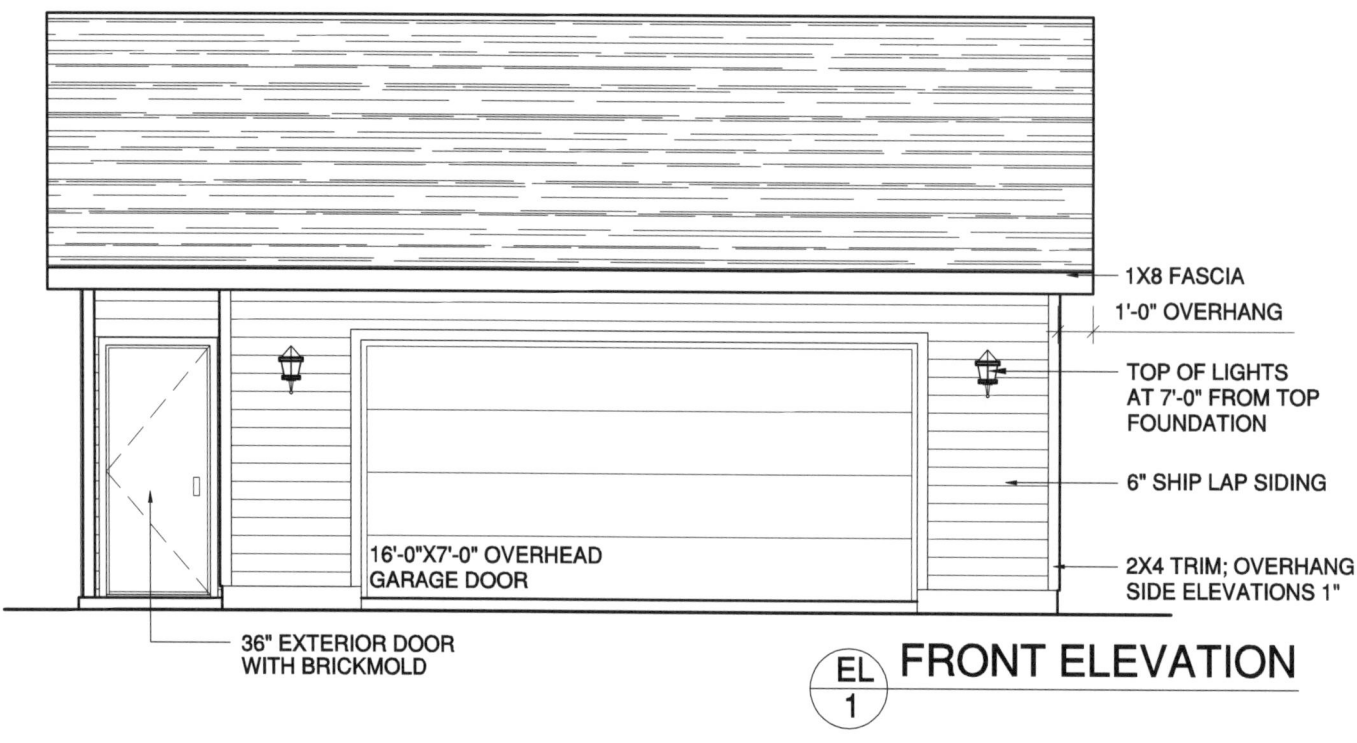

FRONT ELEVATION (EL 1)

- 1X8 FASCIA
- 1'-0" OVERHANG
- TOP OF LIGHTS AT 7'-0" FROM TOP FOUNDATION
- 6" SHIP LAP SIDING
- 2X4 TRIM; OVERHANG SIDE ELEVATIONS 1"
- 16'-0"X7'-0" OVERHEAD GARAGE DOOR
- 36" EXTERIOR DOOR WITH BRICKMOLD

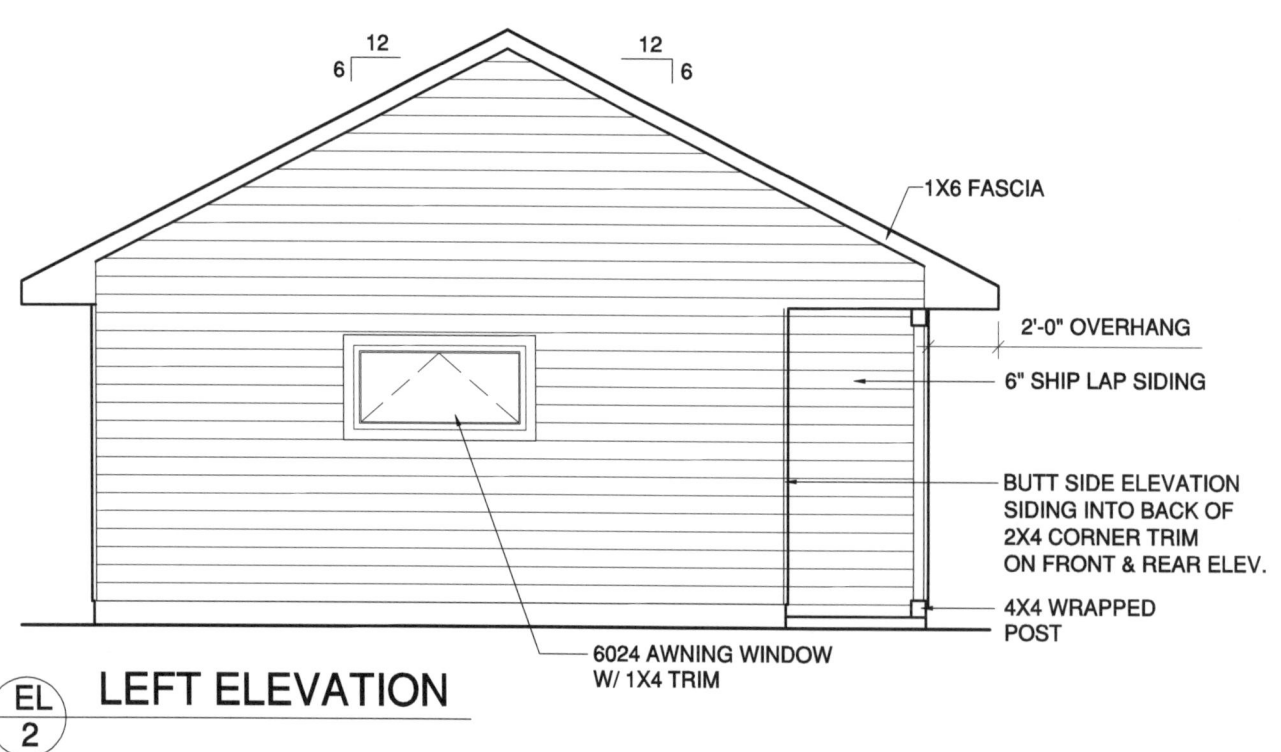

LEFT ELEVATION (EL 2)

- 6/12 roof pitch
- 1X6 FASCIA
- 2'-0" OVERHANG
- 6" SHIP LAP SIDING
- BUTT SIDE ELEVATION SIDING INTO BACK OF 2X4 CORNER TRIM ON FRONT & REAR ELEV.
- 4X4 WRAPPED POST
- 6024 AWNING WINDOW W/ 1X4 TRIM

CARLTON | Elevations | Scale: 3/16" = 1'-0"

REAR ELEVATION (EL/3)

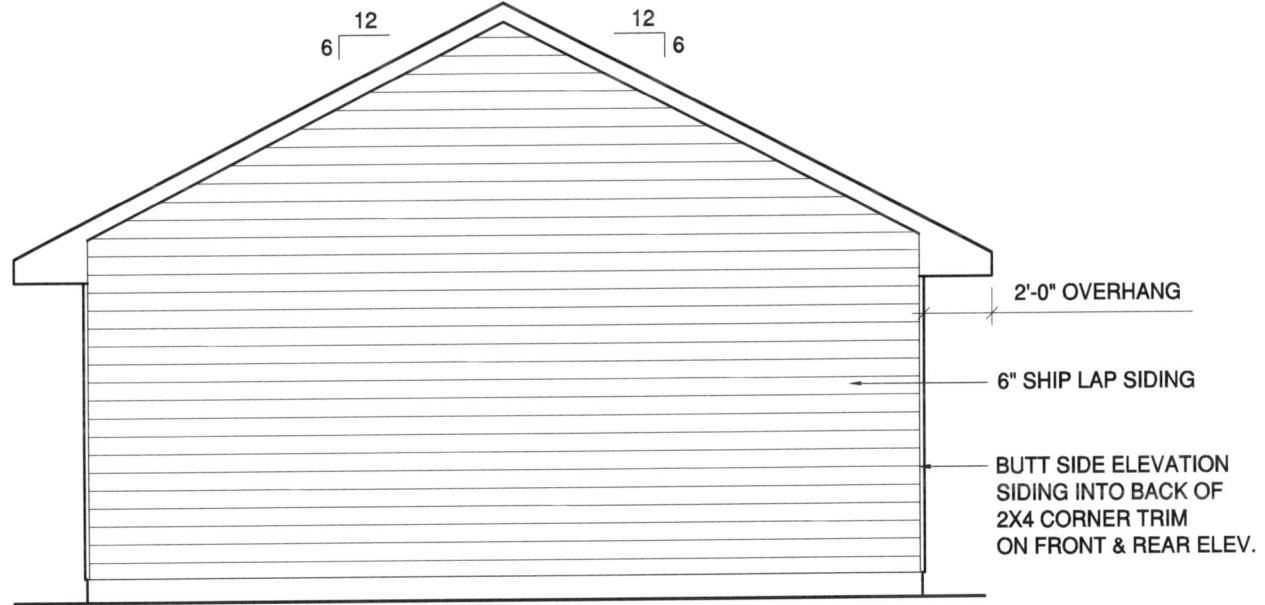

RIGHT ELEVATION (EL/4)

www.homedepot.com 121

Carlton — Sections and Details

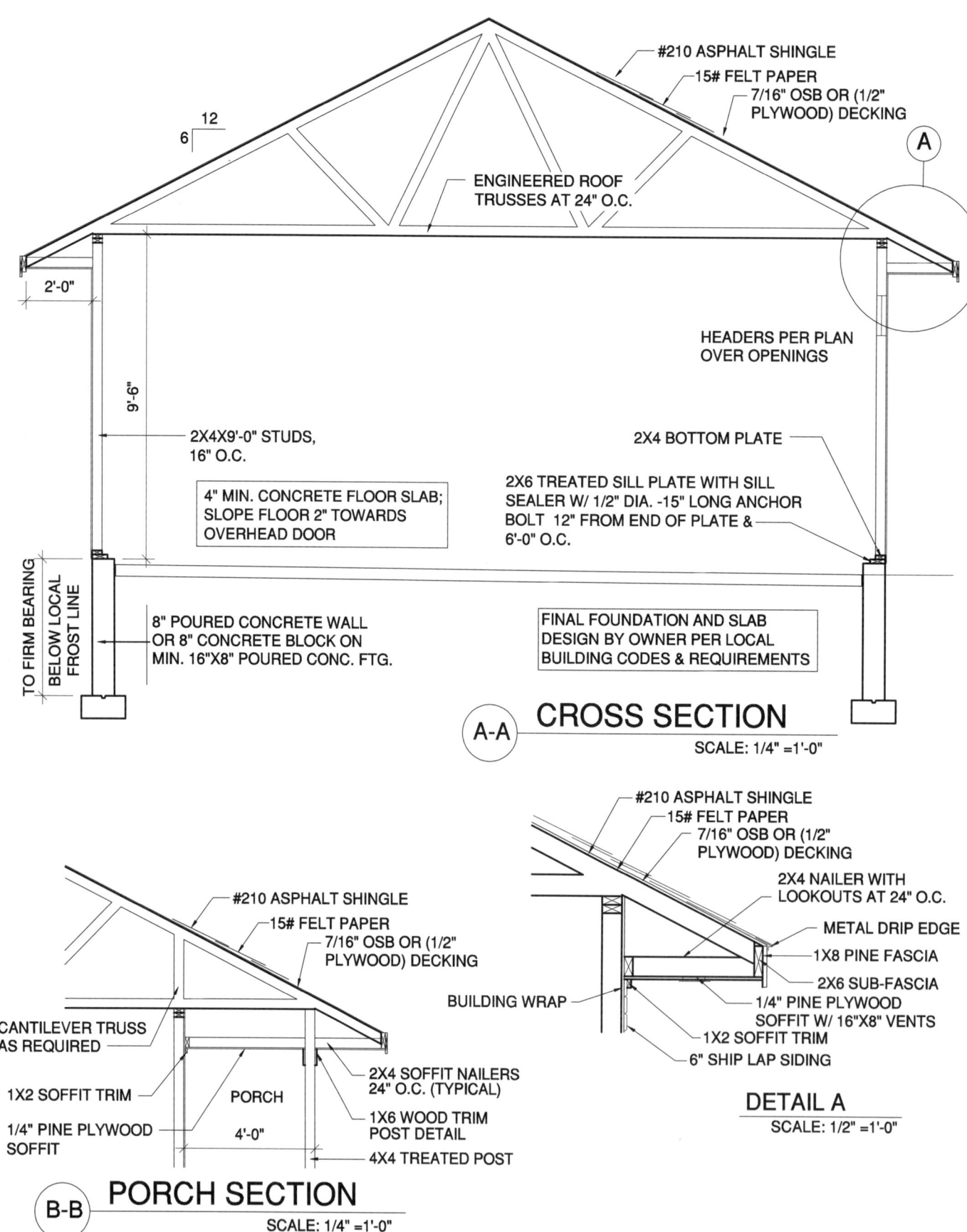

CARLTON — Material List

ROOF

Item	Location	Qty	UM
3 - Tab Shingles 20 Yr.	Shingle	34	BN
15-lb. Asphalt Rfg. Felt	Roofing Paper	5	RL
7/16" OSB (Ply.)	Roof Decking	34	EA
Galv. Drip Edge	Above Fascia	13	EA
Engineered Roof Trusses	Roof	1	Set
2x4 - 12' Std. & Btr.	Truss Bracing	10	EA
2x4 - 12' Std. & Btr.	Rake Block	2	EA
2x4 - 12' Std. & Btr.	Soffit Nailer	6	EA
2x4 - 12' Std. & Btr.	Lookout	5	EA
2x4 - 16' Std. & Btr.	Ladder Rake	8	EA
2x6 - 16' Std. & Btr.	Sub-Fascia	4	EA
1x6 - 12' #2 & Btr. S4S	Fascia	6	EA
1x8 - 12' #2 & Btr. S4S	Fascia	6	EA
5# 6d Galv. Nails	General Framing	4	EA
5# 8d Ctd. Box Nails	General Framing	4	EA
5# 10d Bright Box Nails	General Framing	4	EA
5# 6d Galv. Box Nails	General Framing	2	EA
5# 6d Galv. Finish Nails	General Finish Trim	1	EA
5# 8d Galv. Finish Nails	General Finish Trim	1	EA
5# 1-1/4"Roofing Nails	Shingle	4	EA
10 oz. - Paintable Caulk	Flashing	4	TB

WALL FRAMING

Item	Location	Qty	UM
2x4 - 10' Std. & Btr.	Stud	112	EA
2x4 - 12' Std. & Btr.	Plate	14	EA
2x4 - 16' Std. & Btr.	Plate	11	EA
2x6 - 16' Treated	Bottom Sill Plate	7	EA
2x12 - 8' Std. & Btr.	Header	1	EA
2x12 - 12' Std. & Btr.	Header	4	EA
1-3/4"x14"x16'-9" LVL Hdr.	Garage Door	2	EA
7/16" OSB (Ply.)	Wall Sheathing	32	EA
3-1/2"x50'x1/4" Sill Sealer	Sill Plate	3	RL
40"x 97' Building Paper	Wall	4	RL
5# 1/2" Galv. Roofing Nails	Building Paper	3	EA
5# 16d Galv. Nails	General Framing	4	EA
5# 8d Ctd. Box Nails	General Framing	2	EA
5# 10d Bright Box Nails	General Framing	3	EA

EXTERIOR TRIM & ACCESSORIES

Item	Location	Qty	UM
1x6 - 10' Ship Lap Siding	Siding	210	EA
2x4 - 10' Std. & Btr.	Corner Trim	5	EA
2x6 - 8' Std. & Btr.	Ovh. Gar. Dr. Jamb	2	EA
2x6 - 16' Std. & Btr.	Ovh. Gar. Dr. Head	1	EA
1x4 - 10' Std. & Btr.	Window Trim	7	EA
1/4" Plywood (Sanded)	Soffit Material	7	EA
1x4 - 10' Std. & Btr. (Rip-1x2)	Soffit Trim	3	EA
1x6 - 6' Std. & Btr.	Post Trim	1	EA
4x4 - 12' Treated	Post	1	EA
14"x6" Metal Soffit Vent	Soffit	4	EA
5# 6d Galv. Finish Nails	General Fin. Trim	5	EA
5# 8d Galv. Finish Nails	General Fin. Trim	4	EA
10 oz. - Paintable Caulk	Ledger	4	TB
16'x7' Ovh. Gar. Dr. W/Hrdwr.	Garage Door	1	EA
36"x80" Exterior LH Door	Service Door	1	EA
6024 Awning Window	Window	1	EA
Lockset/Deadbolt	Service Door	1	EA
1-1/4"x2" Brickmold	Service Door	7	EA
4" - 10' "Z" Flashing	Door/Window	3	EA

CHAPTER 4

THE ADAMS

HPM-1008

Brick arches and keystone details complement the simple yet sleek lines of this easy-to-build two-car garage. Two separate openings create a style and elegance not found in the garages of most neighborhoods. A window and another door offer additional light and access.

Dimensions for this garage are 22' X 22'. 484 sq. ft.

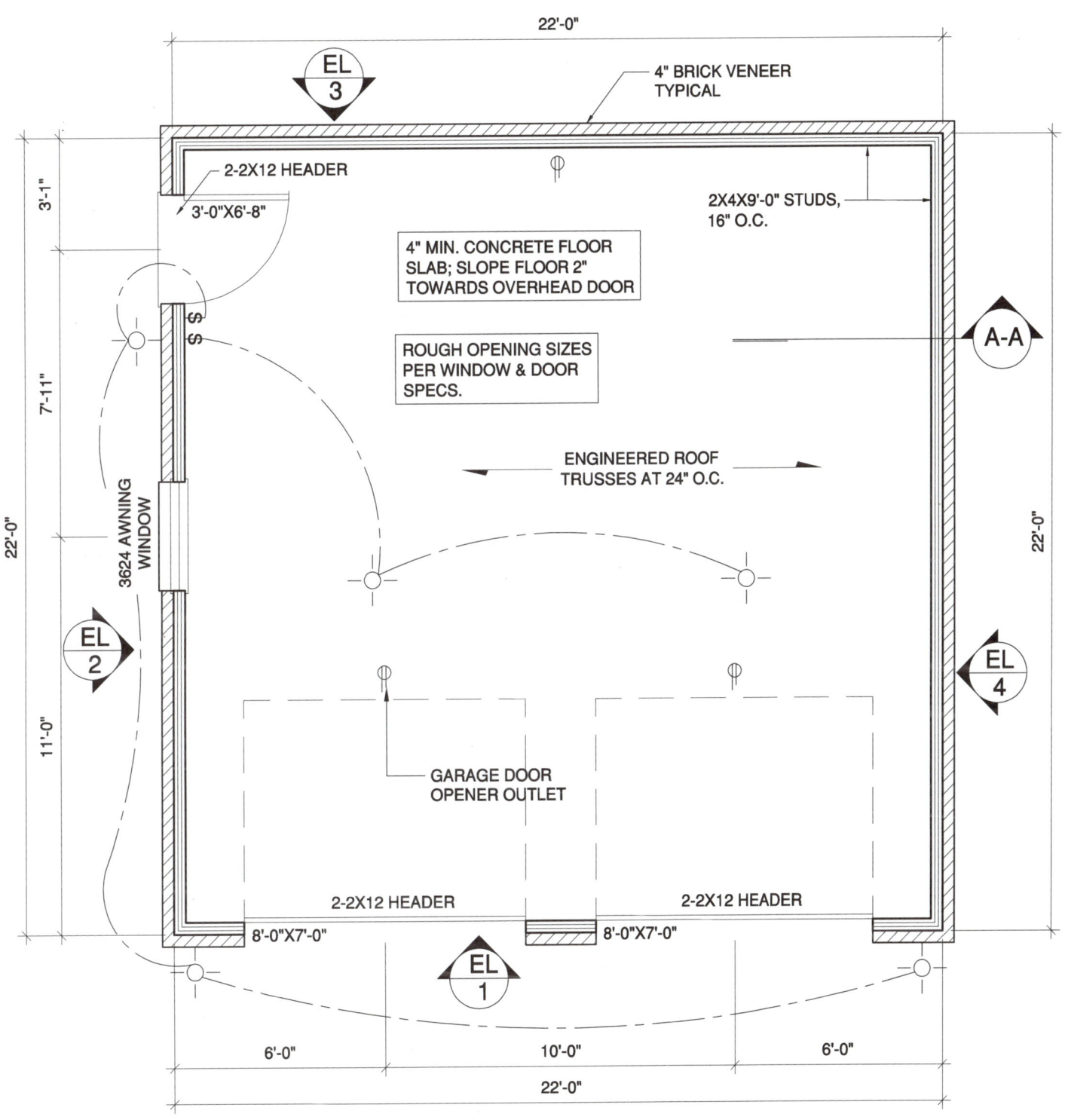

ADAMS
Foundation Plan
Scale: 1/4" = 1'-0"

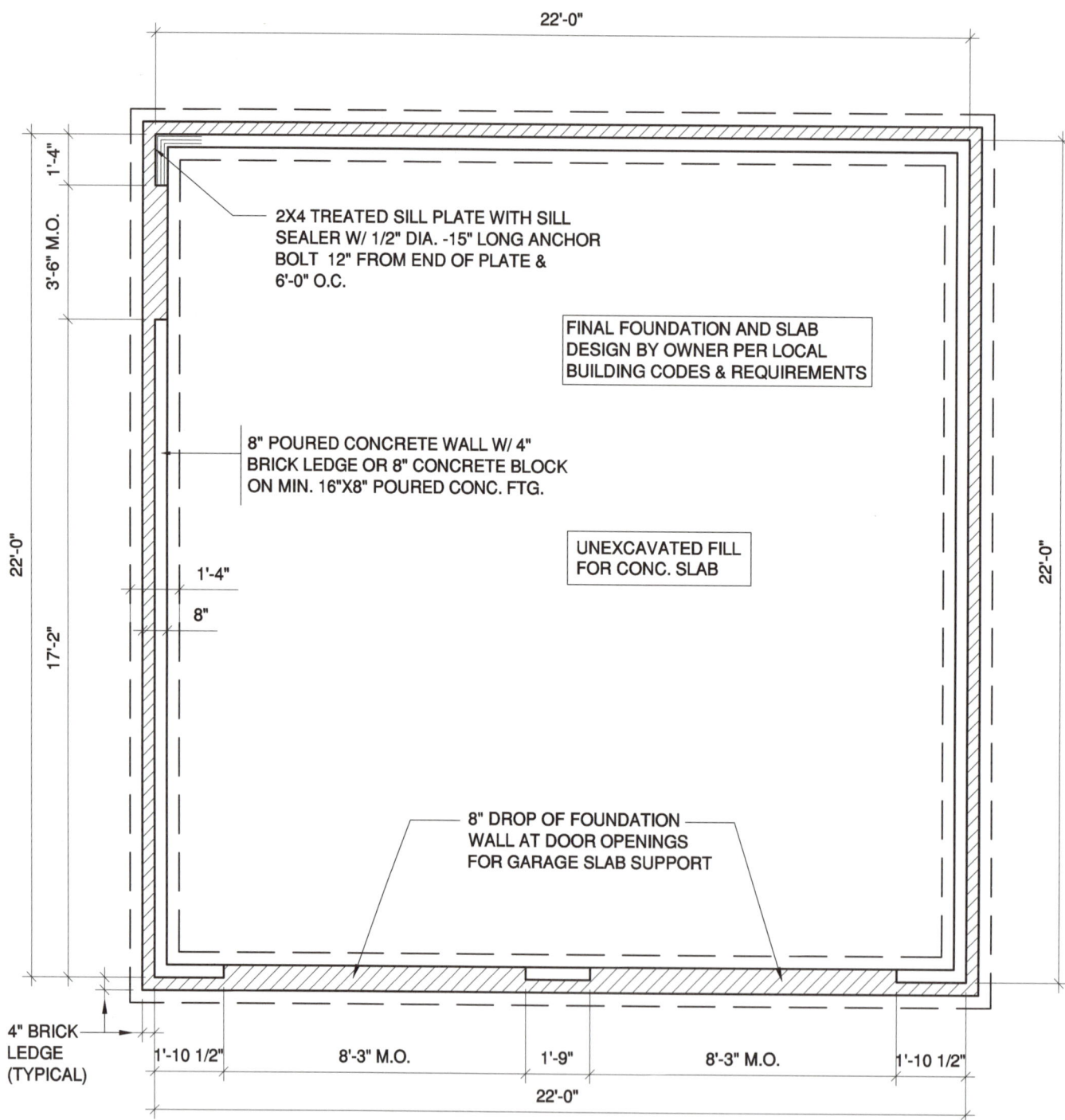

ADAMS — Elevations

Scale: 3/16" = 1'-0"

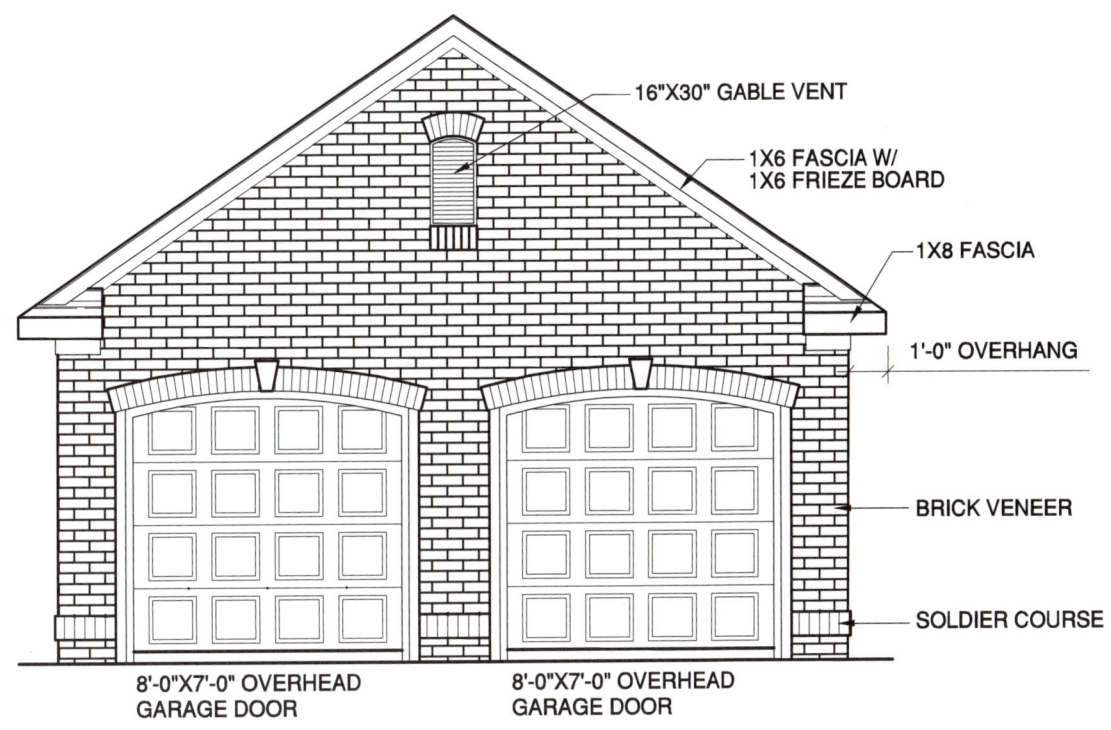

FRONT ELEVATION (EL/1)

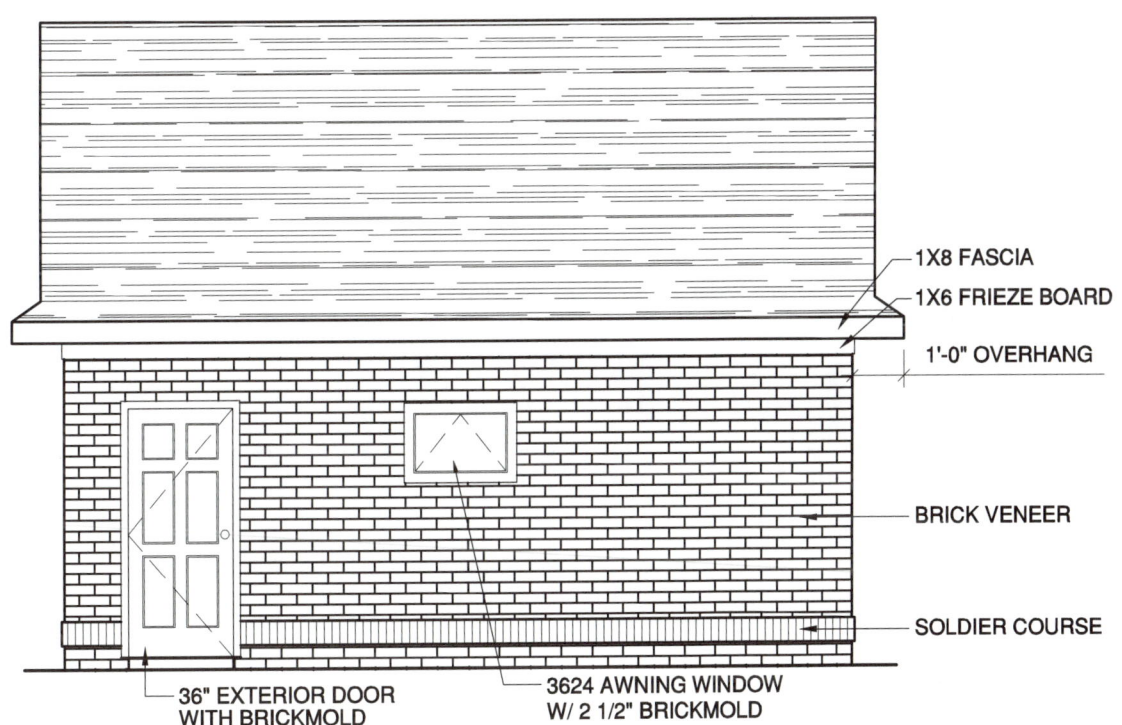

LEFT ELEVATION (EL/2)

www.homedepot.com

ADAMS — Elevations

Scale: 3/16" = 1'-0"

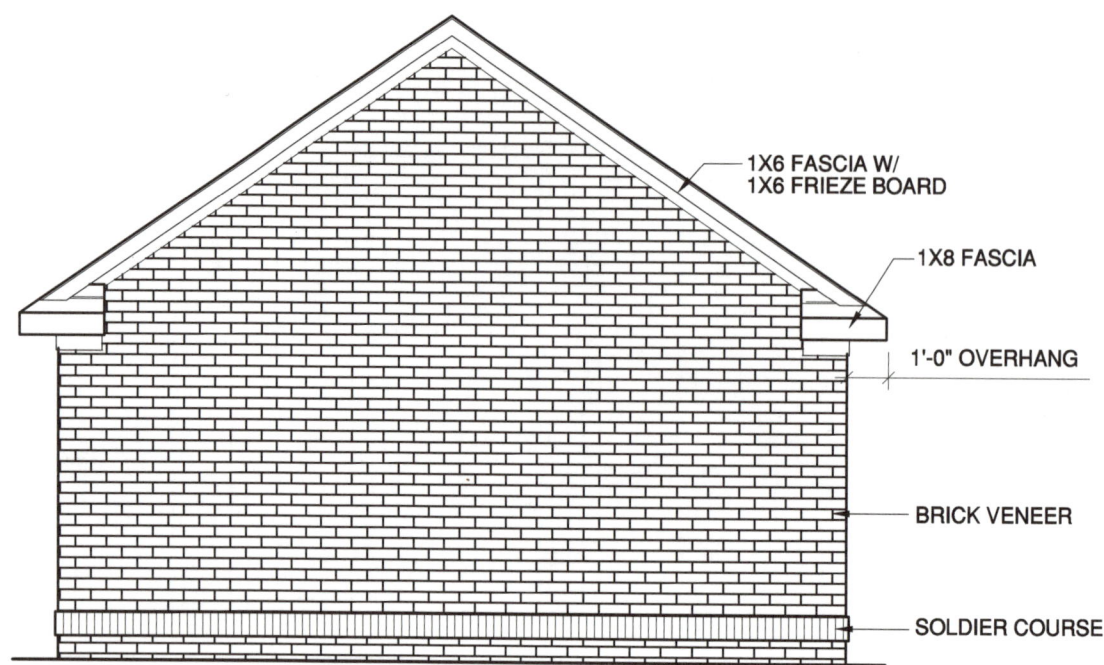

REAR ELEVATION (EL 3)

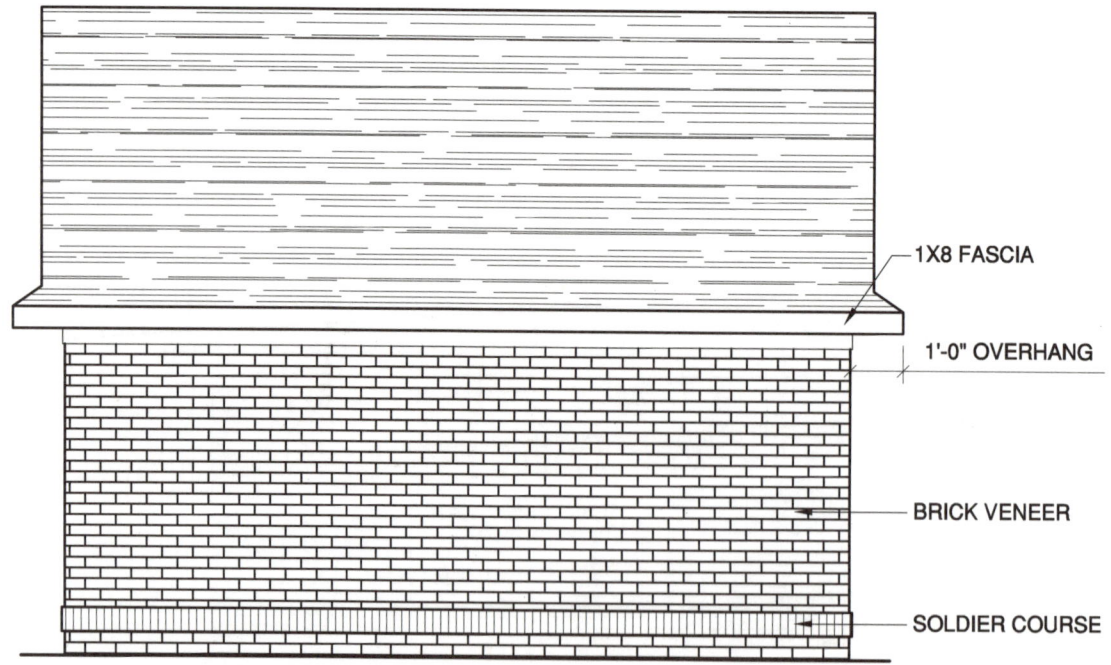

RIGHT ELEVATION (EL 4)

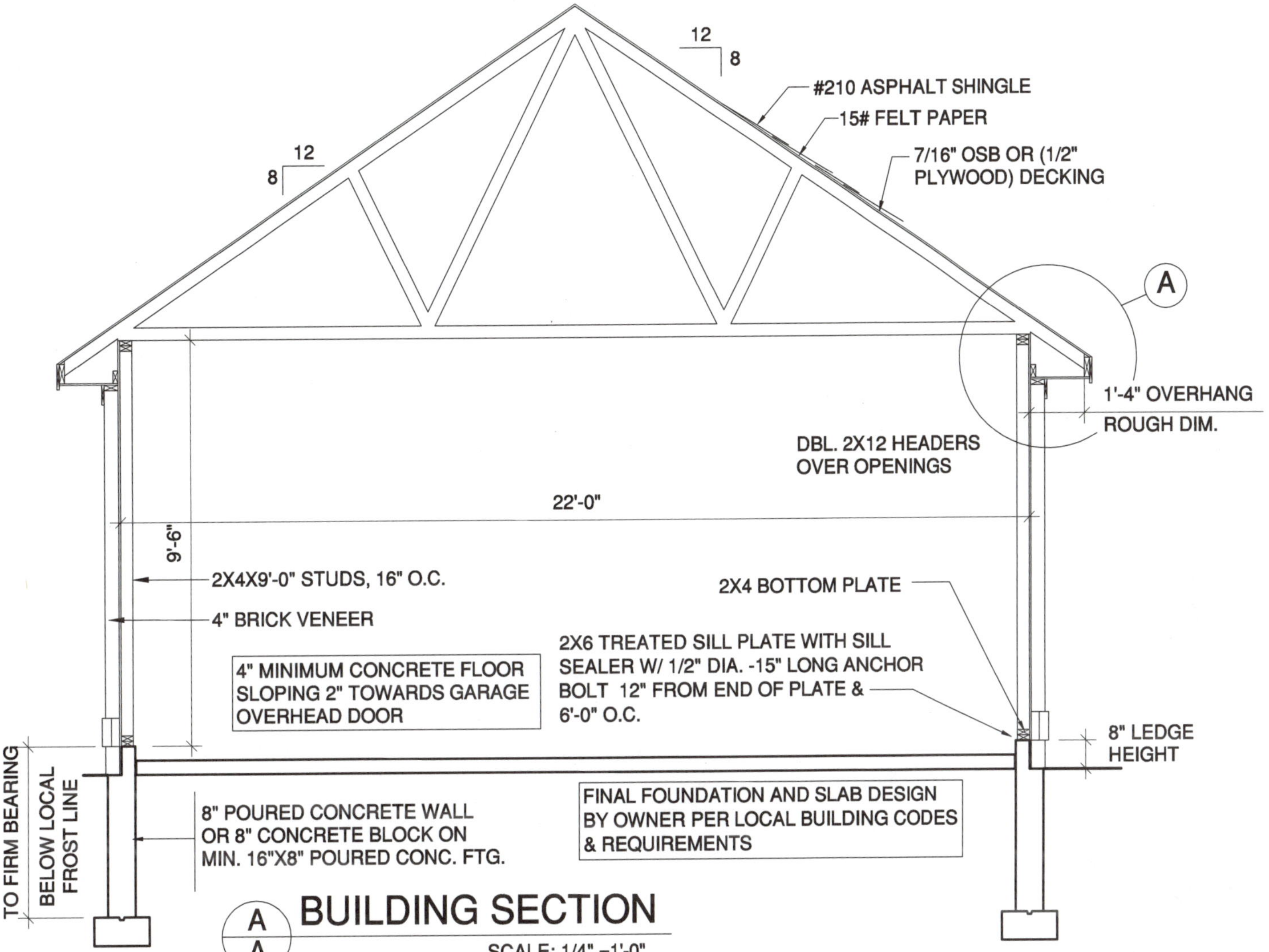

ADAMS — Section and Detail

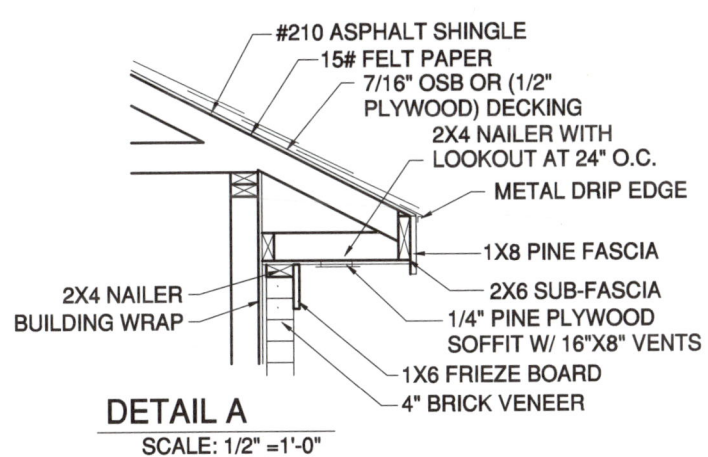

BUILDING SECTION
SCALE: 1/4" = 1'-0"

Callouts:
- #210 ASPHALT SHINGLE
- 15# FELT PAPER
- 7/16" OSB OR (1/2" PLYWOOD) DECKING
- 12 / 8 (roof slope, both sides)
- 1'-4" OVERHANG ROUGH DIM.
- DBL. 2X12 HEADERS OVER OPENINGS
- 22'-0"
- 9'-6"
- 2X4X9'-0" STUDS, 16" O.C.
- 4" BRICK VENEER
- 2X4 BOTTOM PLATE
- 2X6 TREATED SILL PLATE WITH SILL SEALER W/ 1/2" DIA. -15" LONG ANCHOR BOLT 12" FROM END OF PLATE & 6'-0" O.C.
- 4" MINIMUM CONCRETE FLOOR SLOPING 2" TOWARDS GARAGE OVERHEAD DOOR
- 8" LEDGE HEIGHT
- 8" POURED CONCRETE WALL OR 8" CONCRETE BLOCK ON MIN. 16"X8" POURED CONC. FTG.
- FINAL FOUNDATION AND SLAB DESIGN BY OWNER PER LOCAL BUILDING CODES & REQUIREMENTS
- TO FIRM BEARING
- BELOW LOCAL FROST LINE

DETAIL A
SCALE: 1/2" = 1'-0"

- #210 ASPHALT SHINGLE
- 15# FELT PAPER
- 7/16" OSB OR (1/2" PLYWOOD) DECKING
- 2X4 NAILER WITH LOOKOUT AT 24" O.C.
- METAL DRIP EDGE
- 1X8 PINE FASCIA
- 2X6 SUB-FASCIA
- 1/4" PINE PLYWOOD SOFFIT W/ 16"X8" VENTS
- 1X6 FRIEZE BOARD
- 4" BRICK VENEER
- 2X4 NAILER
- BUILDING WRAP

www.homedepot.com

ADAMS Material List

ROOF

Item	Location	Qty	UM
3 - Tab Shingles 20 Yr.	Shingle	25	BN
15-lb. Asphalt Rfg. Felt	Roofing Paper	4	RL
7/16" OSB (Ply.)	Roof Decking	24	EA
Galv. Drip Edge	Above Fascia	14	EA
Engineered Roof Trusses	Roof	1	Set
2x4 - 12' Std. & Btr.	Truss Bracing	4	EA
2x4 - 12' Std. & Btr.	Sof. Nlr./Lookout	7	EA
2x4 - 14' Std. & Btr.	Truss Bracing	4	EA
2x4 - 16' Std. & Btr.	Rake/Blk./Bxg.	10	EA
2x6 - 16' Std. & Btr.	Sub-Fascia	5	EA
1x6 - 12' #2 & Btr. S4S	Fascia	6	EA
1x8 - 12' #2 & Btr. S4S	Fascia	5	EA
5# 16d Galv. Nails	General Framing	4	EA
5# 8d Ctd. Box Nails	General Framing	4	EA
5# 10d Bright Box Nails	General Framing	4	EA
5# 6d Galv. Box Nails	General Framing	2	EA
5# 6d Galv. Finish Nails	General Fin. Trim	1	EA
5# 8d Galv. Finish Nails	General Fin. Trim	1	EA
5# 1-1/4" Roofing Nails	Shingle	4	EA
10 oz. - Paintable Caulk	Flashing	4	TB

WALL FRAMING

Item	Location	Qty	UM
2x4 - 10' Std. & Btr.	Stud	100	EA
2x4 - 12' Std. & Btr.	Plate	12	EA
2x4 - 16' Std. & Btr.	Plate	9	EA
2x6 - 16' Treated	Bottom Sill Plate	6	EA
2x12 - 8' Std. & Btr.	Header	2	EA
2x12 - 10' Std. & Btr.	Header	4	EA
7/16" OSB (Ply.)	Wall Sheathing	28	EA
3-1/2"x50'x1/4" Sill Sealer	Sill Plate	2	RL
40"x 97' Building Paper	Wall	3	RL
5# 1/2" Roofing Nails	Building Paper	3	EA
5# 16d Galv. Nails	General Framing	4	EA
5# 8d Ctd. Box Nails	General Framing	2	EA
5# 10d Bright Box Nails	General Framing	3	EA

EXTERIOR TRIM & ACCESSORIES

Item	Location	Qty	UM
2x6 - 8' Std. & Btr.	Ovh. Gar. Dr. Jamb	4	EA
2x6 - 8' Std. & Btr.	Ovh. Gar. Dr. Head	2	EA
1x4 - 10' Std. & Btr.	Window Trim	9	EA
1/4" Plywood (Sanded)	Soffit Material	5	EA
2x4 - 12' Std. & Btr.	Brick Frieze Nlr.	10	EA
1x6 - 12' Std. & Btr.	Brick Frieze	10	EA
14"x6" Metal Soffit Vent	Soffit	4	EA
16"x30" Gable Vent	Gable End	1	EA
5# 6d Galv. Finish Nails	General Fin. Trim	5	EA
5# 8d Galv. Finish Nails	General Fin. Trim	4	EA
10 oz. - Paintable Caulk	Ledger	4	TB
8'x7' Ovh. Gar. Dr.	Garage Door	2	EA
36"x80" Exterior LH Dr.	Service Door	1	EA
3624 Awning Window	Window	1	EA
Lockset/Deadbolt	Service Door	1	EA
1-1/4"x2" Brickmold	Service Door	9	EA
4" - 10' "Z" Flashing	Window/Door	3	EA
Brick	Exterior	821	SF
Mortar	Brick	47	CF

The Marquis

HPM-1009

Stucco walls, arched garage door openings, and ornamental details add interest to this unique garage and shed combination. You'll have plenty of room to park two cars, as well as store equipment, complete projects or get a head start on your gardening in the attached shed space. Double doors in this versatile space make it easy to move large objects in and out.

Dimensions for this garage/shed are 28' X 22'.
Garage 484 sq. ft., shed 96 sq. ft. Total 580 sq. ft.

Marquis

Plan View

Scale: 3/16" = 1'-0"

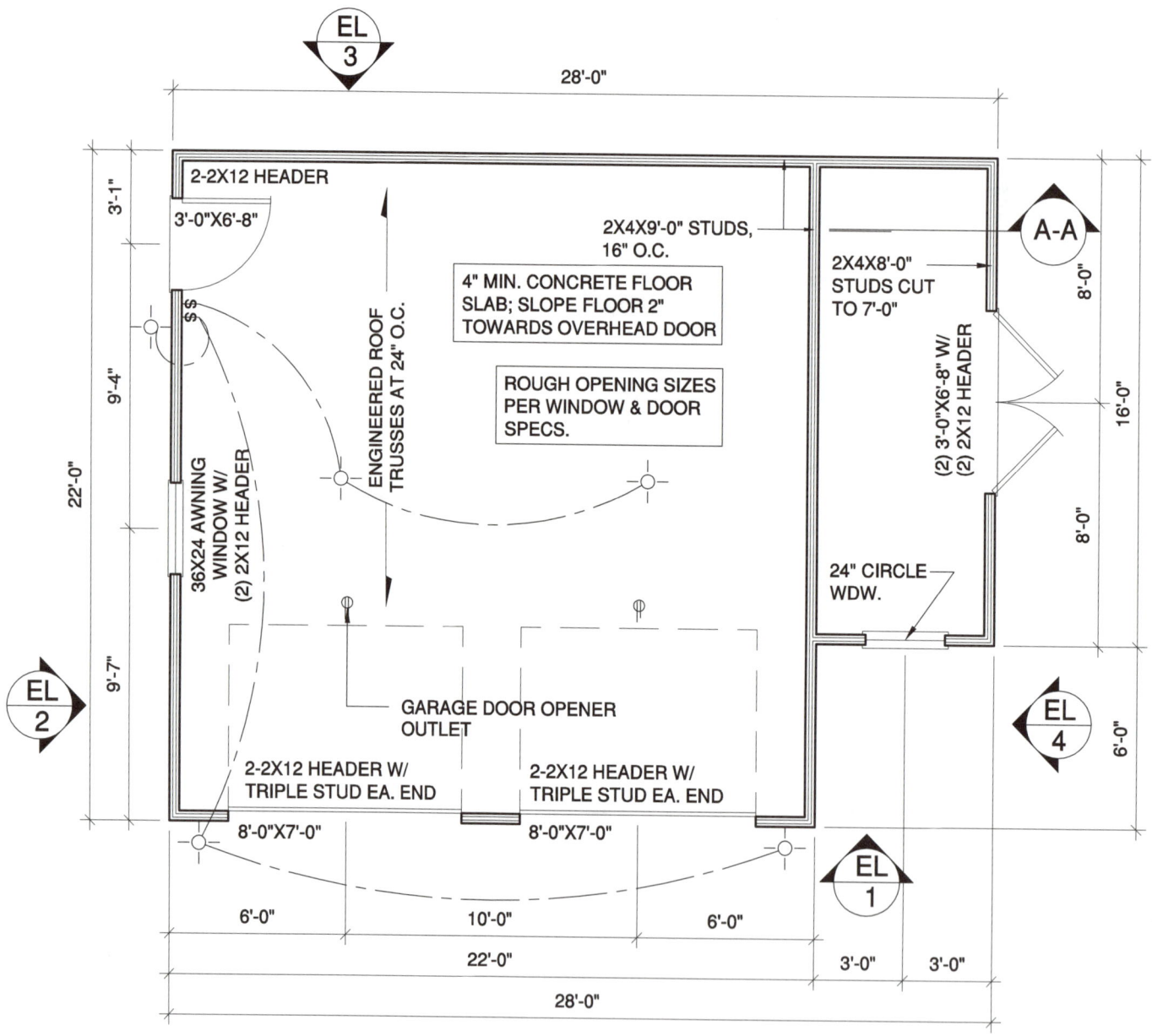

132   www.DreamIt-BuildIt.com

MARQUIS — Foundation Plan

Scale: 3/16" = 1'-0"

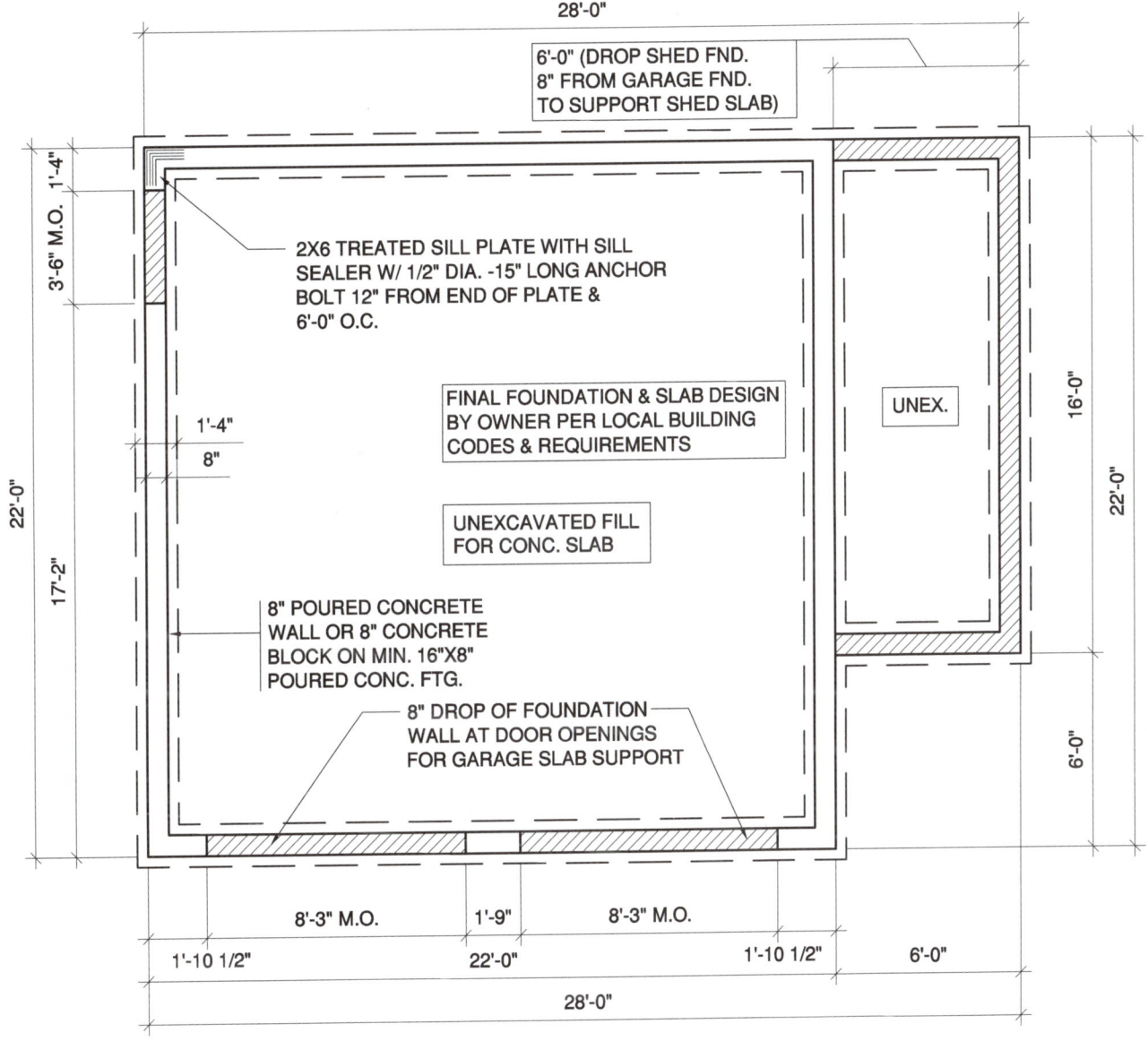

www.homedepot.com 133

MARQUIS — Elevations

Scale: 3/16" = 1'-0"

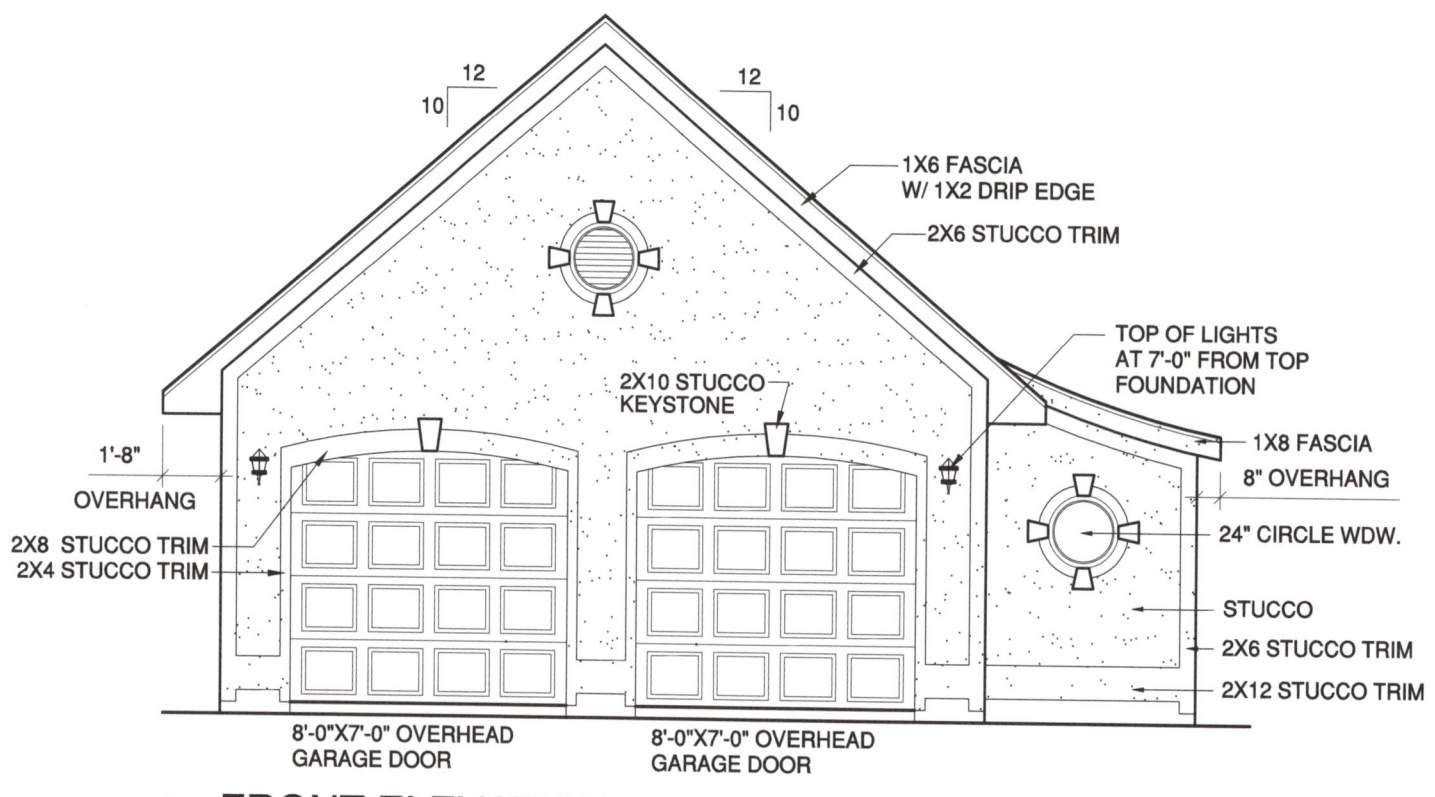

FRONT ELEVATION (EL/1)

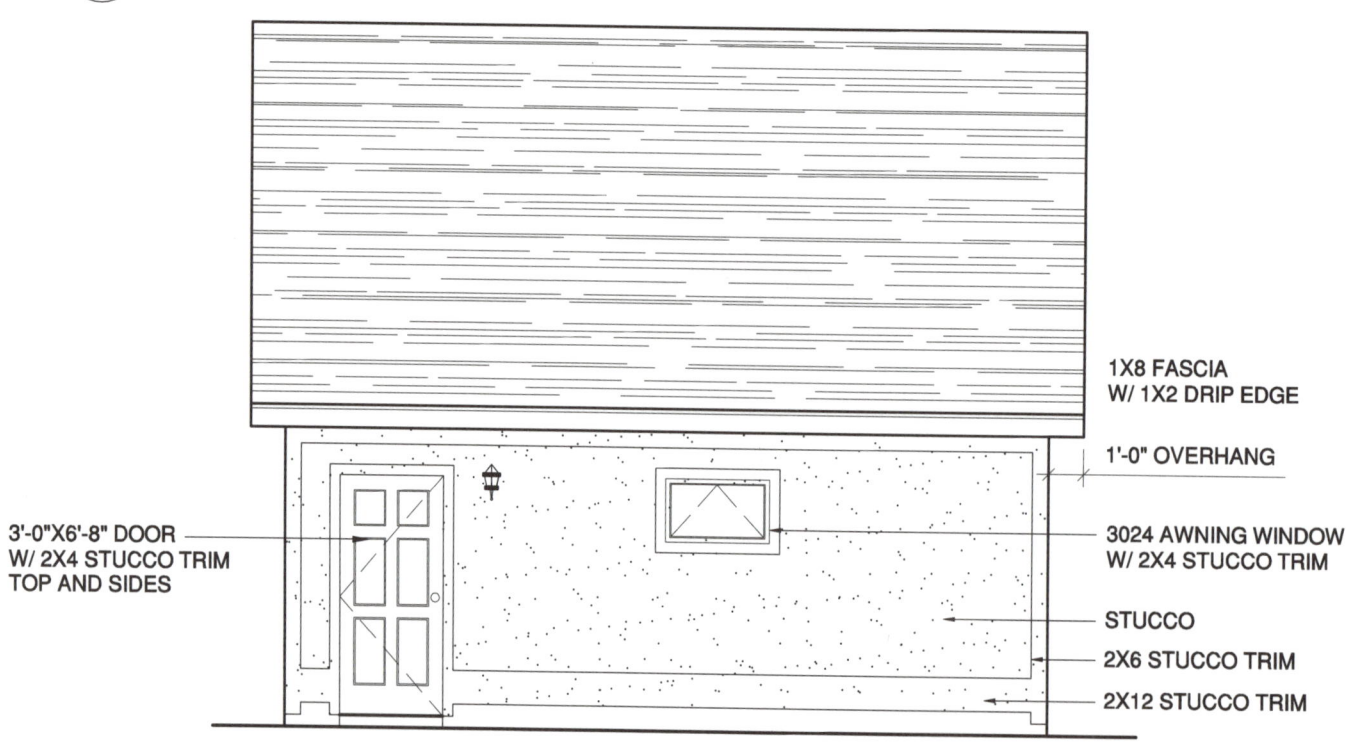

LEFT ELEVATION (EL/2)

134 www.DreamIt-BuildIt.com

MARQUIS — Elevations

Scale: 3/16" = 1'-0"

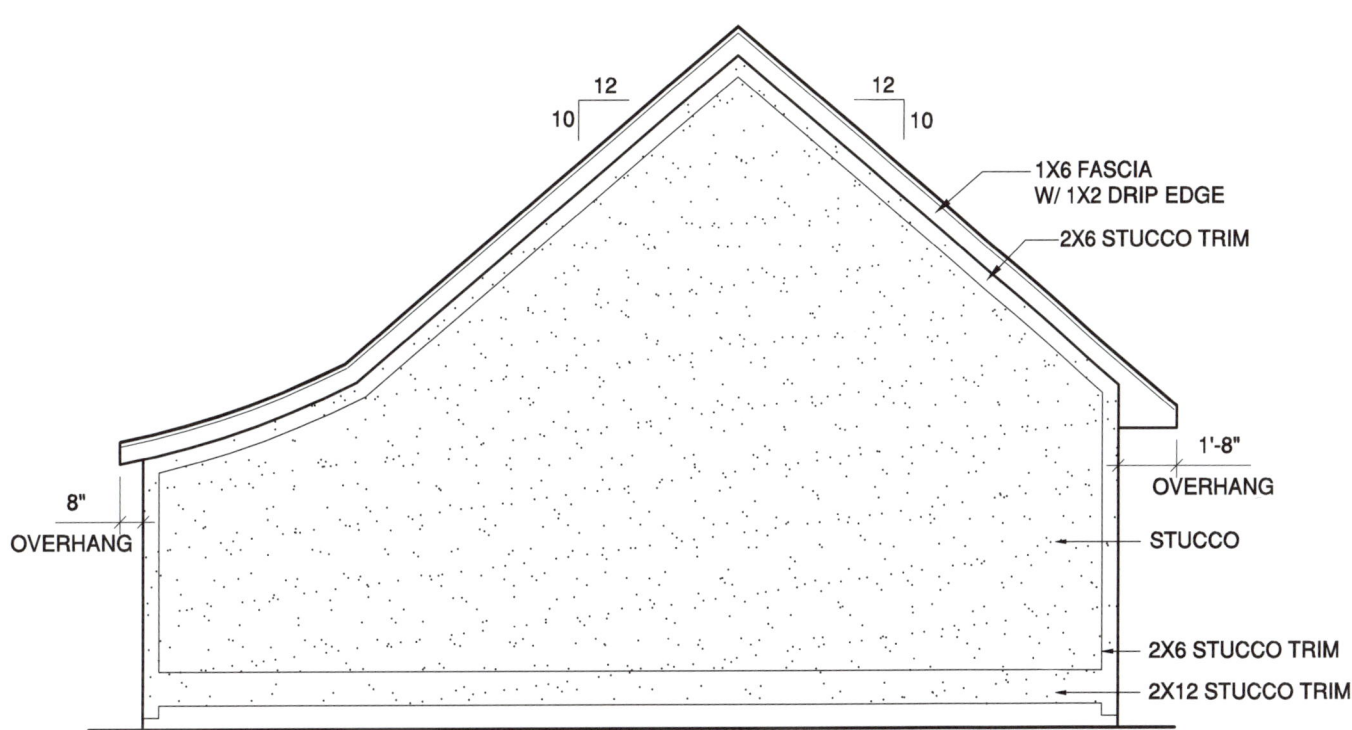

- 1X6 FASCIA W/ 1X2 DRIP EDGE
- 2X6 STUCCO TRIM
- 1'-8" OVERHANG
- 8" OVERHANG
- STUCCO
- 2X6 STUCCO TRIM
- 2X12 STUCCO TRIM

EL/3 REAR ELEVATION

- 1'-0" OVERHANG
- (2) 3'-0" X 6'-8" DOORS W/ 2X4 STUCCO TRIM
- STUCCO
- 2X6 STUCCO TRIM
- 2X12 STUCCO TRIM

EL/4 RIGHT ELEVATION

www.homedepot.com

Marquis — Section and Details

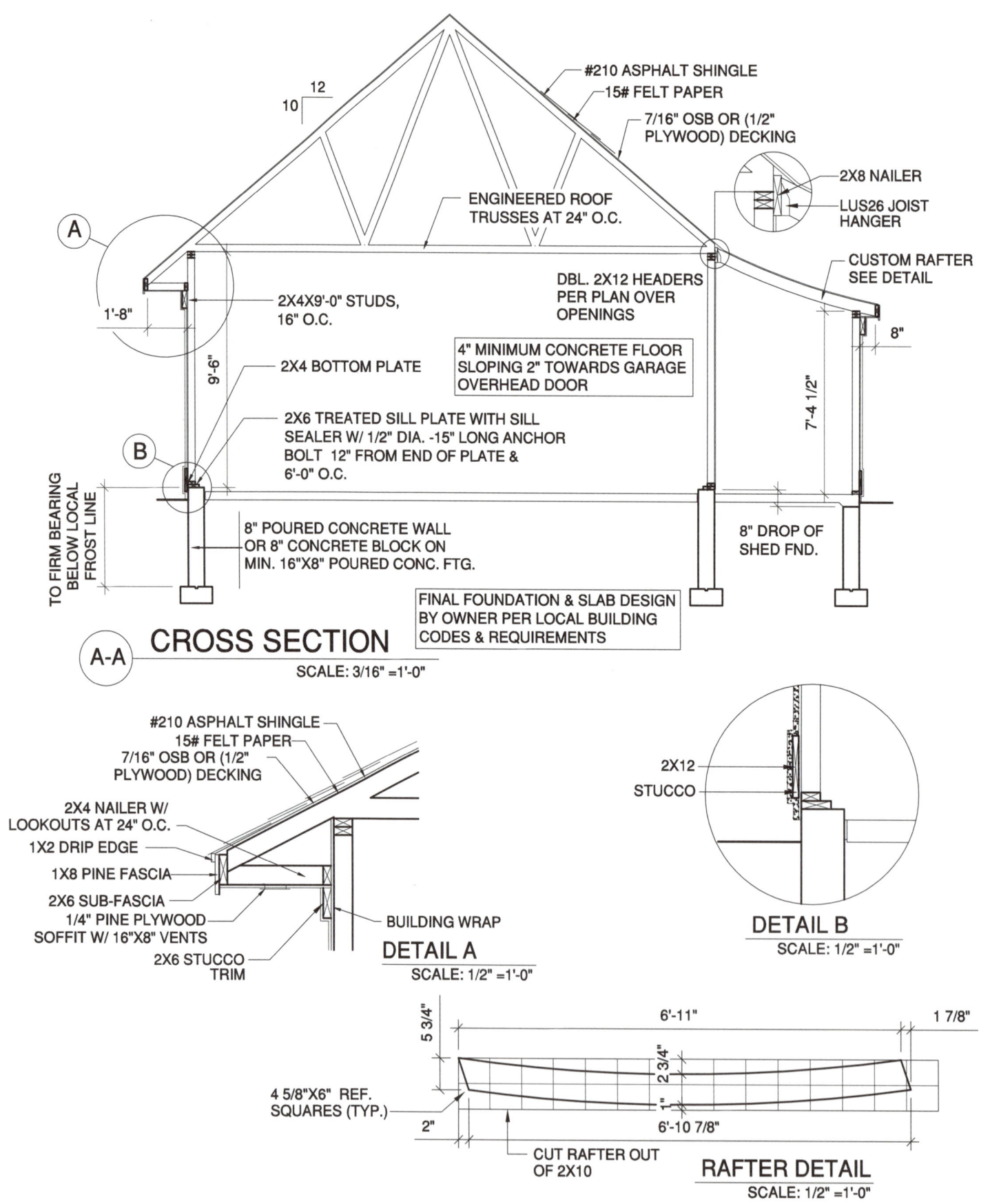

MARQUIS Material List

ROOF

Item	Location	Qty	UM
3 - Tab Shingles 20 Yr.	Shingle	30	BN
15-lb. Asphalt Rfg. Felt	Roofing Paper	5	RL
7/16" OSB (Ply.)	Roof Decking	30	EA
Galv. Drip Edge	Above Fascia	14	EA
Engineered Roof Trusses	Roof	1	Set
2x8 - 16' Std. & Btr.	Nailer	1	EA
2x10 - 8' Std. & Btr.	Rafter	13	EA
Joist Hanger (LUS26)	Rafter	9	EA
2x4 - 12' Std. & Btr.	Truss Bracing	4	EA
2x4 - 12' Std. & Btr.	Sof. Nlr./Lookout	9	EA
2x4 - 14' Std. & Btr.	Truss Bracing	4	EA
2x4 - 20' Std. & Btr.	Rake/Blk./Gable	9	EA
2x6 - 16' Std. & Btr.	Sub-Fascia	4	EA
1x6 - 12' #2 & Btr. S4S	Fascia	7	EA
1x8 - 12' #2 & Btr. S4S	Fascia	5	EA
1x12 - 12' #2 & Btr. S4S	Fascia	2	EA
5# 16d Galv. Nails	General Framing	4	EA
5# 8d Ctd. Box Nails	General Framing	4	EA
5# 10d Bright Box Nails	General Framing	4	EA
5# 6d Galv. Box Nails	General Framing	2	EA
5# 6d Galv. Finish Nails	General Fin. Trim	1	EA
5# 8d Galv. Finish Nails	General Fin. Trim	1	EA
5# 1-1/4" Roofing Nails	Shingle	4	EA
10 oz. - Paintable Caulk	Flashing	4	TB

WALL FRAMING

Item	Location	Qty	UM
2x4 - 8' Std. & Btr.	Stud	38	EA
2x4 - 10' Std. & Btr.	Stud	104	EA
2x4 - 12' Std. & Btr.	Plate	14	EA
2x4 - 16' Std. & Btr.	Plate	11	EA
2x4 - 16' Treated	Bottom Sill Plate	2	EA
2x6 - 16' Treated	Bottom Sill Plate	6	EA
3 1/2"x50'x1/4" Sill Sealer	Sill Plate	3	RL
2x12 - 8' Std. & Btr.	Header	5	EA
2x12 - 10' Std. & Btr.	Header	4	EA
7/16" OSB (Ply.)	Wall Sheathing	36	EA
40"x 97' Building Paper	Wall	4	RL
5# 1/2" Roofing Nails	Building Paper	3	EA
5# 16d Galv. Nails	General Framing	4	EA
5# 8d Ctd. Box Nails	General Framing	2	EA
5# 10d Bright Box Nails	General Framing	3	EA

EXTERIOR TRIM & ACCESSORIES

Item	Location	Qty	UM
80# One Coat Stucco	Wall	95	EA
Furred Stucco Netting	Wall	3	RL
1/2"x10' Casing Bead	Window/Door	13	EA
5 1/2" #7 Fnd. Sill Screen	Sill	11	EA
2x6 - 8' Std. & Btr.	Ovh. Gar. Dr. Jamb	4	EA
2x6 - 8' Std. & Btr.	Ovh. Gar. Dr. Head	2	EA
1/4" Plywood (Sanded)	Soffit Material	5	EA
14x6 Metal Soffit Vent	Soffit	4	EA
24" Round Gable Vent	Gable End	1	EA
2x4 - 8' Std. & Btr.	Stucco Trim	11	EA
2x6 - 12' Std. & Btr.	Stucco Trim	19	EA
2x8 - 12' Std. & Btr.	Stucco Trim	2	EA
2X12 -12' Std. & Btr.	Stucco Trim	9	EA
1x4 -10' Std. & Btr. (Rip-1x2)	Drip Edge	12	EA
5# 6d Galv. Finish Nails	General Fin. Trim	5	EA
5# 8d Galv. Finish Nails	General Fin. Trim	4	EA
10 oz. - Paintable Caulk	Ledger	4	TB
8x7 Ovh. Gar. Dr. W/Hrdwr.	Garage Door	2	EA
36"x80" Exterior LH Door	Service Door	1	EA
(2) 36"x80" Exterior Door	Shed	1	EA
30x24 Awning Window	Window	1	EA
24" Circle Window	Window	1	EA
Lockset/Deadbolt	Service Door	1	EA
Lockset/Deadbolt/Pin	Shed Door	1	EA
2x10 - 8' Std. & Btr.	Keystone	1	EA
4"- 10' "Z" Flashing	Window/Door	4	EA

CHAPTER 4

THE WINDSONG

HPM-1007

This unique two-car garage is ideal for the owner of a boat or a recreational or oversized vehicle. The larger stall offers a 12' x 12' opening, while the smaller stall has a 9' x 8' standard, one-car opening.

Dimensions for this garage are 32' X 28'. 848 sq. ft.

Windsong — Plan View

Scale: 3/16" = 1'-0"

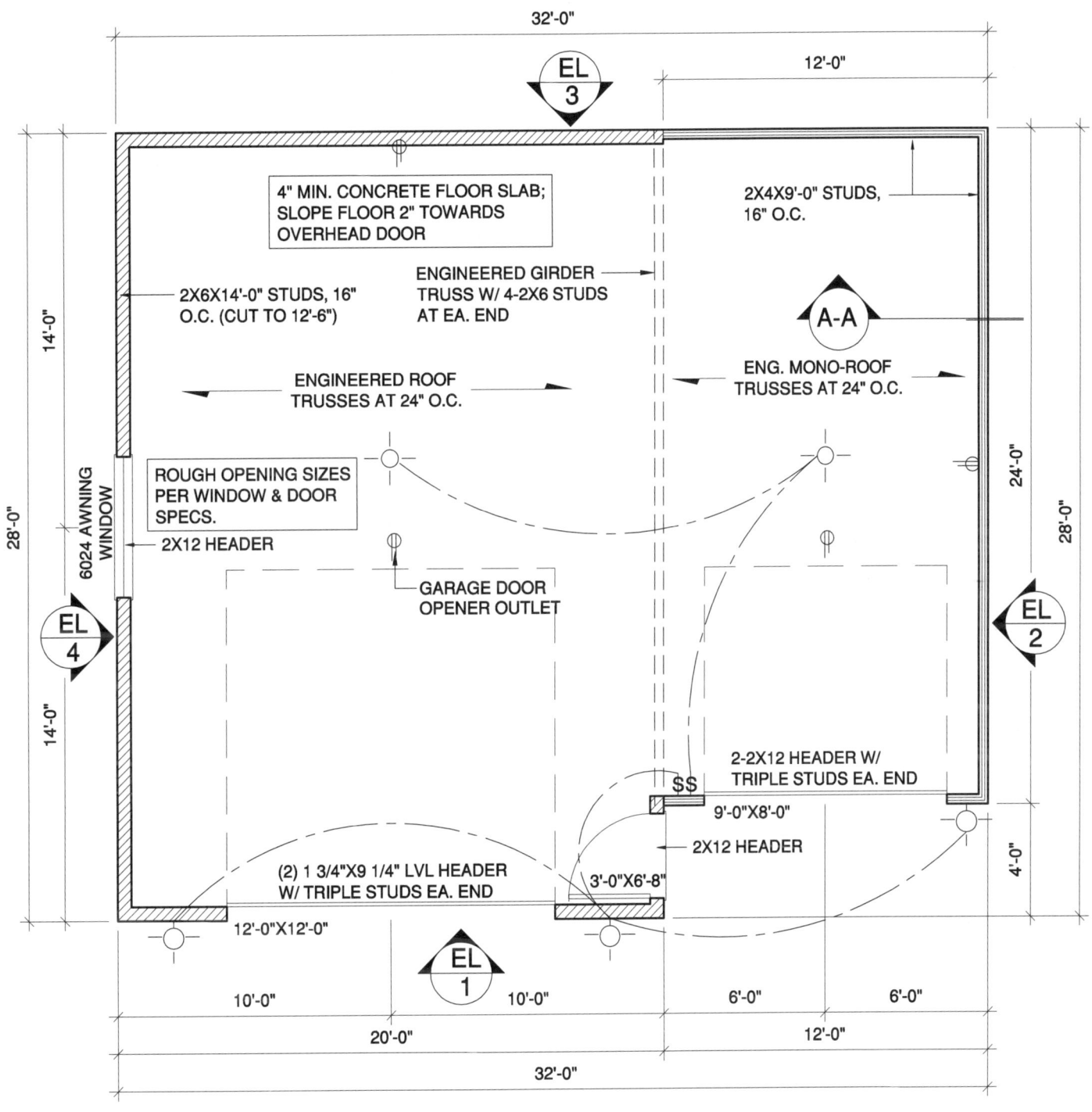

www.homedepot.com 139

WINDSONG — Foundation Plan

Scale: 3/16" = 1'-0"

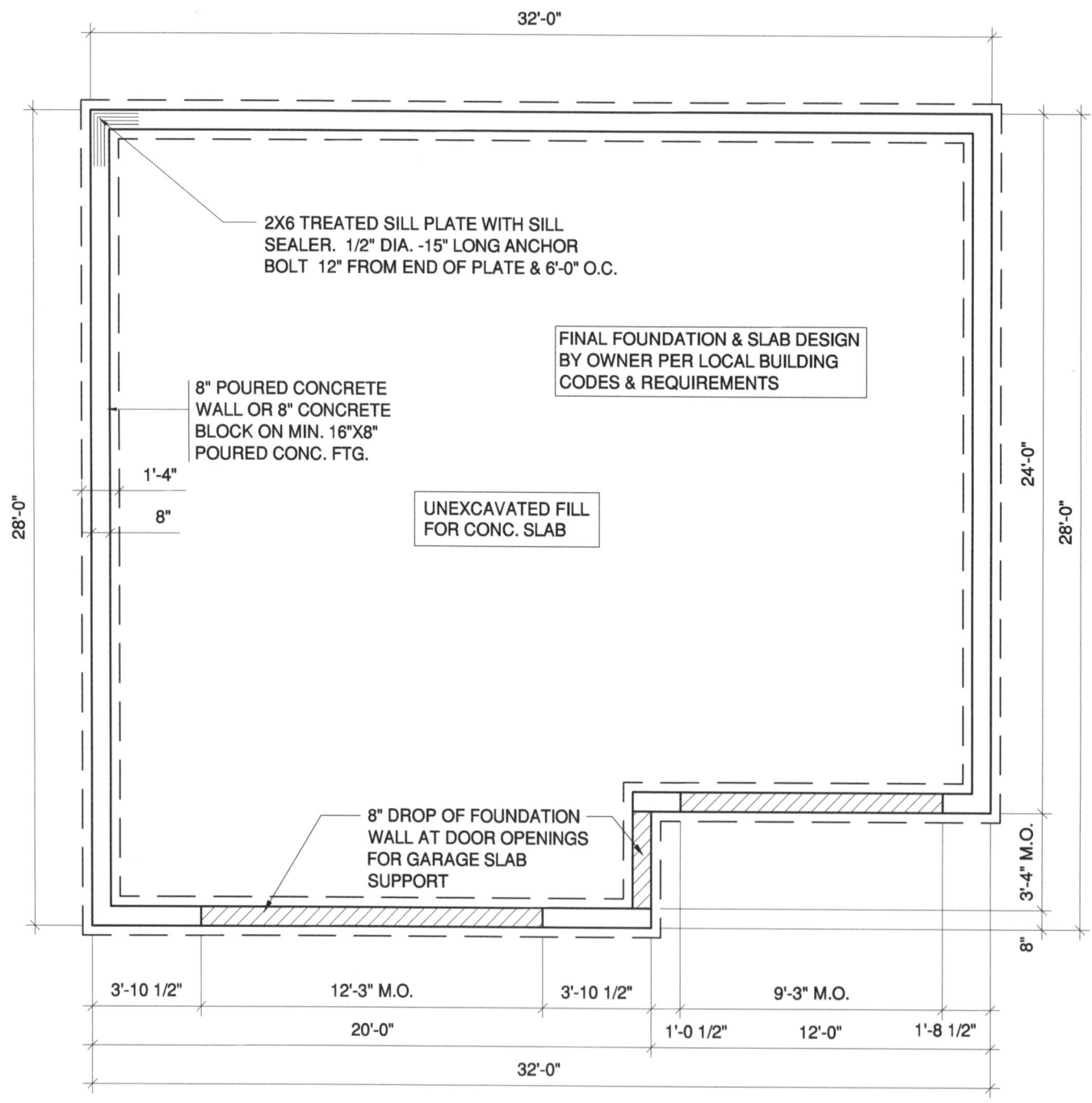

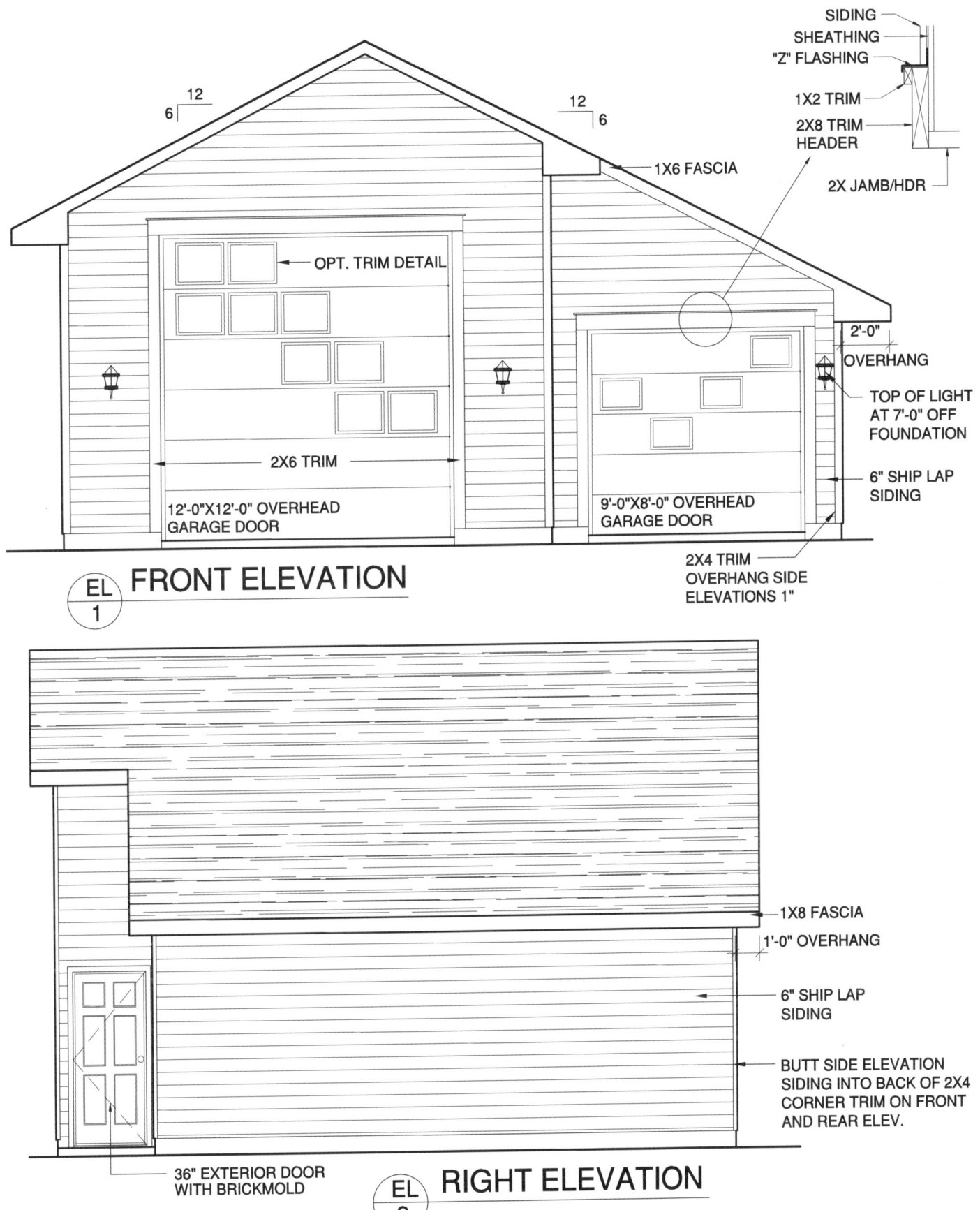

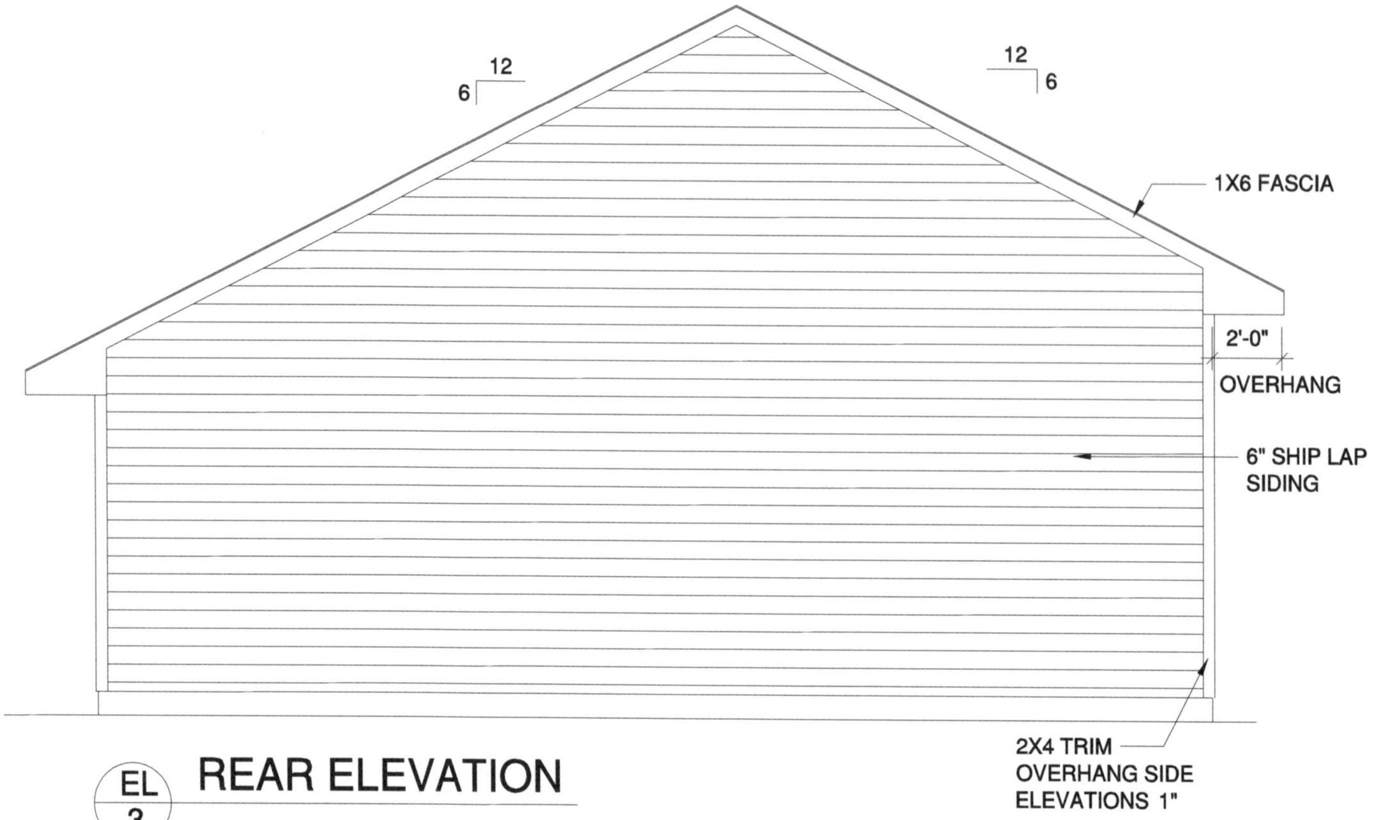

WINDSONG — Elevations

Scale: 3/16" = 1'-0"

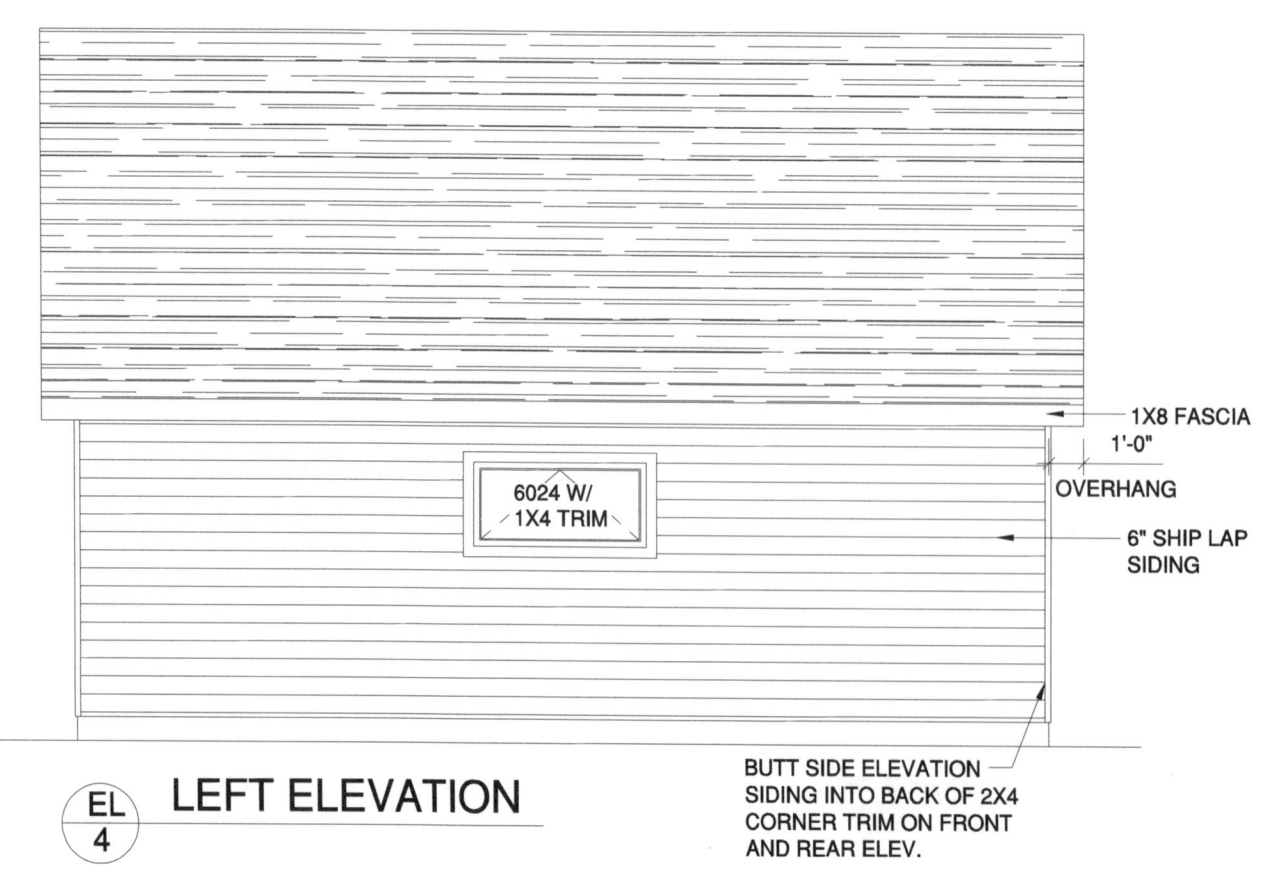

REAR ELEVATION (EL/3)

- 12/6 roof pitch
- 1X6 FASCIA
- 2'-0" OVERHANG
- 6" SHIP LAP SIDING
- 2X4 TRIM OVERHANG SIDE ELEVATIONS 1"

LEFT ELEVATION (EL/4)

- 6024 W/ 1X4 TRIM
- 1X8 FASCIA
- 1'-0" OVERHANG
- 6" SHIP LAP SIDING
- BUTT SIDE ELEVATION SIDING INTO BACK OF 2X4 CORNER TRIM ON FRONT AND REAR ELEV.

Windsong
Section and Details

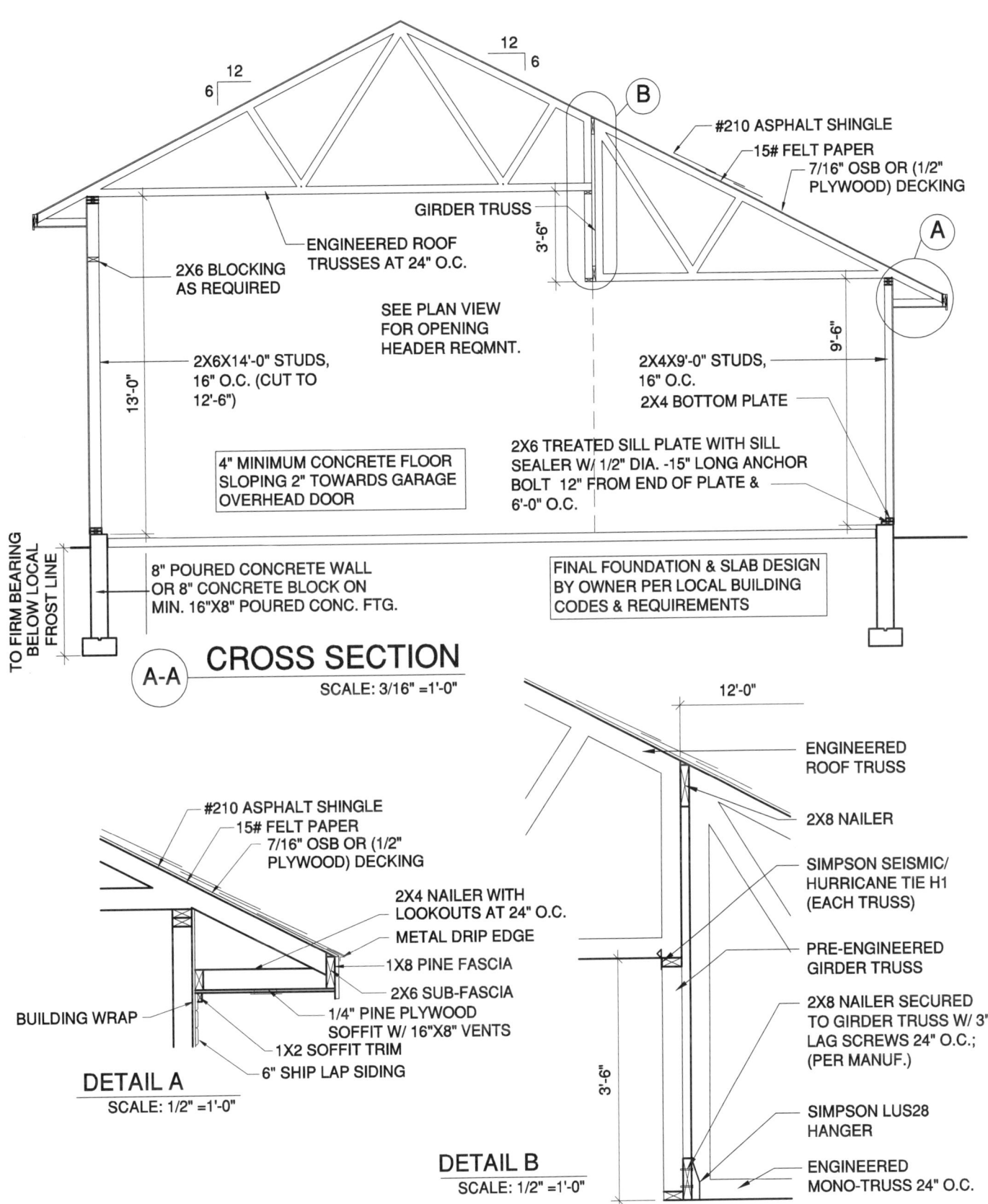

www.homedepot.com 143

WINDSONG Material List

ROOF

Item	Location	Qty	UM
3 - Tab Shingles 20 Yr.	Shingle	39	BN
15-lb. Asphalt Rfg. Felt	Roofing Paper	6	RL
7/16" OSB (Ply.)	Roof Decking	38	EA
Galv. Drip Edge	Above Fascia	14	EA
Engineered Roof Trusses	Roof	1	Set
2x4 - 12' Std. & Btr.	Truss Brcg./Rake	6	EA
2x4 - 12' Std. & Btr.	Lookout/Sof. Nlr.	10	EA
2x4 - 16' Std. & Btr.	Truss Brace/Rake	11	EA
2x4 - 20' Std. & Btr.	Rake/Blocking	4	EA
2x6 - 16' Std. & Btr.	Sub-Fascia	4	EA
2x8 - 16' Std. & Btr.	Truss Nailer	4	EA
Joist Hanger (LUS28)	Mono Truss	13	EA
Seismic/Hurricane Tie (H1)	Girder Truss	13	EA
5/16" Lag Screws	Nailer	26	EA
5/16"x 1/2" Washer	Nailer	26	EA
1x6 - 12 #2 & Btr. S4S	Fascia	6	EA
1x8 - 12 #2 & Btr. S4S	Fascia	8	EA
5# 16d Galv. Nails	General Framing	4	EA
5# 8d Ctd. Box Nails	General Framing	4	EA
5# 10d Bright Box Nails	General Framing	4	EA
5# 6d Galv. Box Nails	General Framing	2	EA
5# 6d Galv. Finish Nails	General Fin. Trim	1	EA
5# 8d Galv. Finish Nails	General Fin. Trim	1	EA
5# 1-1/4" Roofing Nails	Shingle	4	EA
10 oz. - Paintable Caulk	Flashing	4	TB

WALL FRAMING

Item	Location	Qty	UM
2x4 - 10' Std. & Btr.	Stud	54	EA
2x6 - 14' Std. & Btr.	Stud	92	EA
2x6 - 14' Std. & Btr.	Blocking	6	EA
2x4 - 12' Std. & Btr.	Plate	16	EA
2x4 - 16' Std. & Btr.	Plate	12	EA
2x6 - 16' Treated	Bottom Sill Plate	8	EA
2x12 - 8' Std. & Btr.	3' Ext. Dr. Header	1	EA
2x12 - 10' Std. & Btr.	9' Gar. Dr. Header	2	EA
2x12 - 12' Std. & Btr.	Window Header	1	EA
1-3/4"x9-1/4"x14" LVL Hdr.	12' Gar. Dr. Header	2	EA
7/16" OSB (Ply.)	Wall Sheathing	55	EA
40"x 97' Building Paper	Wall	6	RL
3-1/2"x50'x1/4" Sill Sealer	Sill Plate	3	RL
5# 1/2" Roofing Nails	Building Paper	3	EA
5# 16d Galv. Nails	General Framing	4	EA
5# 8d Ctd. Box Nails	General Framing	2	EA
5# 10d Bright Box Nails	General Framing	3	EA

EXTERIOR TRIM & ACCESSORIES

Item	Location	Qty	UM
1x6 - 10' Ship Lap Siding	Siding	360	EA
2x4 - 10' Std. & Btr.	Corner Trim	2	EA
2x4 - 12' Std. & Btr.	Corner Trim	2	EA
2x4 - 16' Std. & Btr.	Corner Trim	1	EA
2x6 - 8' Std. & Btr.	Ovh. Gar. Dr. J./Trim	4	EA
2x6 - 10' Std. & Btr.	Gar. Dr. Head	1	EA
2x6 - 12' Std. & Btr.	Gar. Dr. J./Hd./Trim	5	EA
2x8 - 14' Std. & Btr.	Garage Dr. Trim	1	EA
2x8 - 16' Std. & Btr.	Garage Dr. Trim	1	EA
1x4 - 10' Std. & Btr.	Window Trim	2	EA
1/4" Plywood (Sanded)	Soffit Material	7	EA
1x4 - 10' Std. & Btr. (Rip-1x2)	Soffit Trim	4	EA
14"x6" Metal Soffit Vent	Soffit	4	EA
5# 6d Galv. Finish Nails	General Fin. Trim	5	EA
5# 8d Galv. Finish Nails	General Fin. Trim	4	EA
10 oz. - Paintable Caulk	Ledger	4	TB
9'x8' Ovh. Gar. Dr.	Garage Door	1	EA
12'x12' Ovh. Gar. Dr.	Garage Door	1	EA
36"x80" Exterior LH Dr.	Service Door	1	EA
6024 Awning Window	Window	1	EA
Lockset/Deadbolt	Service Door	1	EA
1-1/4"x2" Brickmold	Service Door	3	EA
4" - 10' "Z" Flashing	Window/Door	4	EA

THE MORTON

HPM-1010

Need a place to shelter your car and store oversized, seasonal or outdoor items? This functional carport shelters one vehicle and provides compartmentalized storage space at the back. Behind double doors, a central storage space is anchored by built-in shelves. The carport attaches to an existing wall of your home and can be custom designed with the same siding and roof pitch.

Dimensions for this carport are 12' X 24'. 288 sq. ft.

MORTON — Plan View

Scale: 1/4" = 1'-0"

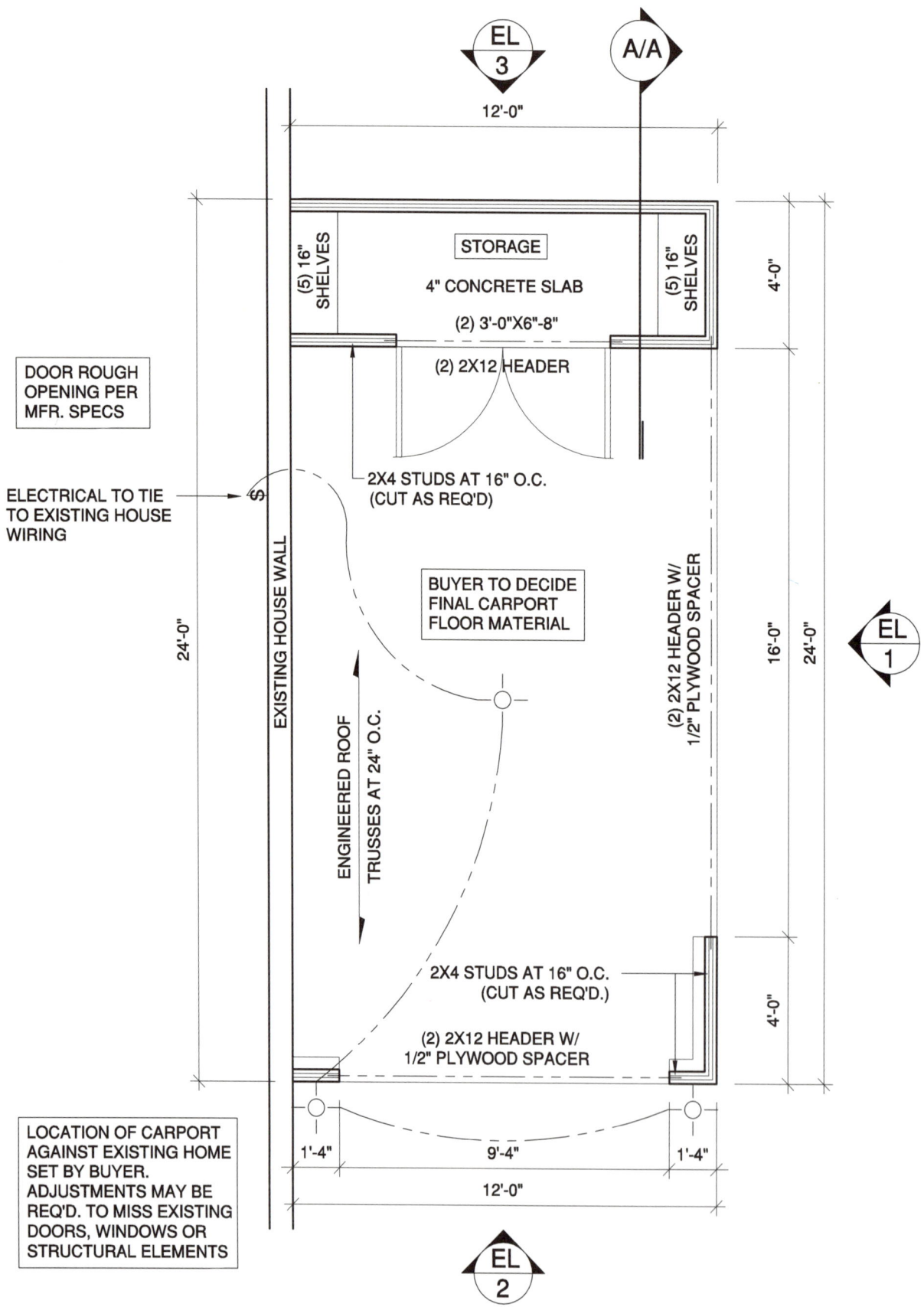

146 www.DreamIt-BuildIt.com

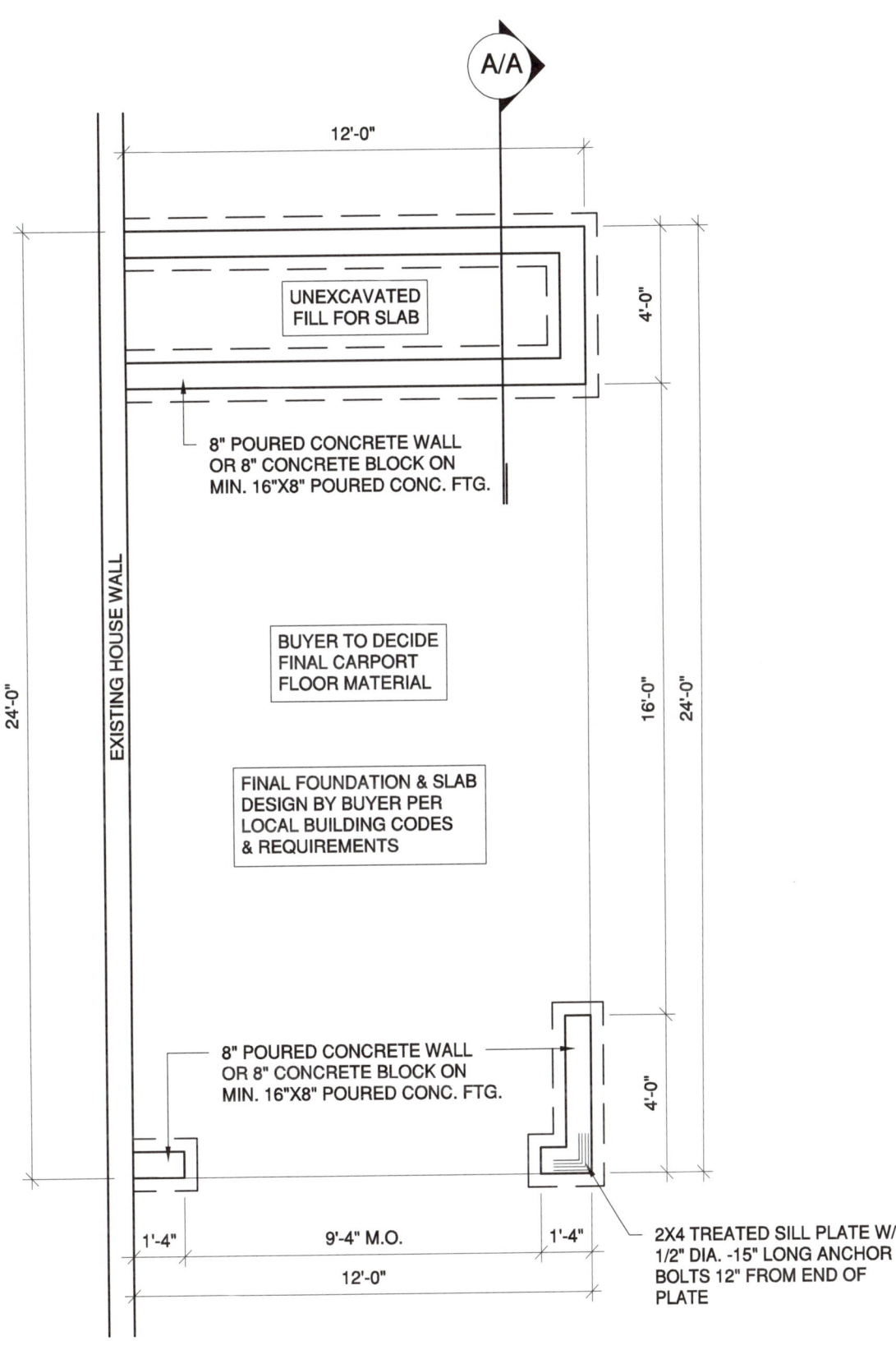

MORTON — Elevation

Scale: 1/4" = 1'-0"

EXTERIOR MATERIALS SHOWN AS NOTED. MATCHING MATERIALS TO EXISTING HOUSE ARE AT BUYER'S DISCRETION. LOCATION OF CARPORT AGAINST EXISTING HOUSE SET BY BUYER. ADJUSTMENTS MAY BE REQ'D. TO MISS EXISTING DOORS, WINDOWS OR STRUCTURAL ELEMENTS.

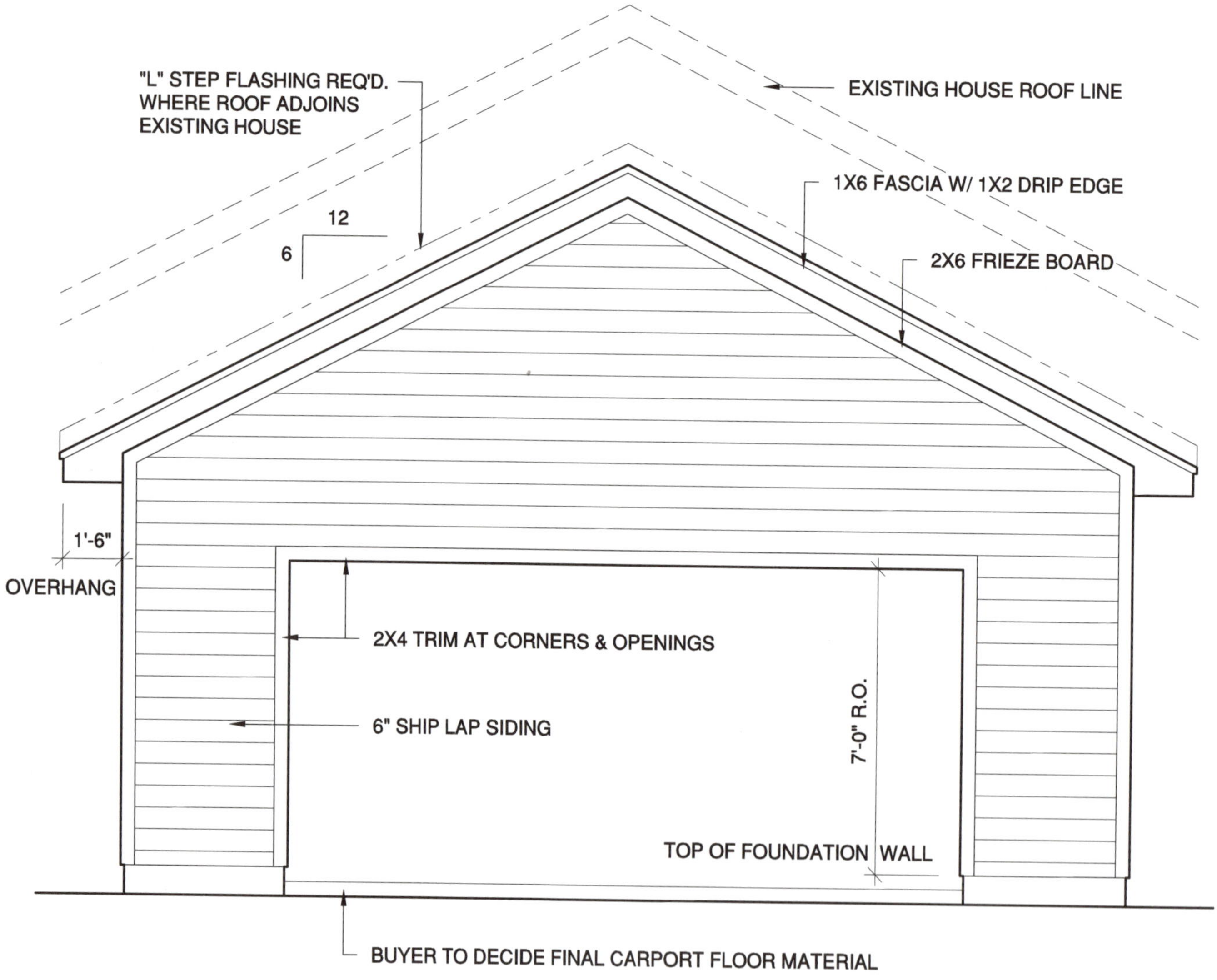

"L" STEP FLASHING REQ'D. WHERE ROOF ADJOINS EXISTING HOUSE

EXISTING HOUSE ROOF LINE

1X6 FASCIA W/ 1X2 DRIP EDGE

2X6 FRIEZE BOARD

12 / 6

1'-6" OVERHANG

2X4 TRIM AT CORNERS & OPENINGS

6" SHIP LAP SIDING

7'-0" R.O.

TOP OF FOUNDATION WALL

BUYER TO DECIDE FINAL CARPORT FLOOR MATERIAL

EL/1 **RIGHT ELEVATION**

MORTON — Elevations

Scale: 1/4" = 1'-0"

EXTERIOR MATERIALS SHOWN AS NOTED. MATCHING MATERIALS TO EXISTING HOUSE ARE AT BUYER'S DISCRETION. LOCATION OF CARPORT AGAINST EXISTING HOUSE SET BY BUYER. ADJUSTMENTS MAY BE REQ'D. TO MISS EXISTING DOORS, WINDOWS OR STRUCTURAL ELEMENTS.

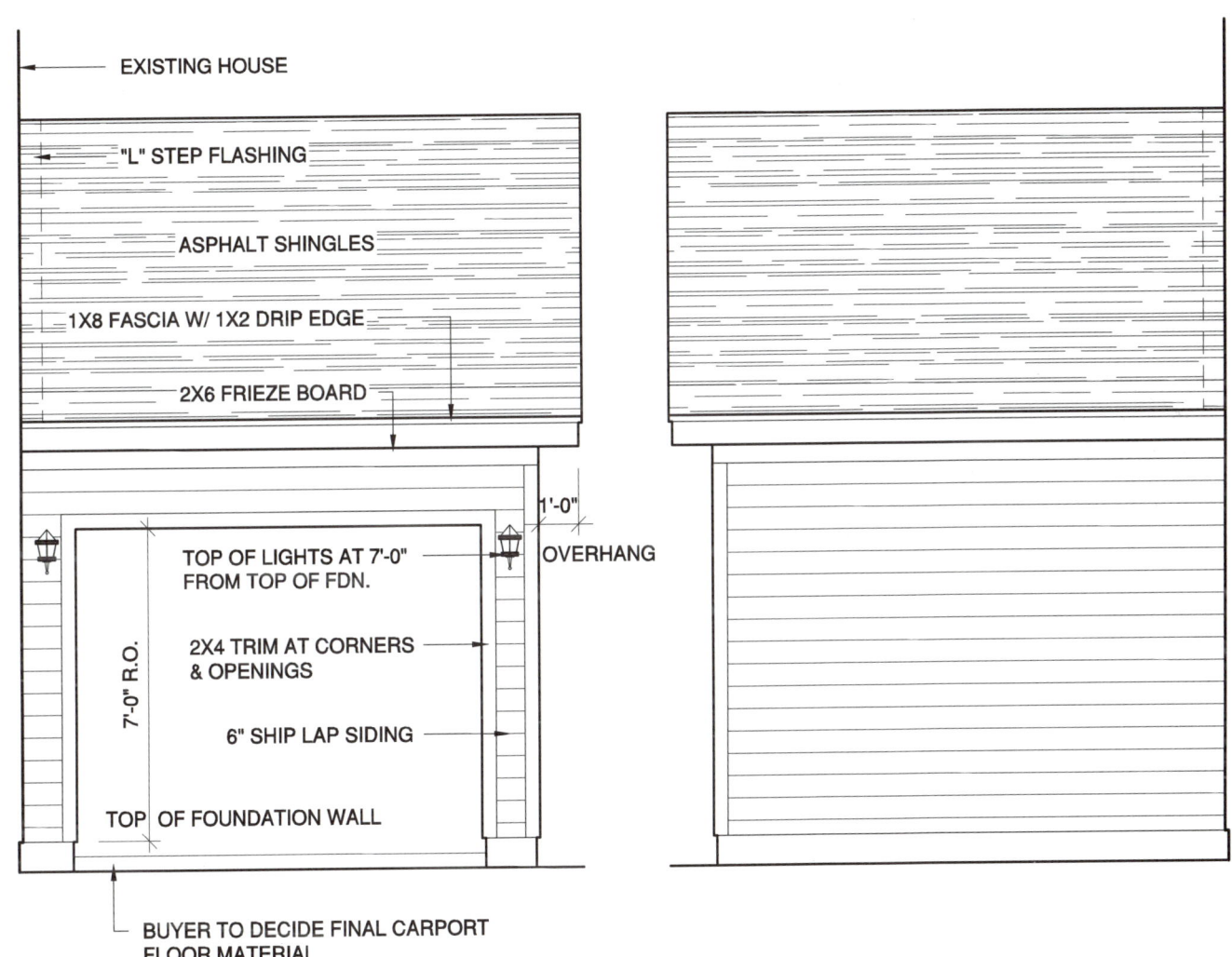

FRONT ELEVATION (EL/2)

REAR ELEVATION (EL/3)

www.homedepot.com

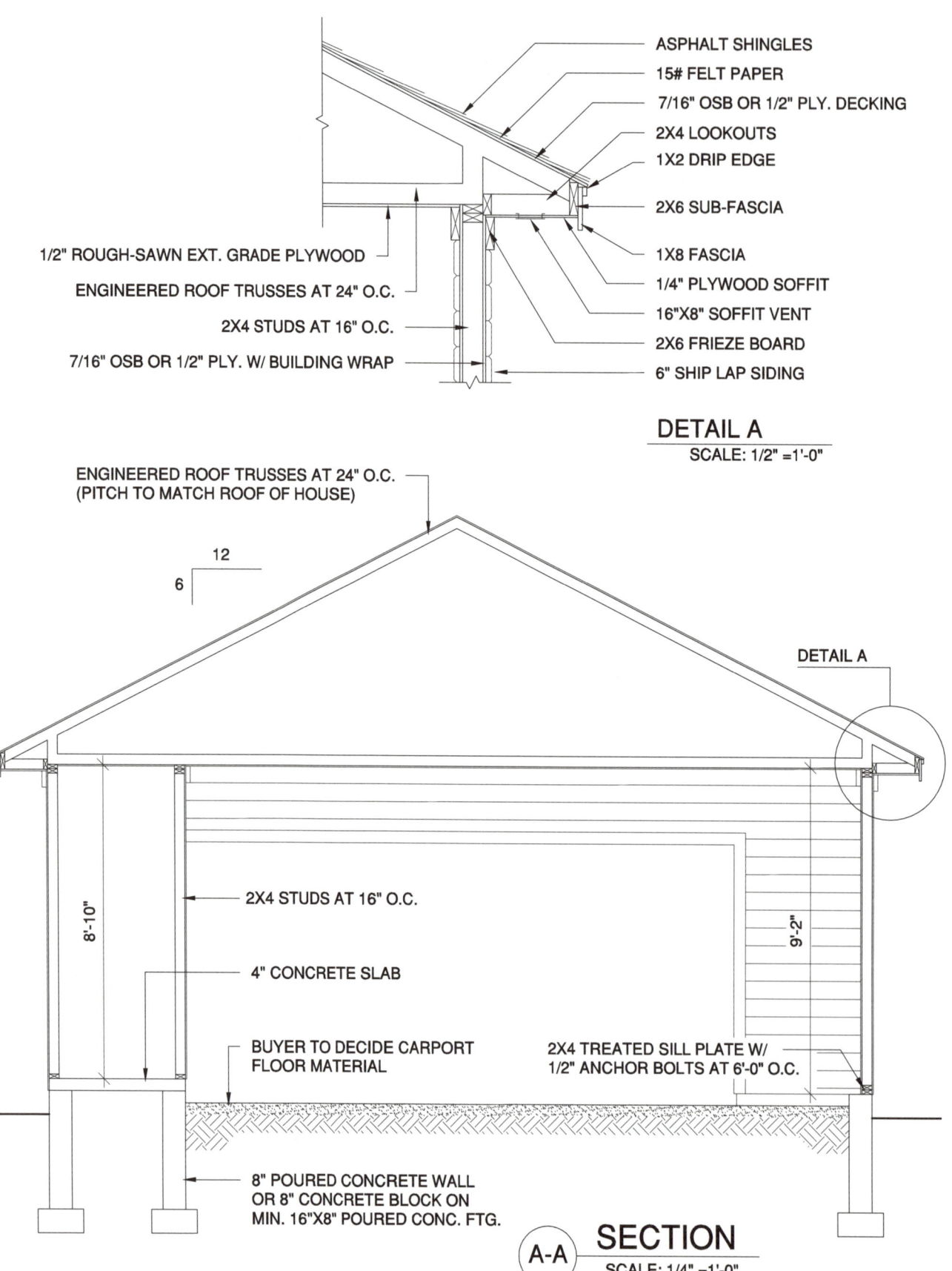

MORTON Material List

ROOF

Item	Location	Qty	UM
3 - Tab Shingles 20 Yr.	Shingle	14	BN
15-lb. Asphalt Rfg. Felt	Roofing Paper	2	RL
7/16" OSB (Ply.)	Roof Decking	14	EA
1/2" RS Exterior Plywood	Carport Ceiling	9	EA
Galv. Drip Edge	Above Fascia	6	EA
"L" Flashing -10' Roof -Wall	Roof/House	4	EA
Engineered Roof Trusses	Roof	1	Set
2x4 - 12' Std. & Btr.	Truss Brcng./Block	5	EA
2x4 - 12' Std. & Btr.	Lookout/Sof. Nailer	4	EA
2x4 - 16' Std. & Btr.	Ladder Rake	4	EA
2x6 - 14' Std. & Btr.	Sub-Fascia	2	EA
1x6 - 12' #2 & Btr. S4S	Fascia	3	EA
1x8 - 12' #2 & Btr. S4S	Fascia	3	EA
5# 16d Galv. Nails	General Framing	4	EA
5# 8d Ctd. Box Nails	General Framing	4	EA
5# 10d Bright Box Nails	General Framing	4	EA
5# 6d Galv. Box Nails	General Framing	2	EA
5# 6d Galv. Finish Nails	General Fin. Trim	1	EA
5# 8d Galv. Finish Nails	General Fin. Trim	1	EA
5# 1-1/4" Roofing Nails	Shingle	4	EA
10 oz. - Paintable Caulk	Flashing	4	TB

WALL FRAMING

Item	Location	Qty	UM
2x4 - 10' Std. & Btr.	Stud	54	EA
2x4 - 12' Std. & Btr.	Plate	6	EA
2x4 - 16' Std. & Btr.	Plate	4	EA
2x4 - 16' Treated	Bottom Sill Plate	3	EA
2x12 - 8' Std. & Btr.	Header	2	EA
2x12 - 10' Std. & Btr.	Header	2	EA
2x12 - 20' Std. & Btr.	Header	2	EA
1/2" CDX - 5 Ply. Plywd.	Header Spacer	1	EA
7/16" OSB (Ply.)	Wall Sheathing	16	EA
3-1/2"x50'x1/4" Sill Sealer	Sill Plate	1	RL
40"x 97' Building Paper	Wall	2	RL
5# 1/2" Roofing Nails	Building Paper	3	EA
5# 16d Galv. Nails	General Framing	4	EA
5# 8d Ctd. Box Nails	General Framing	2	EA
5# 10d Bright Box Nails	General Framing	3	EA

EXTERIOR TRIM & ACCESSORIES

Item	Location	Qty	UM
1x6 - 10' Ship Lap Siding	Siding	120	EA
2x4 - 10' Std. & Btr.	Crnr. Trim/Dr. Trim	24	EA
2x6 - 16' Std. & Btr.	Frieze	10	EA
1/4" Plywood (Sanded)	Soffit Material	3	EA
1x4 - 10' Std. & Btr. (Rip-1x2)	Soffit Trim	3	EA
14"x6" Metal Soffit Vent	Soffit	4	EA
5# 6d Galv. Finish Nails	General Fin. Trim	5	EA
5# 8d Galv. Finish Nails	General Fin. Trim	4	EA
10 oz. - Paintable Caulk	Ledger	4	TB
(2) 36"x80" Ext. Door	Service Door	1	EA
Lockset/Deadbolt/Pin	Service Door	1	EA
4" - 10' "Z" Flashing	Door/Window	4	EA
1x4 - 6' Board	Hook Strip	10	EA
3/4" OSB Sq. Edge (Ply.)	Shelf	2	EA

CHAPTER 4

THE CLINTON

HPM-1011

Keep your automobiles out of the elements and your outdoor belongings organized in this handsome two-car carport. Two deep storage spaces sit at the back of the 28-ft.-long shelter; each space can be closed off to conceal valuable items or unfinished work.

Dimensions for this carport are 22' X 28'. 616 sq. ft.

CLINTON — Plan View

Scale: 1/4" = 1'-0"

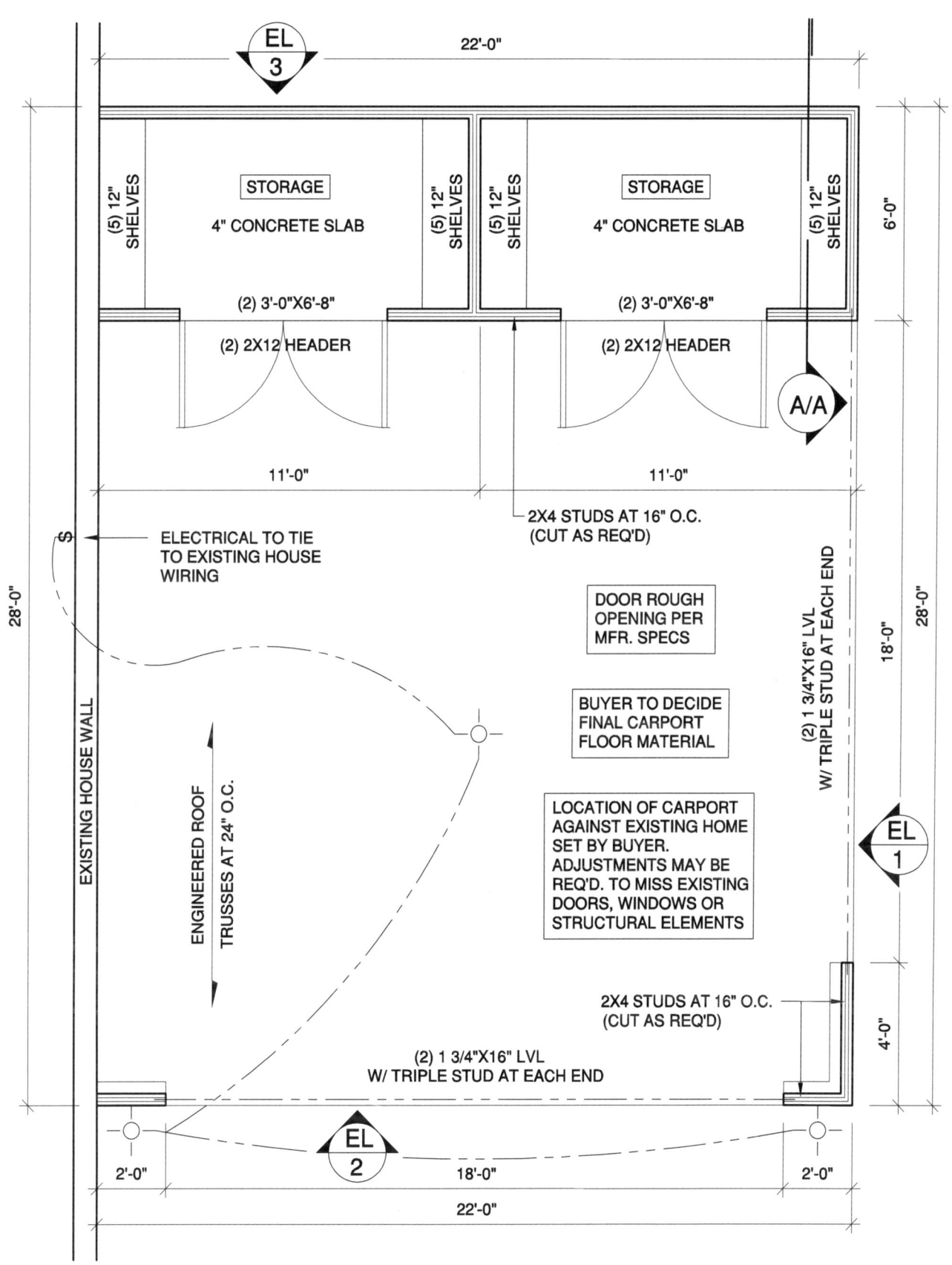

www.homedepot.com — 153

CLINTON — Foundation Plan

Scale: 1/4" = 1'-0"

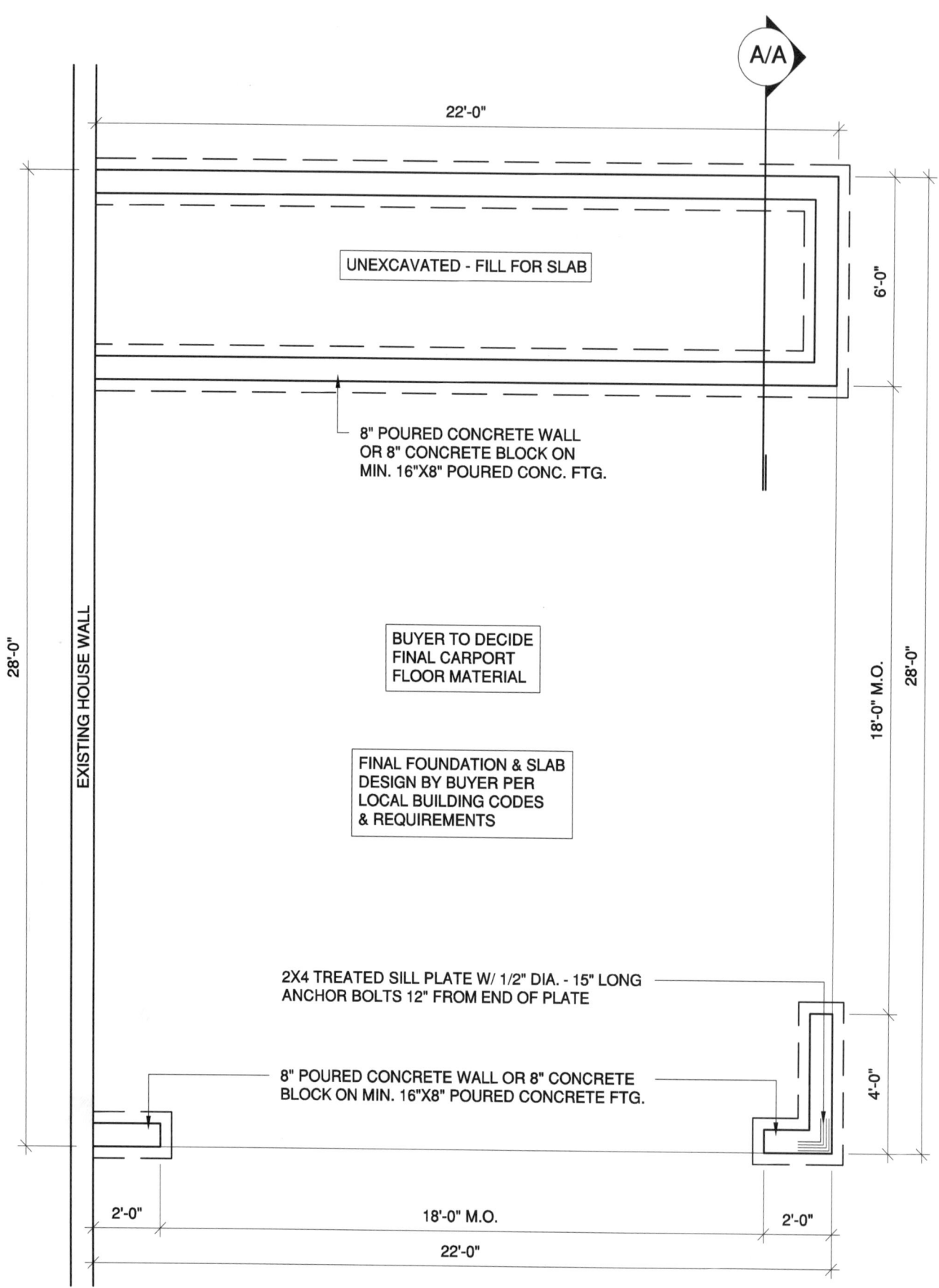

CLINTON — Elevation

Scale: 1/4" = 1'-0"

EXTERIOR MATERIALS SHOWN AS NOTED. MATCHING MATERIALS TO EXISTING HOUSE ARE AT BUYER'S DISCRETION. LOCATION OF CARPORT AGAINST EXISTING HOUSE SET BY BUYER. ADJUSTMENTS MAY BE REQ'D. TO MISS EXISTING DOORS, WINDOWS OR STRUCTURAL ELEMENTS.

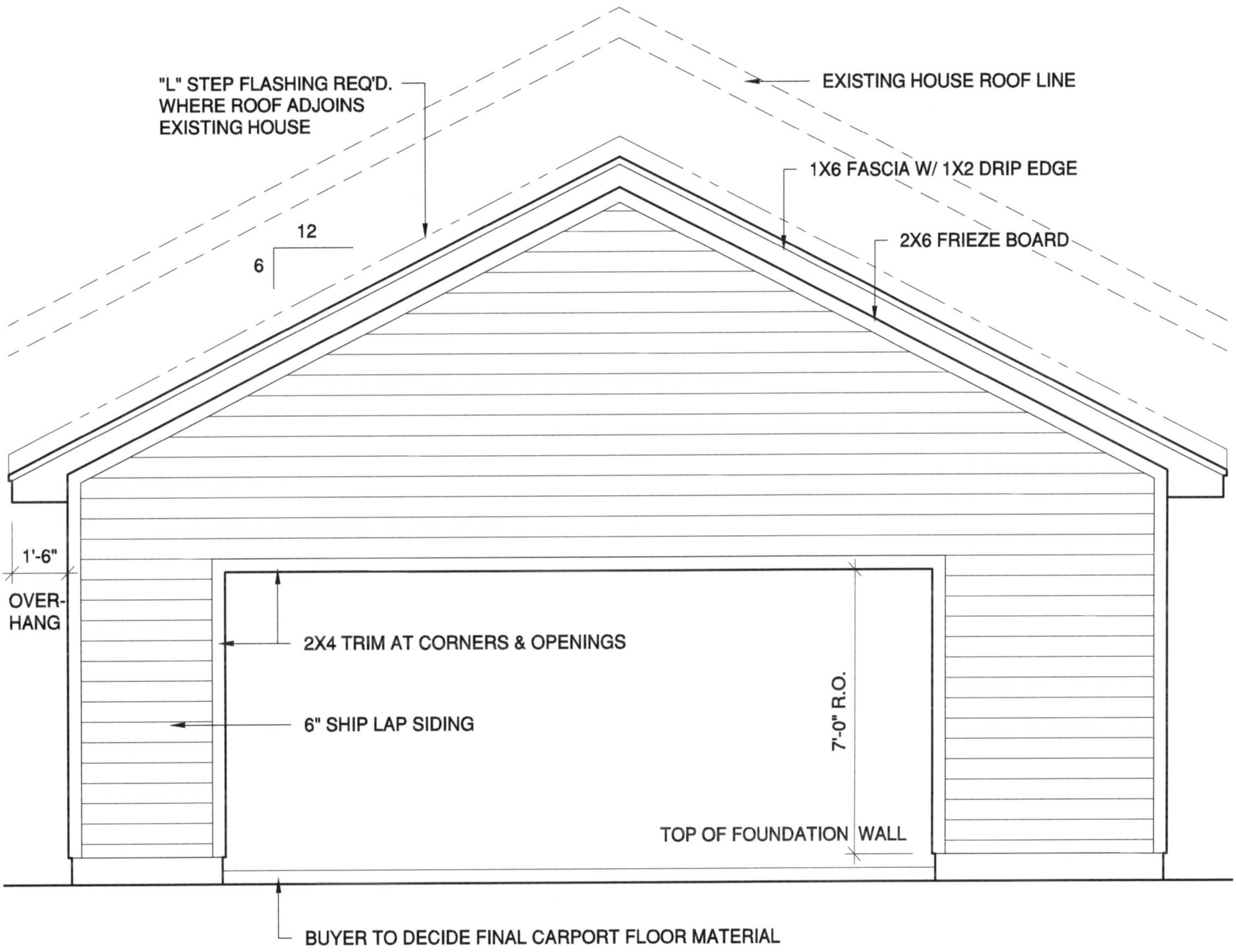

- "L" STEP FLASHING REQ'D. WHERE ROOF ADJOINS EXISTING HOUSE
- EXISTING HOUSE ROOF LINE
- 1X6 FASCIA W/ 1X2 DRIP EDGE
- 2X6 FRIEZE BOARD
- 12 / 6
- 1'-6" OVERHANG
- 2X4 TRIM AT CORNERS & OPENINGS
- 6" SHIP LAP SIDING
- 7'-0" R.O.
- TOP OF FOUNDATION WALL
- BUYER TO DECIDE FINAL CARPORT FLOOR MATERIAL

EL/1 **RIGHT ELEVATION**

CLINTON — Elevations

Scale: 3/16" = 1'-0"

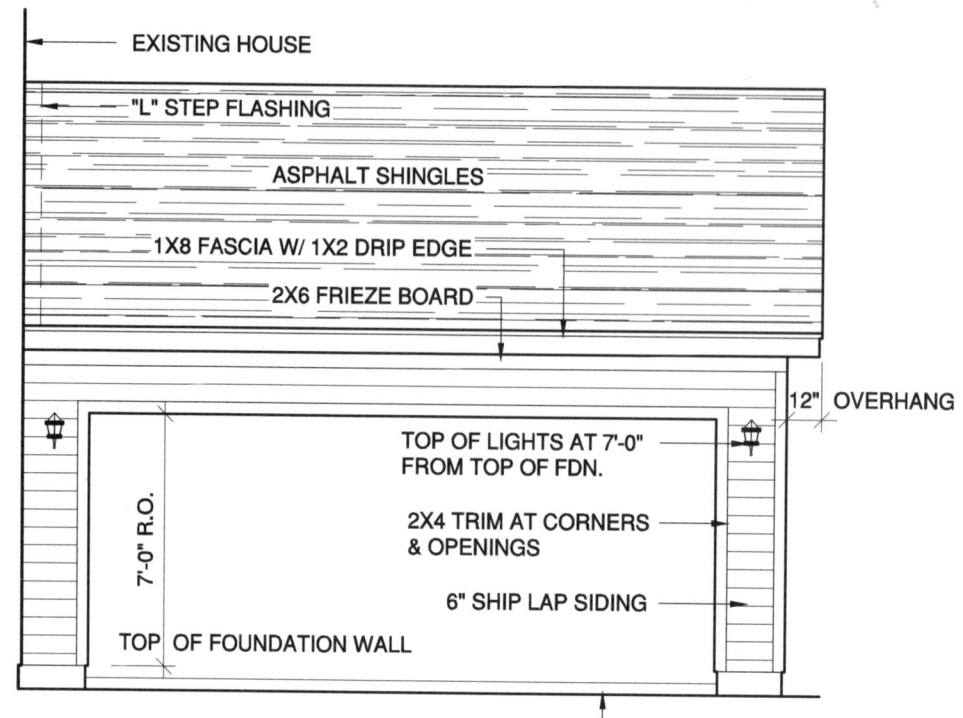

FRONT ELEVATION (EL/2)

EXTERIOR MATERIALS SHOWN AS NOTED. MATCHING MATERIALS TO EXISTING HOUSE ARE AT BUYER'S DISCRETION. LOCATION OF CARPORT AGAINST EXISTING HOUSE SET BY BUYER. ADJUSTMENTS MAY BE REQ'D. TO MISS EXISTING DOORS, WINDOWS OR STRUCTURAL ELEMENTS.

REAR ELEVATION (EL/3)

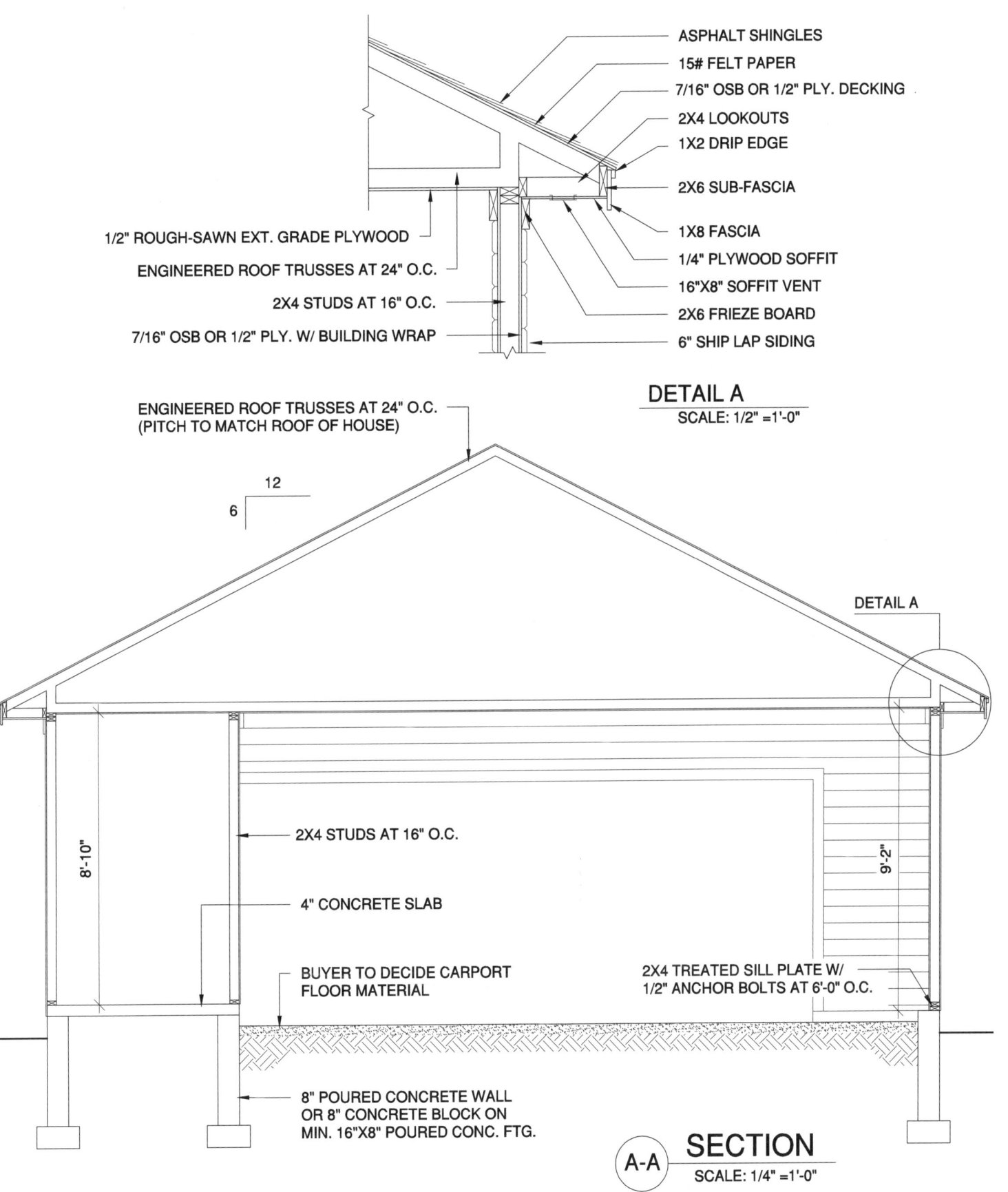

CLINTON Material List

ROOF

Item	Location	Qty	UM
3 - Tab Shingles 20 Yr.	Shingle	27	BN
15-lb. Asphalt Rfg. Felt	Roofing Paper	4	RL
7/16" OSB (Ply.)	Roof Decking	28	EA
1/2" RS Exterior Plywood	Carport Ceiling	10	EA
Galv. Drip Edge (1x2 - 10')	Above Fascia	9	EA
"L" Flashing - 10' Roof-Wall	Roof/House	4	EA
Engineered Roof Trusses	Roof	1	Set
2x4 - 12' Std. & Btr.	Lookout/Sof. Nailer	7	EA
2x4 - 16' Std. & Btr.	Truss Brcng./Block	9	EA
2x4 - 20' Std. & Btr.	Ladder Rake	4	EA
2x6 - 12' Std. & Btr.	Sub-Fascia	4	EA
1x6 - 12' #2 & Btr. S4S	Fascia	4	EA
1x8 - 12' #2 & Btr. S4S	Fascia	5	EA
5# 16d Galv. Nail	General Framing	4	EA
5# 8d Ctd. Box Nail	General Framing	4	EA
5# 10d Bright Box Nail	General Framing	4	EA
5# 6d Galv. Box Nail	General Framing	2	EA
5# 6d Galv. Finish Nails	General Fin. Trim	1	EA
5# 8d Galv. Finish Nails	General Fin. Trim	1	EA
5# 1-1/4" Roofing Nails	Shingle	4	EA
10 oz. - Paintable Caulk	Flashing	4	TB

WALL FRAMING

Item	Location	Qty	UM
2x4 - 10' Std. & Btr.	Stud	100	EA
2x4 - 12' Std. & Btr.	Plate	9	EA
2x4 - 16' Std. & Btr.	Plate	7	EA
2x4 - 16' Treated	Bottom Sill Plate	4	EA
2x12 - 8' Std. & Btr.	Header	4	EA
1-3/4"x16"x19' LVL	Header	4	EA
7/16" OSB (Ply.)	Wall Sheathing	25	EA
3-1/2"x50'x1/4" Sill Sealer	Sill Plate	2	RL
40"x 97' Building Paper	Wall	3	RL
5# 1/2" Roofing Nails	Building Paper	3	EA
5# 16d Galv. Nails	General Framing	4	EA
5# 8d Ctd. Box Nails	General Framing	2	EA
5# 10d Bright Box Nails	General Framing	3	EA

EXTERIOR TRIM & ACCESSORIES

Item	Location	Qty	UM
1x6 - 10' Ship Lap Siding	Siding	160	EA
2x4 - 10' Std. & Btr.	Crnr. Trim/Dr. Trim	30	EA
2x6 - 16' Std. & Btr.	Frieze	10	EA
1/4" Plywood (Sanded)	Soffit Material	4	EA
1x4 - 10' Std. & Btr. (Rip-1x2)	Soffit Trim	5	EA
14"x6" Metal Soffit Vent	Soffit	4	EA
5# 6d Galv. Finish Nails	General Fin. Trim	5	EA
5# 8d Galv. Finish Nails	General Fin. Trim	4	EA
10 oz - Paintable Caulk	Ledger	4	TB
(2) 36"x 80" Exterior Door	Service Door	2	EA
Lockset/Deadbolt/Pin	Service Door	2	EA
4" - "Z" Flashing	Door/Window	5	EA
1x4 - 10' Boards	Hook Strip	20	EA
3/4" OSB Sq. Edge (Ply.)	Shelf	5	EA

Picture Credits

4	Raynor Worldwide
5	Jean-Claude Hurni
8	Jean-Claude Hurni
9	Jean-Claude Hurni
10	*(upper)* Handy Home Products
	(lower) Jean-Claude Hurni
11	Jean-Claude Hurni
12	*(upper)* Jean-Claude Hurni
	(lower) Jean-Claude Hurni
13	Handy Home Products
14	Handy Home Products
15	*(upper)* Kloter Farms, Inc./Fred Bird Photography
	(lower) Kloter Farms, Inc./Fred Bird Photography
16	*(upper)* Jason Miller
	(lower) Jean-Claude Hurni
17	Jean-Claude Hurni
18	Raynor Worldwide
19	*(upper)* Garages by Opdyke
	(lower) Garages by Opdyke
20	*(upper)* Jean-Claude Hurni
	(lower) Garages by Opdyke
21	*(upper)* Raynor Worldwide
	(lower) Garages by Opdyke
28	*(upper left)* Handy Home Products
	(lower left) Garages by Opdyke
	(lower center) Garages by Opdyke
	(right) Jean-Claude Hurni
29	Jean-Claude Hurni
35	Hickory Dickory Decks
37	Jean-Claude Hurni
38	Summerwood.com
39	Garages by Opdyke
40	Jamaica Cottage Shop
42	Summerwood.com
43	Handy Home Products
44	Suntuf/Elizabeth Benham
45	Limestone Trail Company Ltd.
47	*(upper)* Knape & Vogt Manufacturing
	(lower left, lower right) Werner Co.
48	Jean-Claude Hurni

Front cover: Jean-Claude Hurni

Glossary

Anchor bolt
A J-shaped bolt used mainly to fasten sill plates to the concrete piers or foundation slab of a shed or garage. The curved end of the bolt is embedded in the concrete. The threaded section projecting upward attaches to the sill plate.

Baluster
Vertical member of porch railings, usually made from 2x2 lumber and fastened to rails spanning two or more posts.

Batterboard
A wooden assembly made up of two stakes and a third board spanning horizontally between them; used with mason's line to lay out shed piers and garage foundations.

Blocking
Lengths of 2x4 fastened between joists to add support and structural rigidity on long spans.

Decay resistant
Refers to wood that is either naturally resistant to rot—such as cedar and redwood—or treated with chemicals to be rot-resistant.

Detail
Part of a shed or garage plan showing a cutaway section of a particular view and revealing hidden structural elements.

Dimensional lumber
Graded for strength, this wood is intended for the understructure of a shed or garage; it ranges in nominal size from 2 to 4 inches in width and is at least 2 inches thick.

Downspout
A pipe, made of metal or vinyl, that channels water running off the roof into the gutter to the ground away from the foundation.

Drip edge
A board, typically 1x2, or length of metal or vinyl installed along the roof line; one edge slips under the roofing material and the other covers the fascia to channel water into the gutter and keep water from seeping under the roofing material.

Easement
A section of property that must be left accessible for others to use.

Elevation
Part of a shed or garage plan that shows a side view. Included in the view are dimensions, materials and, in some cases, a detail of the view.

Face-nail
To drive a nail through the face of one board into another, with the nail perpendicular to the surface.

Fascia
A length of lumber, typically 1x8, installed to cover the exposed ends of roof rafters; often covered with aluminum or vinyl.

Footing
The wide concrete base under a concrete pier; serves to hold the pier firmly in place.

Framing connector
Metal hardware that is used to connect structural members to form a stronger joint than is possible with conventional fasteners.

Frost line
The depth below grade to which the ground freezes in winter.

Galvanized
A process by which fasteners are coated with zinc to prevent oxidization due to contact with moisture. Hot-dipped galvanized fasteners are the highest quality.

Grade
The slope or incline of the ground; usually expressed in vertical inches per horizontal foot.

Ground-fault circuit interrupter (GFCI)
An electrical device that shuts off power to a circuit when current leakage is detected. Usually required in outdoor wiring.

Gutter
A trough, made of metal or vinyl, fastened to the fascia below the eave, designed to carry water running off the roof to a downspout.

Height limit
A zoning bylaw that sets a limit on the height of a structure on your property.

Lot-coverage limit
A legal restriction governing what proportion of your property a structure can cover.

On center
The span from the center of one supporting member to the center of another. Abbreviated on deck plans as "o.c."

Overhead
A structure built over a doorway or landing for shade or privacy.

Pier
A cylindrical concrete foundation member set below ground level to support a shed.

Plan view
A view of the shed or garage structure seen from directly above, indicating mainly the dimensions of the structure's perimeter.

Pressure-treated
A process by which chemical preservatives are forced into lumber under pressure, making it resistant to decay and insect damage.

Setback
A legal restriction governing how close to your property line a structure can be built.

Single-hung window
A two-sash window in which only one sash, usually the interior bottom one, moves up and down.

Site plan
A complete map of a lot indicating the position of all structures, including the proposed shed or garage.

Soffit
The underside of the eave, usually finished with wood, vinyl or metal panels; vents in the soffit enable air to circulate under the roof.

Span
The distance from the center of one supporting member to the center of another.

Stucco
A siding material made of a mixture of portland cement, lime, sand and water.

Toenail
To fasten two wood pieces together with a nail driven in at an angle.

Understructure
The supporting structure of a shed or garage, made up of the piers or foundation and joists.

Z flashing
Sheet metal or vinyl specially cut and formed to fit over doors and windows to prevent water from seeping behind door and window frames.